The Vanishing Middle Class

The Vanishing Middle Class

Prejudice and Power in a Dual Economy

Peter Temin

The MIT Press
Cambridge, Massachusetts
London, England

This book was set in Sabon LT Std by Toppan Best-set Premedia Limited. Printed and bound in the United States of America.

Library of Congress Cataloging-in-Publication Data

Names: Temin, Peter, author.
Title: The vanishing middle class : prejudice and power in a dual economy / Peter Temin.
Description: Cambridge, MA : MIT Press, 2017. | Includes bibliographical references and index.
Identifiers: LCCN 2016035191 | ISBN 9780262036160 (hardcover : alk. paper)
Subjects: LCSH: Income distribution--United States. | Middle class--United States--Economic conditions. | Minorities--United States--Economic conditions. | Equality--United States. | United States--Economic conditions--2009- | United States--Economic policy--2009-
Classification: LCC HC110.I5 T455 2017 | DDC 339.2/208900973--dc23 LC record available at https://lccn.loc.gov/2016035191

10   9   8   7   6   5   4   3   2   1

For Charlotte
My wife, companion, and muse for fifty years

Contents

Introduction

Growing income inequality is threatening the American middle class, and the middle class is vanishing before our eyes. There are fewer people in the middle of the American income distribution, and the country is dividing into rich and poor. Our income distribution has changed from looking like a one-humped camel to looking like a two-humped camel with a low part in between. We are still one country, but the stretch of incomes is fraying the unity of the nation.

The middle class was critical to the success of the United States in the twentieth century. It provided the manpower that enabled the nation to turn the corner to victory in two world wars in the first half of the century, and it was the backbone of American economic dominance of the world in the second half. But now the average worker has trouble finding a job, and the earnings of median-income workers have not risen for forty years. (The median income is the middle income, where as many people earn more as earn less; it was about $60,000 in 2014 for a family of three.) If America is to remain strong in the twenty-first century, something has to be done.[1]

This problem is complicated by the influence of American history. Slavery was an integral part of the United States at its beginning, and it took a protracted and bloody Civil War to eliminate it. Too many African Americans still are not fully integrated into the mainstream of American society. While progress has been made, our neighborhoods and schools remain largely segregated by race, and African Americans as a whole are poorer than white Americans.

The combination of inequality and racial segregation is problematic for the health of our democracy. For example, it should be the right of any citizen to vote in a democracy. Slaves of course did not vote, and attempts continue to this day to keep African Americans from voting, including a number of high-profile cases of alleged illegal obstruction that have gone to the courts. In addition, black people are far more likely than white people to be arrested and sent to prison in the American War on Drugs.

Poor whites also have suffered in various ways, but they have remained mostly quiescent and invisible in political debates and decisions. Traditionally, poor white Americans have not voted much, due to the restrictions used to discourage black voting like requiring picture IDs, and widespread beliefs that political parties are all the same and politicians do not care about them. Their frustration and despair at being left out of recent economic growth has resulted in an array of stresses and self-destructive behaviors that have raised the death rates for middle-aged white Americans. Anger at their circumstances is being channeled into politics in 2016. This anger is likely to affect American politics for a long time.

These developments were revealed dramatically in a recent study by the Pew Research Center. The change is shown in figure 1, where total national income is divided into three groups: the middle class with upper and lower groups. The middle class, defined as households earning from two-thirds to double the median American household income, went from earning over three-fifths of total national income in 1970 to earning only just over two-fifths in 2014. The lines in figure 1 were horizontal before 1970, but they are continuing their movements after 2014.

Figure 1 shows that the income share lost by the middle class went to people earning more than double the median income. In short, the rich got richer, the poor did not disappear, and the middle class shrank sharply. We know from the work of Thomas Piketty in *Capital in the Twenty-First Century* that inequality has been increasing since 1970.[2] Now we see that the income distribution is hollowing out. We are on our way to become a nation of the rich and the poor with only a few people in the middle.

This book provides a way to think about this growing disparity of incomes between rich and poor. I argue that American history and politics have a lot to do with how our increasing inequality has been distributed. While our rapidly changing technology, prominently in finance and electronics, is an important part of this story, it is far from the whole tale. Our troubled racial history of slavery and its aftermath also plays an important part in how this growing divide is seen.

English settlers began coming to North America in the seventeenth century. They started in Plymouth, Massachusetts, and Jamestown, Virginia, and spread along the Atlantic seaboard. They found abundant and

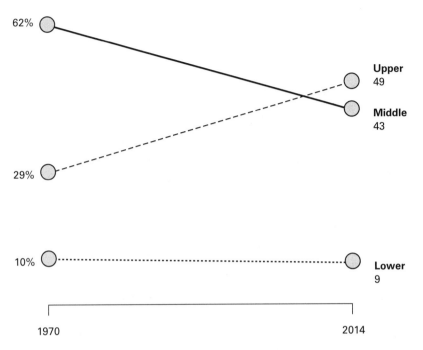

Figure 1
Percent of aggregate U.S. household income. *Note:* The assignment to income tiers is
based on size-adjusted household incomes in the year prior to the survey year. Shares may
not add up to 100 percent due to rounding.
Source: Pew Research Center 2015

fertile land to farm, but there were not enough settlers and labor to farm
as much land as they wanted. The resident Native Americans resisted
working for the English occupiers and were decimated by European dis-
eases. The settlers encouraged other people to come farm their land, and
European and African population movements were attracted in very
unequal ways. Europeans were encouraged to come by themselves or as
indentured servants who became independent farmers, while Africans
were brought against their will by slave traders.

Europeans gained great prosperity first from agriculture and then from
industry, while Africans were condemned to slavery. Cotton was the key
to economic growth in the early nineteenth century—grown by African
slaves in the South and manufactured into cloth by Europeans in the
North. Slavery was abolished by the Civil War that remains unresolved in
the minds of many white Southerners. European immigration was
restricted after the First World War, and six million African Americans

moved north during what was called the Great Migration as a result. In recent years, immigration from Mexico and other nearby Latin American countries has increased rapidly, and Latinos also are concentrated in the lower group shown in figure 1. Public discussion of the working poor focuses on African Americans, but it sometimes refers to them simply as "them," including Latinos as well.

African Americans also have become the focus of policy debates at both state and federal levels. Politicians who oppose government welfare expenses used to identify the recipients as black; however, since the Civil Rights Movement of the 1960s, politicians use code words instead. While nearly half of black Americans are included the "poorer" group in figure 1, most poor people in fact are not black. There are not enough African Americans for them to be the majority. Poor whites also are affected by the withdrawal of social services, but they have been largely invisible in policy discussions. As Bob Dylan said in a song at Martin Luther King's 1963 March on Washington, "The poor white remains / On the caboose of the train / But it ain't him to blame / He's only a pawn in their game."[3]

Race and class are distinct, but they have interacted in complex ways from the U.S. slavery era that ended in 1865; to Ronald Reagan announcing his 1980 presidential campaign in Philadelphia in Mississippi, where three civil rights workers had been murdered in 1964; to Donald Trump's equally indirect claim to "Make America Great Again" in his 2016 presidential campaign—where "great" is a euphemism for "white." The Civil Rights Movement changed the language of racism without reducing its scope. As incomes become more and more unequal, racism becomes a tool for the rich to arouse poor whites to feel superior to blacks and distract them from their economic plight.

Figure 1 is both simple and complex. It is simple because it summarizes a great deal of empirical research in a memorable way. It is complex because it is the result of economics, history, politics, and technology. To weave these varied strands into a coherent intellectual fabric, I use an economic model. A model is a simple version of a complex reality that reveals interactions between the strongest forces. It also facilitates the introduction of other forces into the model to make a more comprehensive representation of a complex reality.

I employ an economic model that was created over sixty years ago—and continues to be taught in economics classes today—to integrate the various strands of this narrative into a coherent story. This model continues to provide insights into the process of economic development even though it is clear enough to be understood by those who are not students of economics.

Economists identify this model by its creator, W. Arthur Lewis; it is known as the Lewis model. More descriptively, it also is known as the original model of a *dual economy*. A dual economy exists when there are two separate economic sectors within one country, divided by different levels of development, technology, and patterns of demand. This definition reflects the use of the Lewis model in the field of economic development, and I adapt it in this book to describe current conditions in the United States, the richest large country in the world.

This is less paradoxical than it sounds because the political policies that grow out of our dual economy have made the United States appear more and more like a developing country. Anyone who stirs out of his or her house knows about the problems of deteriorating roads and bridges in our country. And if you are not rich enough to send your children to private schools or to live in an expensive suburb known for having good public schools, you may know also about the current crisis in education.

Education was the key to American prosperity in the twentieth century. It is not too much to claim that we lived through an "American Century" because we had a long tradition of education that was the envy of the world. Claudia Goldin and Lawrence Katz made that point in *The Race between Education and Technology*.[4] Education is doubly important in the story told here. First, education is the key path for people to move from the poorer sector of the dual economy to the richer. And second, anyone interested in the continued economic success of the United States in the twenty-first century must want to fix our schools to preserve the prosperity of the country and its growth over time.

While this seems compelling to most people, the politics that emerge from our dual economy prevent us from acting sensibly to reconstruct our ailing educational system. As we will see, we now have two systems of education, one for each sector of the dual economy. Schools for the richer sector vary in quality, and the best of them are well within the American historical experience. By contrast, schools for the poorer sector are failing. Attempts to fix these schools have been known primarily for their spectacular failures.

The legacy of slavery hangs over attempts to provide every child with an education. It was illegal to educate black people under slavery, and politicians today neglect education of the poor by implicitly invoking this racist history. Urban pockets of poverty are deprived of good education by coded messages that invoke race to justify neglect or worse toward them. African Americans are condemned for violent actions, but they are largely the results—not the causes—of educational failure. Local school-district control was the key to good education during American expansion, but it has become a barrier to good education in recent decades.[5]

Even when black students get a good education, they often have trouble finding jobs that will move them up in the economy. Factory jobs have been disappearing for a generation; that is the main driver of the declining line in figure 1. The implication is that an educated black graduate in today's American economy has to make a leap to get into the higher-income group—a leap that is doubly hard. It typically requires even more education, and there is resistance to hiring bright young black people for high-paying jobs. The changing shape of the economy appears to have locked a large percentage of African Americans into a subordinate position, from which only the best and the brightest can hope to escape. Latinos who came to the United States seeking good jobs, like African Americans who left the post–Civil War South in the Great Migration, are in similar trouble.

This description will become clearer as we explore the implication of our model and history. We also will learn what the possibilities are for a political change that will make our efforts more fruitful. While no one can predict the future, we hope for changes that will improve the varied underpinnings of our economy and society. As we will see, the rich of the twenty-first century are trying to kill the goose that laid all those golden eggs in the twentieth century. The question is how we can alter the bad trajectory we are on.

The discussion in this book is divided into four parts. I describe and adapt the Lewis model in part I, showing both the implications of the model and its application to the United States today. One implication of the Lewis model is that the upper sector tries to keep wages low in the poorer sector. We can see that in many ways. For example, the *Boston Globe* recently tried to reduce the expense of delivering the newspaper. Most of us do not think about how the paper gets to our door in the morning, but paper delivery has evolved into a grueling nocturnal marathon for low-income workers who work invisibly at the edge of the economy. Delivery drivers are classified as independent contractors rather than employees; they therefore do not get guaranteed health care or retirement savings. They work 365 days a year for pay that makes ordinary jobs look good, and they have to find a replacement if they need to take a day off. Many of them work at another job during the day to support their families. More and more working people are being forced into working conditions like these.[6]

I resolve an apparent paradox in the second part. How can one sector of the economy impose its will on the other part in a democracy? Why don't the numerous poor vote the fewer rich out of office? The Median Voter Theorem helps pose these questions more precisely and indicates where answers may lie. An alternate view known as the Investment Theory of Politics reveals how democracy operates in our dual economy.

I start part II with the effects of race and gender on our decisions and progress to the role of the richest Americans in our politics. Their actions are most visible in a few Midwestern states. Hedge fund managers in Indiana drummed up support for Governor Mike Pence who wants to cut government spending, abandon the state's pension system, and weaken or destroy public-employee unions. This agenda is more advanced in Wisconsin where Governor Scott Walker started earlier and has gone further to allow corporations to contribute directly to political parties and to replace the state's nonpartisan government accountability board with commissions made up of partisan appointees. And in neighboring Michigan, Governor Rick Snyder ignored warnings about lead in the drinking water of Flint, a town that is poor and black. Since the effect of lead poisoning of black kids will have harmful effects over many years, some observers have been calling Flint a case of "environmental racism."[7]

This is the program of the very rich who have been allowed to dominate government policies by a succession of legislative and court decisions. The democracy that aspired to guarantee the right to vote for every person has been undermined in the last generation by a political structure where income matters more than demography. Income matters in varied ways, and campaign spending affects both votes and who can vote. The decisions creating the new politics have been justified by indirect racism that castigates poor people as "others," meaning black or brown. Despite the absence of directly racist statements, it is worth noting that the states that rejected the free expansion of Medicare under the Affordable Care Act are mostly former members of the Confederacy.

Part III of this book applies the insights of parts I and II to specific policy areas, organized around two popular oxymorons: "majority minority" and "private public." The largest unseen policy is the growth of mass incarceration in the period demarcated in figure 1. Starting from President Nixon's declaration of a War on Drugs, the American rate of incarceration has grown from the level of other modern democracies to one previously seen only in totalitarian countries. By the twenty-first century, one in three black men could expect go to jail. Blacks are not the majority of prisoners even so—one out of six Hispanic men and one out of seventeen white men can expect to go to jail—but the War on Drugs has eroded the black community. Phrased differently, 22 percent of black males aged 35 to 44 had been in prison in 2001, compared to 10 percent of Hispanic males and 4 percent of white males in this age group.[8]

Many poor black families have a member or know a relative or neighbor who has gone to jail. Too many black mothers are condemned to be single parents struggling to raise their children alone. And many black boys attending school know they have a good chance of being stopped by police, maybe even arrested, and ending up in jail. How can such a child think of the future when his present is so hard?

Families of single parents are poorer than intact families. They live in poor areas, typically in cities, where the schools are bad. Government decisions over the past generation have constructed a bifurcated school system, one for prosperous suburban whites who go on to college and one for urban black and brown people who are preoccupied with the threat of jail. The suburban schools are well funded from local taxes, while the urban tax base has shrunk under the economic burden placed on individuals and families by mass incarceration.

The combination of these policies has created a vicious cycle where black men are in jail, black women are under strain, and black children are deprived of a good education. The boys have few gainful opportunities and many contacts with the police; many may end up in jail, perpetuating this system. Politicians debate the value of investing more in urban schools if the students often drop out and go to jail—failing to recognize this is the outcome of a system of mass incarceration and complex public funding arrangements. This cycle is what Michelle Alexander called *The New Jim Crow.*[9]

Public investment in our cities also has been neglected. The infrastructure of cities, from roads and bridges to public transportation, has deteriorated to the point where it approaches the dilapidated conditions formerly found only in the developing countries that Lewis described. And debts of individuals, both from failed mortgages and bad education, have mushroomed to a size where they impede consumer spending and delay a full recovery from the financial crisis of 2008.

I close in part IV by comparing the American experience to that of other prosperous countries to show opportunities for change that are possible if we want to alter our current policies. Some countries have followed our pattern of rapidly increasing income inequality. Other countries have moderated this development by instituting programs to help ordinary people keep up at least partially with the advancing income at the top of their societies. The trend of separating rich and poor within a country can be damped down by policies that address the problems outlined in this book.

But in America, the Lewis model of a dual economy applies. It shows why the upper sector wants to keep wages low in the lower sector—and that is exactly what has been happening in the United States for the last forty years. This book draws on economics, politics, and history to explain how our changing technology affects us all, and why we cannot design a better country as if our previous history had not taken place. Our initial economic growth was supported by slavery, and we fought a bloody Civil War to end slavery. The legacy of history has driven us to a position where American society has divided into two distinct sectors. We need to understand this existing economic structure to think how we can weave our diverse nation's disparate parts into some kind of unified fabric in the future.

I have been thinking about the issues raised here for a decade, ever since I wrote a paper on income inequality with Frank Levy. Then my wife and I taught a course titled The New Jim Crow at the Harvard Institute for Learning in Retirement and formed a racial justice group there. I wrote a paper on these themes, which I now have expanded into this book.[10] I thank Robert C. Allen, Stanley L. Engerman, Thomas Ferguson, Rob Johnson, Frank Levy, Linda K. Kerber, Michael J. Piore, and Robert M. Solow for useful comments on this book and the members of seminars at the Harvard Institute for Learning in Retirement, the Economics Department of the University of Michigan, the National Institute for Economic and Social Research (London), the Institute for New Economic Thinking, and the Economic History Seminar at Columbia University for their helpful feedback. I also thank my editor at the MIT Press, Emily Taber, for her detailed and excellent editorial comments and my assistant at MIT, Emily Gallagher, for the many large and small assignments she has helped me with. I thank the librarians at MIT's Dewey Library, named after Davis Rich Dewey, older brother of John Dewey, who I quote later in this book, for help finding the books I needed. Finally, I thank the Institute for New Economic Thinking for financial support and the Russell Sage Foundation for a fellowship as I started on the research that led to this book.[11]

I

An American Dual Economy

1

A Dual Economy

The American middle class is vanishing, as can be seen vividly in figure 1. The middle class's share of total income fell 30 percent in forty-four years. This is a big change for the United States; one that we need to comprehend in order to adapt to or change. We have to look beyond this graph in order to understand what is happening. Why did the Pew Research Center begin its graph in 1970? What can we expect to happen in the near future?

There was good reason to start in 1970. Real wages stopped growing at that time, as shown in figure 2. Wages had grown with the rest of the economy since the end of the Second World War. National production continued to grow after 1970, but wages did not. Somehow wages were disconnected from what we all regarded as economic growth.

This disconnect has been noticed widely. John Edwards, a presidential candidate, observed in 2004, "We shouldn't have two different economies in America: one for people who are set for life, they know their kids and their grand-kids are going to be just fine; and then one for most Americans, people who live paycheck to paycheck."[1]

Where did the rest of the national product go? Not to the lower group shown in figure 1. It went instead to the upper group as shown in figure 3. This well-known graph comes from Thomas Piketty, author of *Capitalism in the Twenty-First Century*, and his colleagues who have developed data for the richest 1 percent of the population for many countries as far back as the data allow. The top group in figure 1 contains 20 percent of the population, and the path of what is called the "one percent" shows the pattern. Chrystia Freeland calls this group "the plutocrats." A graph of the next 19 percent looks like figure 3, albeit not quite as steep. And a graph of college graduates—representing something close to the top 30 percent of the population—shows that the educational premium has risen as well. The higher one goes in the income distribution, the more rapid

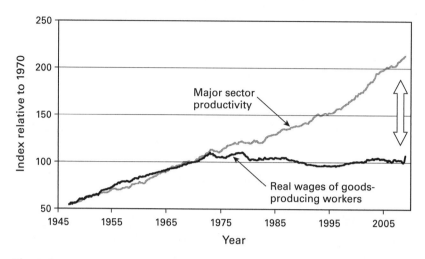

Figure 2
Productivity and average real earnings
Source: Bickerton and Gourevitch 2011, using data from the US Bureau of Labor Statistics

the growth of incomes in recent decades, and the pattern of differential growth extends to the upper 20 percent of the income distribution.[2]

Graphs like figures 2 and 3 have become common since the global financial crisis of 2008, although the two curves often are discussed by different people. The decline in the growth of workers' compensation has been cited as a cause of the 2008 financial crisis as workers borrowed on the security of their houses to sustain their rising consumption that rising incomes had supported before 1980. And the growth of high incomes has been the stuff of recent political discussions as fundraising looms ever more important in American politics.

I argue here that the disparity between the lines in these figures has increased to the point where we should think of a *dual economy* in the United States. The upper sector represented in figure 1 contains 20 percent of the population. Their fortunes have separated from the rest of the county; the low-wage sector contains the remaining 80 percent whose income is not growing. I analyze this disparity using this simple theory, and I examine the important role that race plays in political choices that affect public policies in this dual economy.

W. Arthur Lewis, a professor at the University of Manchester in England, proposed a theory of economic development in a paper

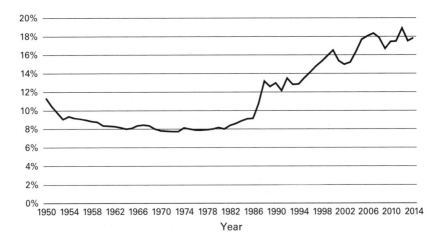

Figure 3
Top 1 percent income share in the United States
Source: http://www.wid.world/

published in 1954. He noted that development did not progress only country by country, but also by parts of countries. Economic progress was not uniform, but spotty. Ports where merchants organized trade in and out of a county might well grow rich before the country as a whole. Parts of a country might grow apart as a result. Lewis wanted to generalize from examples like this to learn how the parts of such an economy related to each other.[3]

Lewis assumed that developing countries often have what has come to be called a dual economy. He termed the two sectors, "capitalist" and "subsistence" sectors. The capitalist sector was the home of modern production using both capital and labor. Its development was limited by the amount of capital in the economy. The subsistence sector was composed of poor farmers where the population was so large relative to the amount of land or natural resources that the productivity of the last worker put to work—called the "marginal product" by economists—was close to zero. The addition of another farmer would not add to the total production. The new worker would be like a fifth wheel on your car.

Lewis followed the practice of economists by summarizing whatever differences there might be in parts of an economy into just two sectors.

To take the example of a port and the countryside, Lewis saw the port as the capitalist sector and the countryside as the sector of subsistence farmers. He assumed there were lots of farmers on limited land, so that meant they were poor farmers. His model is not applicable to every country with a port or an industrial area, but only to countries in which the rest of the economy is characterized by a surplus of workers.

Lewis was thinking of countries in Asia, Africa, and Latin America where there were many farmers engaged in small-scale agriculture and only a few areas where long-distance trade or industrial production was taking place. China was perhaps the largest country he considered. It had expanding trade and production areas on its coast where it was communicating with European and American traders, and it had desperately poor farmers in the center of the country who were producing barely enough for their families to get by. Smaller Asian countries also were dual economies, and several of them grew rapidly in the 1960s and 1970s as they expanded to bring almost the whole population into the capitalist sector. Japan, Korea, and Malaysia are known for these "growth miracles."[4]

Lewis noted that wages in the capitalist sector were higher than in the subsistence sector because work in the port or factory was aided by capital and required more skills than farming. In addition, capitalists constantly were seeking to hire more workers to expand production. He argued that wages in the capitalist sector were linked to the farmers' earnings because capitalists needed to attract workers to their sector by offering a premium over farming wages to induce farmers and farmworkers to leave their familiar homes and activities.

Lewis argued that this linkage gave capitalists an incentive to keep down the wages of subsistence workers. Business leaders in the capitalist sector want to keep their labor costs low. The wages they need to offer are the sum of the basic low wage plus the premium offered to attract low-wage workers to their sector. The business leaders cannot influence the premium, but they can work to keep wages in the subsistence sector low.

Since this is an important part of the Lewis model, it is worth quoting his words. He said, "The fact that the wage level in the capitalist sector depends upon earnings in the subsistence sector is sometimes of immense political importance, since its effect is that capitalists have a direct interest in holding down the productivity of the subsistence workers." Going further and equating capitalists with imperialists, he continued, "The imperialists invest capital and hire workers; it is to their advantage to keep wages low, and even in those cases where they do not actually go out of their way to impoverish the subsistence economy, they will at least very seldom be found doing anything to make it more productive."[5]

The dynamics of this dual economy came from the expansion of the capitalist sector. Capital initially was scarce, giving rise to isolated locations of factory employment. Savings initially were low because subsistence workers consume all or close to all of their incomes. Savings increased as profits and rents grew in the capitalist sector, and the reinvestment of profits to purchase or construct more capital led to the expansion of the capitalist sector. Although the capitalist sector initially appeared as a series of islands, they can be seen as one sector due to the mobility of capital that equalized the earnings from capital. Not every island needed to have the same average productivity, but profits from the last bit of investment in each case—again, marginal profit to economists—would be the same. If a new machine or productive unit was added, it would be equally productive on any island.

Lewis assumed that the difference between the two sectors was not simply in their incomes, but also in their thought processes. Subsistence workers think only of surviving, or living day to day, from paycheck to paycheck. Businessmen in the capitalist sector are maximizing profits and trying to do so by finding the best place and activity to invest. That is the process that results in the marginal profit being the same in different parts of the capitalist sector of a dual economy.[6]

This model received a lot of attention when it was published, and Lewis was honored with a Nobel Prize in Economics for it in 1979. He noted the link between wages in the two sectors without detailing the transition from one to the other. Some years later, other economists proposed that the transition be considered a rational choice by the worker. They extended Lewis's assumption of economic rationality from the capitalist to the subsistence sector. They argued that a farmer thinking of moving to the city was attracted by the wage available in the city, which was substantially higher than the wage he was earning in the countryside. He would leave if his *expected wage* in the city would be larger; the expected wage is the product of the wage differential and the probability that the worker would find a high-paying job in the city. The farmer was assumed to anticipate both the higher wage and the difficulty of obtaining a job that paid this wage.[7]

The economists recognized that the effort to transfer into the capitalist sector was neither certain nor swift. It was not enough to move to the city; the aspiring worker had to find a good job. We know that this was hard to do from the massive slums that surround all big cities in developing countries. These slums are full of migrants who came to the city and then failed to find a good job. The economists recognized this difficulty by noting that the migrant only had a probability—hardly a certainty—of finding a job in the capitalist sector.

Many factors influenced the fortunes of the aspiring migrants, from their prior education to their personality, from who they knew in the city to pure luck in meeting new people. The economists did not ignore these individual traits; they summarized the mostly unobservable characteristics and events into a probability distribution. And they implicitly saw this distribution as the sum of many underlying influences more or less randomly distributed among the migrants, yielding a bell-shaped probability distribution.[8]

What then determined the average probability of finding a good job in the city? The many determinants of the average can be divided into supply and demand. The supply of new jobs will be increased if the growth of the capitalist sector is rapid. And the demand for new jobs in the capitalist sector will be increased if it is easy for farmers to go to the city and try their chances. These factors clearly vary from time to time and place to place.

The names for the sectors that Lewis chose were transformed into urban and rural sectors in articles using the Lewis model to analyze developing countries. I transform them further as I apply the Lewis model to the United States today. I observe the division of the American economy into two separate groups in a different way than the typical division of urban and rural, but very much in the spirit of Lewis's model. I distinguish workers by the skills and occupations of the two sectors. The first sector consists of skilled workers and managers who have college degrees and command good and even very high salaries in our technological economy. I call this the FTE sector to highlight the roles of finance, technology, and electronics in this part of the economy. The other group consists of low-skilled workers who are suffering some of the ills of globalization. I call this the low-wage sector to highlight the role of politics and technology in reducing the demand for semi-skilled workers.

The wages in the two sectors then can be seen in figures 2 and 3. Figure 2 shows the stagnation of average wages for the last generation. The workers with stagnant wages are the analogue of Lewis's subsistence sector, although these workers earn well above what we think of as the earnings of actual subsistence farmers. (Lewis noted that wages typically were above that primitive threshold even in subsistence farming.)

Figure 3 shows the wages of the top earners in the FTE sector. As noted already, the wages of others in this sector have risen in the last generation, although not at the same rate as the top 1 percent.[9]

The division between the two sectors divides the economy unevenly. The FTE sector includes about 20 percent of the population, while the low-wage sector contains the other 80 percent. These numbers come from the Pew Research Center's report that contains figure 1. The middle group contains households earning from two-thirds to twice the median income, that is, from $40,000 to $120,000 for a family of three in 2014.

The middle and lower groups of families were 50 and 30 percent respectively of the population. The proportions in the three groups have changed a bit over time. There were 10 percent more people in the middle class in 1970, 60 percent instead of 50 percent, and they were better off as the figure illustrates. The other groups were each about 5 percent smaller in 1970, and the population gains in the upper and lower groups accentuate the division between the two sectors of the dual economy.

Whites and Asians were less likely to be in the lower group and more likely to be in the upper group than the national average. Blacks and Latinos were more likely to be in the lower group and less likely to be in the upper group. Blacks became less likely to be in the lower group over time, although blacks today still are far less likely than whites or Asians to be in the upper group. African Americans were advancing into the middle class before the financial crash of 2008, but they have been frustrated since then by losing housing capital and good jobs. Latinos were more likely to be in the lower group over time. Recent immigrants from Mexico and other Latin American countries are in danger of being trapped in the low-wage sector.[10]

It may make these numbers more meaningful to think of our population as being roughly divided between groups that were here before 1970 and groups that have come to America since then. In the group that has been here longer, white Americans dominate both the FTE sector (the upper group in figure 1) and the low-wage sector, while African Americans are located almost entirely in the low-wage sector. In the group of recent immigrants, Asians predominantly entered the FTE sector, while Latinos joined African Americans in the low-wage sector. Asian immigrants are only slightly more than 5 percent of the population, while Latino immigrants have grown to around 17 percent and now are more numerous than African Americans.

Phrased differently, the FTE sector is largely white, with few representatives from other groups. The low-wage sector is more varied, with a mix of whites, blacks, and Latinos ("browns"). The low-wage sector is about 50 percent white, with the other half composed more or less equally of African Americans and Latino immigrants.

Figure 1 reveals the changes in incomes before taxation. When taxes and government benefits are subtracted and added, the resulting pattern of differential growth is softened but not eliminated. Family income for working families has stayed constant since the 1970s, but the disposable income of these families has risen as a result of increasing tax incentives and benefits for working people. The contrast between the two sectors is not erased by shifting to disposable income, but the division between them is reduced. The United States still has the most unequal distribution of after-tax income in the world for people under age 60, that is, for working people. Retail stores catering to the vanishing middle class are failing.[11]

The rising inequality of income has led to an increase in the inequality of wealth in America. People with high incomes save more of their income than poorer people, and high earned income resulted in high capital growth. The wealth share of the top tenth of the top 1 percent has tripled since 1978 and now is near 1916 and 1929 levels. The share of the middle class fell from 35 percent of national wealth to 23 percent in 2012. The middle-class share of wealth is lower than the middle-class share of income in figure 1, and it suffered a similar fall.[12]

The link between the two parts of the modern dual economy is education, which provides a possible path that the children of low-wage workers can take to move into the FTE sector. This path is difficult, however, and strewn with obstacles that keep the numbers of children who make this transition small. Thirty percent of Americans have graduated from college, and this provides an upper bound of membership in the FTE sector, but a college education does not by itself guarantee a high and rising income. The choice of major, the state of the business cycle, and other less intangible personal characteristics affect the relation between education—called human capital by economists—and income. Just as relocating to the city in the original Lewis model did not guarantee the migrant farmworker would find a good urban job, a college graduate today is not certain to find a job in the FTE sector.

In addition, the path to the FTE sector is difficult because education requires a change of attitude as well as an increase in knowledge. This follows the Lewis model where people in the two sectors of the economy are assumed to think differently. Subsistence farmers think only of surviving for another season, while capitalists maximize profits over a longer period.[13]

Education has a long payoff and requires attention over many years before its benefits are apparent. This difficulty may be seen within the FTE sector as similar to the issues in saving for retirement or persuading children to continue piano lessons. In addition, the gains from education are varied, and the educational system needs to be structured to help students learn many dimensions of knowledge. Problems in the education system that result from politics and societal decisions are in addition to the problems of individual students.

Many people in the low-wage sector see the gains that accrue from moving into the FTE sector, but they know that any attempt entails risks. Despite all the efforts that low-wage-earning parents can muster for their children, there is only a small probability that their children will be able to complete this long transition and achieve the desired move into the FTE sector. This probability is determined by the FTE sector's limitation of schools funding and by the attitudes of individual students.

Lewis argued that the size of the capitalist sector (FTE sector in my version) was limited by the amount of capital. Working within a traditional economic framework, Lewis interpreted capital as being factories and infrastructure. Research over the past fifty years since he created his model has expanded this concept; I draw on this research to detail the kind of capital that is needed in the FTE sector in my version of a dual economy. This sector is limited by the availability of three kinds of capital. The first kind is physical capital—machines and buildings—used to produce products that people will buy. The second kind is what economists call human capital, the gains from education. The transition from the low-wage sector to the FTE sector involves education because human capital is needed for almost all jobs in the FTE sector. The third kind of capital is social capital, which means maintaining the widespread trust of others and interpersonal networks that help people get jobs, find opportunities for advancement, and provide feedback on innovative ideas.[14]

Robert Putnam, who popularized the concept of social capital among social scientists, stressed the importance of education in his most recent book, *Our Kids*. This collection of interviews makes the argument that our economy has separated into rich and poor. Putnam identified the division between them as a college education. I argue here that people in the FTE sector, the rich, are less numerous than Putnam implied because not all college graduates find jobs that pay well. Despite this minor difference,

Putnam's vivid interviews provide human examples of many of the points made here.[15]

The FTE sector functions in the long run as standard economic growth models predict. Capital—physical, human, and social—comes from savings and produces more output. It is important to include social capital on both the input and output sides. Trust and networks are important for productivity, and the capital of finance, for example, is not primarily physical capital. This is not the place to try and calculate the productivity of finance, but it clearly is a growing part of national income. The FTE sector retains much of the favored position of white males that characterized earlier growth. Women and blacks have made progress but there is still a long way to go toward equality. They are still underrepresented in positions of wealth and high incomes.[16]

There is an important asymmetry between figures 2 and 3. Significantly fewer people are described in figure 3, but they exert far more political power. One purpose of this book is to describe the framework within which many political decisions are made. Members of the FTE sector are largely unaware of the low-wage sector, and they often forget about the needs of its members. In addition, the top 1 percent exerts disproportionate power within the FTE sector, and its members' political decisions accentuate the differences between the two sectors because they would rather lower their taxes than deal with societal problems, as Lewis argued. Their political power has inhibited full recovery from the crisis of 2008 by preventing fiscal-policy expansion.[17]

The members of the low-wage sector are diverse, but many who aspire to move into the FTE sector through education face growing difficulties. The first reason is the geography of residents. Poverty is concentrated in inner cities, and schools in those areas are famously challenged in their ability to engage students in academic pursuits. Attempts to deal with school problems have led to universal testing, which leads teachers and students to focus on elementary skills. The areas of education that are not tested increasingly are neglected. Gone is the excitement of exploring more advanced areas. Gone is attention to intangible aspects of education that promote social capital. Support for maintaining these obstacles often is presented in the context of keeping African Americans "in their place." While blacks are a minority even in the low-wage sector, the focus on blacks in public and political discussions helps obscure the problems of low-wage whites.[18]

The result is that education, which long ago was a force for improvement of the entire labor force, has become a barrier reinforcing the dual economy. For most young people, education is appropriate for the economy they are growing up in, and the contrast between suburban schools for the FTE sector and urban schools for the low-wage sector is increasing. The decline of racially integrated schools is part of this process, as African Americans and now also Latinos are concentrated in urban schools, and the politics of improving urban schools has become entangled with America's long history of racial politics. The problems of American education cannot be understood without understanding the racial and gender history of the United States. I review this history in chapter 5 to provide background for the analysis of politics today.

2

The FTE Sector

The United States was turbulent in the 1960s. The Civil Rights Movement roiled the South and led President Johnson to lobby Congress to pass the Civil Rights Act of 1964, which forbade discrimination in employment and public accommodations, and the Voting Rights Act of 1965, which authorized the federal government to ban state barriers to African American voting under the Fifteenth Amendment. These acts should not have been necessary, since the constitutional amendments passed just after the Civil War granted African Americans full citizenship. Americans of European descent, however, opposed this sudden equality, and the Civil Rights Movement of the 1960s was an effort to gain full citizenship for blacks. The backlash from this movement was one of the pillars of the subsequent policies, as will become clear later.

At the same time as he fought for these bills, Johnson dramatically expanded American expenditures and forces in Vietnam. Reluctant to raise taxes soon after the Kennedy tax cut of the previous year and lacking congressional support as well, he overheated the economy and put great pressure on the value of the dollar, fixed at that time by the Bretton Woods system that regulated international commerce after the Second World War. The postwar dollar shortage turned into a dollar glut.[1]

President Nixon set himself up in opposition to Johnson. He won election to the presidency through a Southern Strategy that appealed to Southern racism and opposition to the Civil Rights Movement. He abandoned Johnson's War on Poverty and declared a War on Drugs in 1971. He also abandoned the fixed exchange rate of the Bretton Woods system to deal with the strain on the dollar exerted by the expanding war in Vietnam.[2] Nixon switched the United States to a floating exchange rate, transferring responsibility for the domestic economy from the federal government, which controls fiscal policy, to the Federal Reserve System, which controls monetary policy. The Fed had been securing the exchange rate for the previous quarter century, and it had to learn how to fulfill its new role. This process was complicated greatly when the Organization of Petroleum Exporting Countries (OPEC) quadrupled the price of oil in 1973. The resulting "Oil Shock" sent many prices—including exchange rates—in motion.[3]

Anticipation of the Oil Shock led President Nixon to propose "Project Independence" in November 1971. Nixon's emphasis was on domestic production and consumption, and his policy implied that the United States was to remain passive in the face of OPEC provocation. This idea was transformed over the next few years into a more active stance that would seek steady supplies of oil from the Middle East. Nixon also replaced the ailing draft for Army soldiers with the volunteer army at this time, a plan he also started before the Oil Shock. The draft had become difficult as the Vietnam War dragged on, and conservatives argued against the idea of forced service. This was an early step in the privatization of the military.[4]

The Oil Shock also raised the question of how the members of OPEC were going to hold their newly acquired wealth. The highly regulated financial system established at Bretton Woods in the 1940s could not easily absorb this large inflow of cash, and the cash found a temporary home in the arrangement for dollar deposits outside the United States. These dollar deposits in European banks were known as Eurodollars, and they were not heavily regulated by either the United States or Europe. Much of the cash went to Switzerland, where banks were willing to preserve the anonymity of the depositors. The combination of changing prices and large amounts of money seeking a safe home led to demands to deregulate the financial system that stimulated a general push for deregulation and affected policy decisions in the following decades.[5]

The Fed did not know how to contain the price shocks of the 1970s, and "stagflation"—both inflation and unemployment—was the result. President Carter tried to end this monetary chaos by appointing Alfred Kahn to head the Council on Wage and Price Stability and promote deregulation and then, under pressure, Paul Volcker to chair the Federal Reserve System and rein in inflation. Kahn, banned from using the term "recession," famously said, "Let's call our condition a banana." Volcker dramatically raised interest rates sharply and slowed the growth of money. The result was a sharp recession in 1981–1982 with massive unemployment followed by stable prices. Exchange rates fluctuated widely, putting strain on many industries. Banking problems led the government to deregulate Savings and Loan Associations (S&Ls), leading to excessive borrowing and failures of one third of the S&Ls in the 1980s.

In retrospect, the S&L crisis anticipated the financial crisis of 2008. Deregulation led to excessive speculative activity that eventually went bad. It took a decade for the federal government to raise taxes to pay off the $100 billion debt it incurred in paying for guaranteed deposits. It was not seen as a cost of deregulation at the time, even though raising taxes may have cost the first President Bush his job.

The S&L crisis instead was seen as a bump in the road to economic deregulation that would come to be called "neoliberalism." That is one term for it, but its adherents call themselves "conservatives." Both labels reveal their desire to return to the world as they imagine it before the wars and depression of the early twentieth century. Some of them go back even further, starting from the states' rights position of the slave-owning South before the Civil War.

Lewis Powell, a successful corporate attorney, crystalized this ideology and presented a plan of action—a call to arms—in a secret memorandum to the United States Chamber of Commerce contemporaneous with Nixon's actions changing American society. The coincident events of 1971 were tied together when Nixon appointed Powell to the Supreme Court later that year.

The Powell Memo opened: "No thoughtful person can question that the American economic system is under broad attack. This varies in scope, intensity, in the techniques employed, and in the level of visibility." It stated: "The overriding first need is for businessmen to recognize that the ultimate issue may be survival—survival of what we call the free enterprise system, and all that this means for the strength and prosperity of America and the freedom of our people." It argued that business should defend itself vigorously in the press, academically and in Congress and the courts.[6]

The Heritage Foundation was formed in 1973, shortly after Powell's memo. It was supported initially by Richard Mellon Scaife, principal heir to the Mellon banking and oil fortune. Its mission is stated on its website: "The Heritage Foundation is a research and educational institution—a think tank—whose mission is to formulate and promote conservative public policies based on the principles of free enterprise, limited government, individual freedom, traditional American values, and a strong national defense."[7] Charles Koch, owner of a privately held oil firm that has made him and his brother among the wealthiest people in the country, was galvanized by the Powell Memo and formed the Cato Institute, a more academic conservative think tank, a few years later.

The references to "the freedom of our people" by Powell and "individual freedom" by The Heritage Foundation were code words for opposition to unions. They harked back to a mythical past where individual and small factory owners bargained equally about pay and working conditions. This view of the past is totally inaccurate as a description of early industrialization. Laws at that time put workers at a great disadvantage by making it a criminal act to leave a job to search for a better one. Destroying unions in the modern world puts workers again in a grossly inferior position when confronting employers.[8]

The language also harked back to the Declaration of Independence, notably "We believe all men are created equal." Our forefathers may have said "all men," but they really meant all white men. It would not be until the Civil War was fought over this issue that the idea of expanding the idea of equality was even possible. Today, while the appeal to individual freedom has economics as its source, this appeal to an iconic American ideal also has a racial overtone.[9]

Powell also wrote that "few elements of American society today have as little influence in government as the American businessman." Organized lobbying of Congress began at this time, stimulated in part by this statement. Lobbying is expensive to initiate but cheap to maintain, leading to declining average costs and the growth of large lobbying firms. The growth of lobbying firms has made it very difficult for small firms to be heard and for Congress to pass coherent legislation. The overpowering clout of lobbyists led to their being more than 300,000 words in both the Affordable Care Act and the Dodd-Frank Financial Reform Act. These important bills are filled with definitions, qualifications, and exceptions to satisfy not only Congress but also the lobbyists.[10]

In addition to lobbying, businesses and industry associations began to support specialized think tanks. The Heritage Foundation and the Cato Institute were joined by a plethora of think tanks that reflect corporate interests in many fields. The think tanks are tax exempt and need to be careful about explicitly championing government policies. They can, however, support points of view by choosing who to hire and retain in return for tax-exempt contributions by corporate interests. This kind of influence extends from general think tanks like the Brookings Institution, which supports corporate efforts to rebuild damaged cities, to the United States Institute for Peace, which supports defense spending here and abroad.[11]

The conservative American Legislative Exchange Council, known as ALEC, was formed in 1973 in order to influence state legislation. Charles and David Koch founded and funded ALEC as a nonprofit corporation to advance conservative principles of free market, limited government, and individual liberty. ALEC drafts model legislation to achieve these ends and distributes them to state legislation. Around one-fifth of its proposed legislation gets passed somewhere in the country.

ALEC has about two thousand Republican state lawmakers as members. Its task forces recommend model bills to reduce the regulation of business, privatize public services, cut taxes—particularly for wealthy individuals and large companies—and restrict the efforts of unions. ALEC also organizes meetings for members to learn about specific issues along these lines and provides a network where members can meet other political leaders and business representatives.

State legislatures passed 231 ALEC bills in 1995. Almost every state passed at least one ALEC bill, and Virginia passed twenty-one bills that year. The median state passed three ALEC bills, and the mean was five. A statistical analysis showed that the time and resources available to legislators had a large effect on how many ALEC bills were passed. Legislators with the least time to spend passed a dozen more ALEC bills than legislators who had the most time. The most conservative legislature passed five more ALEC bills than the most liberal legislature, and legislatures with the most business-friendly members were able to pass three more ALEC bills than the legislatures that were the friendliest to organized labor. ALEC is one of the ways that the Koch brothers and their supporters affect political outcomes. Started soon after Powell wrote his secret memo, ALEC remains the only well-funded national legislative organization, and its success shows that there are other ways to affect public policy than to elect favorable representatives.[12]

Limited government was first expressed in the deregulation of finance and airlines in the 1970s, and "individual freedom" was code for the destruction of unions. The failure of a bill to reform labor law in 1978 reveals the change in opinion under way. The bill proposed a set of technical changes in labor law that would have preserved the legal framework in which the U.S. labor system operated. Despite the small scale of the bill, business groups mounted a large, inflammatory public campaign against it. The bill passed the U.S. House of Representatives by a vote of 257 to 163 and undoubtedly would have passed the Senate as well, but employers arranged to have it stopped by a filibuster.[13]

The sharp recession started by Volcker's contractionary monetary policy compressed a generation of normal change into a few years. Durable manufacturing firms—pillars of private-sector unionization—were hit first by recession in the 1970s and then by a high dollar in the 1980s that crippled export sales. The Rural Renaissance of the Midwest in the 1970s became a Rust Belt in the 1980s as the low dollar during 1970s stagflation was succeeded by a high dollar in the 1980s.[14]

Unions were left behind as public policy changed. African Americans moved north in preceding decades to join unions to better their wages and working conditions. This long process, known as the Great Migration, lasted from 1915 to 1970, involved about six million migrants, and produced large black populations in the North and West. It began during the First World War when Northern manufacturers were supplying war goods to the Europeans and trying to expand their production. They needed more labor to produce more goods, but immigration was cut off by the war. They encouraged blacks to move from the South to take these jobs.

The process continued after the war when an isolationist reaction led to immigration restrictions. Northern employers needed workers, and blacks were hired. But all was not rosy for the migrating workers. The Great Migration was both a geographic change and a move from the country to the city. As noted by Lewis in his model, this was a big change, and not all new residents in industrial cities fared well. The mixed results are described in *The Warmth of Other Suns*, Isabel Wilkerson's magisterial description of the Great Migration.[15]

But as African Americans tried to join unions in the North, they found that the members of established unions did not want to give them full status in their unions and they were not willing to acknowledge unions of black workers as equals. The sources of this opposition to black workers were many and complex. They started from racial prejudice and the fear of losing their superiority to another group. They also included the difficulty of absorbing rural Southerners into Northern cities as cultures clashed. White Northerners moved out of cities as African Americans moved in during the Great Migration, and the position of union members was part of this enduring American problem.[16]

Lawyers representing the new African American workers shifted their efforts from labor law to constitutional law to get more traction. They supported federal legislation like the Civil Rights Act of 1964 that banned discrimination. And because unions were excluding African Americans, the lawyers supported open shops, not the union shops preferred by unions where everyone was represented by and paid dues to one dominant union. In the 1980s business supporters of open shops drew on these precedents, but they abandoned the quest for labor equality.[17]

Right at this time, in the middle of the economic disturbances of the 1970s, the real wages of workers stopped growing. As shown in figure 2, the economy continued on its upward trajectory while the average wage stagnated. No one noticed this in the 1970s in the midst of both inflation and unemployment. Even if some people saw what was happening, they could not tell immediately if this was only a temporary aberration during stagflation.

Powell's call to arms for business cohered into what is now called a neoliberal philosophy. It is useful to see this new policy direction in terms of the New Federalism that Nixon proposed in 1969 and the Washington Consensus formulated for developing countries in the 1990s. The New Federalism proposed to counter federal control of Roosevelt's New Deal by converting specific grants to states into block grants, that is, shifting control over federal money from federal to state governments where state officials could preserve racial discrimination. Among the recommendations in common with the Washington Consensus are the desire for fiscal discipline in place of Keynesian polices, low marginal tax rates, low tariffs, privatization of state enterprises, and deregulation of private markets. Neoliberals added freedom of contracts, by which they typically mean opposition to labor unions, and they abandoned the postwar mandate to maintain full employment.[18]

Modern conservatives fear the power of the federal government that grew in the world wars and Great Depression, and they oppose the redistribution in a welfare state. They oppose the New Deal and unions as an "excess of democracy," whatever that phrase means. They believe that the free market is equivalent to freedom itself and that regulating markets means surrendering political liberty. They draw their inspiration from Friedrich Hayek and Ayn Rand. There is an implicit political theory there that will be described in more detail in part II.[19]

This conservative philosophy represented a change in the intellectual legacy of the preceding thirty years of war and depression from John Maynard Keynes to Hayek. Keynes championed the role of government in achieving prosperity and well-being for the citizens of a democracy. Hayek focused on individual activity as the source of prosperity, and he rejected government in his most popular book, *The Road to Serfdom*. American economists rejected Keynes in the turbulent 1970s in favor of individual initiatives, and Keynesian macroeconomics was relegated to undergraduate courses. Professional publications amplified Hayek, while economic policymakers still rely on Keynes.[20]

As noted in the introduction, Ronald Reagan announced his 1980 presidential candidacy in Philadelphia, Mississippi, where three young civil-rights workers were murdered in 1964. He did not have to say a word to communicate his opposition to full citizenship of black Americans. His announcement illustrates the shift in political discourse from overt racism to codes in actions and words. Reagan continued this indirection through the implementation of Nixon's New Federalism, which allowed Southern states to continue to exploit the legacy of slavery.

The Reagan administration often is seen as ushering in the neoliberal policy stance because he began his presidency by announcing in his inaugural address that "government is not the solution to our problem; government is the problem." This anarchist position was the result of the arguments from the Heritage Foundation and the Cato Institute. It signaled a sea change in politics that had been engineered by corporate leaders responding to Powell's secret memo. Reagan destroyed the flight controllers' union—the Professional Air Traffic Controllers Organization (PATCO)—at the start of his administration, even though PATCO was the only union that had supported him, signaling his intent to continue the war on unions. But deregulation and the privatization of government functions like the military and prisons started earlier than when he began his first term in 1981 and continued after he left office in 1989.

Reagan lowered top marginal income tax rates for the rich in two tax cuts. He expanded military spending at the same time to threaten the Soviet Union. This combination led to large government deficits despite Reagan's promise to balance the budget. And it confirmed the exception to the small government that he was proposing. The true conservative position was a government that supported the military and did not otherwise care for its citizens.

The second tax cut in 1986 coincided with the beginning of the rise in the share of income going to the top 1 percent of the population shown in figure 3. This rise also was a consequence of the wage stagnation revealed in figure 2. Stagnant wages were not maintaining workers' share of the growing national income, and some other group's share had to rise. As shown in figures 1 and 3, it was the share of the rich that rose. Reagan's tax reforms emboldened corporate leaders to claim their part of this rise.

The Congressional Budget Office summarized the result: "For households in the top 1 percent of the income distribution, inflation-adjusted after-tax income grew at an estimated average rate of 3.5 percent per year. As a result, inflation-adjusted after-tax income was 200 percent higher in 2011 than it was in 1979 for households in that group. In contrast, households in the bottom quintile experienced inflation-adjusted after-tax income growth of 1.2 percent per year, on average. Consequently, inflation-adjusted after-tax income was 48 percent higher in 2011 than it was in 1979 for that income group."[21]

The most important part of the new program was the deregulation of finance. Instead of bringing the Eurodollar system into the Bretton Woods system, new policies made American finance more like the Eurodollar system. There was a great need for financial help as the gyrations of prices and exchange rates in the 1970s and early 1980s took a fearsome toll on American industry. Resources needed to be shifted from one industry to another, and finance was needed to buy and sell companies in this process. Financial people argued that the great needs of finance required free hands to manage the economic transformation.

The nation's financial sector grew dramatically during the 1980s. Reagan's twin policies of low taxes and high military expenditures meant large government deficits. High interest rates and large international deficits coming from the high dollar stimulated trading in government securities and corporate takeovers, expanding the demand for financial traders, investment bankers, and corporate legal services. After stagnating in the 1970s, the Dow Jones Industrial Index tripled in the 1980s, attracting people to the brokerage industry.[22]

The rising demand for financial services increased the size of the financial sector and the returns to those employed in it. As deregulation created more need for finance as well as more scope for financial innovation, more educated people were attracted to the field. During the Bretton Woods period, banking was highly regulated and did not attract highly educated people. This changed in the tumultuous 1970s, and more educated people entered the financial sector. The increasing human capital in finance explains most of the rise in financial incomes in the 1980s. Wages in finance professions exceeded the educational premium in other industries after that, perhaps because of increasing risks in finance. This part of the economy accounted for one-seventh of the increase in the incomes of the richest people shown in figure 1.[23]

These high returns to people in finance have now become a matter of public concern. Hedge fund managers are handsomely paid whether the returns to their hedge funds are good or lackluster. The top earners made about $1 billion apiece in 2014 and again in 2015 even though their funds did not fare well. These incomes are lightly taxed due to the carried interest exemption, a tax loophole that taxes the income of hedge fund managers as capital gains instead of labor income, as shown dramatically by presidential candidate Mitt Romney's tax returns. He paid taxes of less than 15 percent of his high income (which was smaller than the financial superstars' incomes just described).[24]

The carried interest loophole is only one of the ways that members of the FTE sector reduce the taxes they pay. As congressional leaders were completing a massive tax and spending bill in late 2015, lobbyists descended from those that started in the early 1970s added fifty-four words that preserved a loophole for real estate and Wall Street investors that enabled them to put real estate in trusts to avoid taxes. The carried interest exemption and real estate trust provision are only two examples of tax loopholes initiated and maintained by lawyers and lobbyists for wealthy people.[25]

The rapid growth and high returns in finance raise questions about the role of finance in economic growth. The great changes in trade and production after the end of Bretton Woods clearly required active finance to accommodate, and there is no reason to deny the importance of finance in allowing economies to adapt to new conditions. But the continuing inflation of financial incomes suggests that private gains to financial activity may be exceeding social gains. We may be attracting bright, educated people to finance when their productivity for economic growth would be better employed elsewhere. This suggestion of diminishing returns to finance may only be answered after we have accumulated more evidence.[26]

The highest paid CEOs of nonfinancial corporations earned an order of magnitude less—dropping one zero—than those in finance, around $100 million in 2014. They represent top earners in the technology and electronics part of the FTE sector. The annual earnings limit for the top 1 percent of earners shown in figure 1 is about three orders of magnitude below this—dropping three zeros—at $330,000, and the wealth limit for the top 1 percent is $4 million.[27]

The FTE sector includes the top 20 percent of American earners, including almost all college graduates even though a BA does not provide automatic access to the FTE sector. The top 10 percent of American earners earn incomes in six figures of $100,000 and above.[28] That is a high enough income to live in a good school district, own your house, and drive a new car. It is what we used to call a good middle-class living, although the term "now evokes anxiety, an uncertain future and a lifestyle that is increasingly out of reach."[29] The median worker earns around $40,000, and the dividing line between the FTE and low-wage sector lies in the gap between these two figures.[30]

Workers in this gap struggle to maintain their middle-class life style. The median college teacher of economics, for example, earns around $100,000, which places him or her comfortably in the FTE sector. The median college teacher of English Language and Literature earns only around $60,000, putting him or her perilously close to the median worker in the low-wage sector.[31]

College graduates who are not clearly in the FTE sector may be idealistic or artistic. For example, "John-David Bowman, who teaches Advanced Placement history and a class called Theory of Knowledge in the International Baccalaureate program at Westwood High School in Mesa, AZ, has not had a raise since he was hired, in 2008. He has two bachelor's degrees and a master's degree, and was voted Arizona's Teacher of the Year for 2015." The honor allowed him to shake hands with President Obama at the White House. Still, Bowman said, "I could retire in 20 years, under $50,000."[32] This distinguished high school teacher is and will remain in the low-wage sector if he continues teaching in this setting.

3

The Low-Wage Sector

President Nixon won the election in 1968 with the aid of a Southern Strategy focusing on regional racial tensions and the history of segregation. The Southern Strategy appealed to white Southerners angered by the threat to their power from the Civil Rights Movement and the expansion of the franchise. They were the heirs of slave owners who resorted to Jim Crow policies after Reconstruction ended to preserve their political power. Their policy was to maintain African Americans in the South in a subordinate position.[1]

The low-wage sector—like the FTE sector—was born in 1971 as President Nixon replaced Johnson's War on Poverty with a new War on Drugs and appointed Lewis Powell to the Supreme Court. As the War on Drugs expanded in subsequent decades, it was enforced far more strongly for African Americans than for whites, becoming, in Alexander's widely used term, the "New Jim Crow," revamping and renewing the racist intent of the repressive old anti-black Jim Crow laws that followed Reconstruction in the South. And Nixon's appointment of Powell, author of the memorandum for the Chamber of Commerce described in chapter 2, unified the class interest of Powell with the race interest of white Southerners in a Southern Strategy. Powell was presented as a moderate compared to Rehnquist—appointed to the Supreme Court at the same time—but Powell was part of Nixon's Southern Strategy. Nixon "told Powell of his responsibility to the South, to the Supreme Court, and to the country," in that order. Powell's Supreme Court votes expanded Nixon's Southern Strategy into national policies.[2]

This expansion was in part a response to the massive movement north of African Americans in the previous decades. The Great Migration, as it is known, started in the First World War when immigration was cut off and the demand for American war matériel grew. Business owners were eager to expand production if they could find workers to operate their factories. African Americans moved north to take these jobs, and businessmen were happy to have American workers instead of more European immigrants. The Great Migration continued until 1970 when the events described here began. People in the North found by then that blacks were in their cities and competing with them for jobs.

Rural people sold food to cities in the Lewis model; members of the low-wage sector typically sell services to the FTE sector in this modern reincarnation of the model. They work in fast-food restaurants and clean hospitals and hotels. They drive people around as needed, transport items in factories and stores, work in nonunionized industries and engage in other similar activities that vary too much for robots to take over. Low wages are the result of decreased labor demand coming from improving technology and increased supply coming from globalization in the varied forms of trade, immigration, and moving production offshore.

These varied forces resulted in a change in the demand for specific jobs that created an "hourglass" job profile, as shown in figure 4. Jobs are arranged by wages in the figure, and it can be seen that the jobs in the middle of the range have been disappearing. The number of these jobs fell by 6 percent between 1993 and 2010, while jobs with higher and lower wages rose. This trend has split the American labor market into a

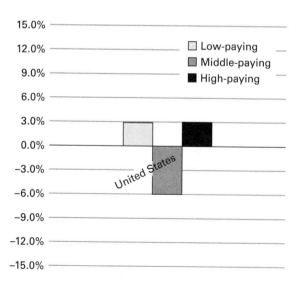

Figure 4
Change in occupational employment shares in low-, middle-, and high-wage occupations in the United States, 1993–2010
Source: Autor and Dorn 2013

low-wage part and a higher-wage part. The division marks the difference between the low-wage sector and the FTE sector of the higher-paid workers. This figure helps explain the decline in the middle class shown in figure 1 by pointing to the changing nature of jobs.

Low-wage workers are laborers and service workers. Middle-wage workers are clerks, operators, and assemblers. Highly paid workers are professionals and managers. A college education is needed to get hired into the top group. It may also be needed for some middle-wage jobs, but these kinds of jobs are disappearing. Lower-paying jobs barely allow workers to maintain the life style they grew up expecting. They do not provide enough income for people to save for retirement, which seems farther away than many current needs. The low-wage sector has very little impact on the progress of the FTE sector.

Figure 4 often is seen as the result of technological change, but technology is only part of the story. Several causes can be distinguished, and they can be divided into domestic and international. All of them are results of decisions made in the nascent FTE sector. Advances in technology and electronics were promoted by government—primarily military—spending. The growing interest in finance shaped firms and industries. Globalization was accelerated by FTE policies opening international capital markets, promoting American foreign investment and American economic influence.

The development of computers in America was an important part of the growth of the FTE sector. Computer capital increasingly substitutes for labor in routine tasks, that is, tasks that can be accomplished by following explicit rules. These factory jobs were the basis of unions in the twentieth century. They also attracted workers in the Great Migration that brought African Americans from the rural South to the urban North. The migration ended in the economic confusion of the 1970s and left the new Northern urban residents scrambling for good jobs as the nature of work changed.

Computers are less able to deal with nonroutine tasks that require problem solving and involve complex and creative thinking, and those that require individual attention to specific people or places. Those jobs can be grouped into professional activities paying well and service jobs paying poorly. The former, well-educated jobs are in the FTE sector. The latter make up the low-wage sector.[3]

The growth of finance has added to problems facing workers by changing the boundaries of companies. In the early twentieth century, a lot of service jobs were performed within large companies. Cleaners, gardeners, drivers, and similar helpers were included on the company payroll. The service workers who worked for large companies tended to be paid more than those that worked in smaller companies, preserving equity among the workers at the large companies.[4]

But as finance expanded in the late 1970s, companies were encouraged to specialize in their core activities, that is, the activities that they were known and patronized for. This would increase their value on the stock market, and outside firms and services could be hired to do menial jobs. The same computers that reduced factory jobs also made it easier to create instructions for service jobs and to monitor them. The company supervisor was replaced by a contract with a separate company that monitored workers. For example, most hotel employees used to work for the hotels they worked in. Today, over 80 percent of a hotel's employees are hired and supervised by a separate management company.[5]

This change in business organization can be accomplished in several ways, through subcontracting, franchising, and supply chains. These are different legal forms, but they all change the relationship between wages and companies. Before, companies and workers considered the equity of the wages that were paid. With all of these forms, wages have been supplanted by prices—the price of hiring the subcontractors and labor suppliers. There may be several tiers between a specific worker and the company where he or she works.

Several conditions are needed to make this new arrangement advantageous. Subcontractors may want to bid low for a service contract, while the parent firm is interested more in the quality of the work. The interests of the subcontractor need to be aligned with those of the parent firm. The alignment can be helped by increased monitoring of the workers, which has become cheaper as a result of the same technology that reduced factory jobs. Tasks need to be precisely defined, and there are now various electronics devices that can monitor individual actions. Parent companies want to avoid being held up by subcontractors who have captured spots in production plans. They seek to hire subcontractors in competitive markets where alternatives are readily available.

These new arrangements work for the company's benefit, but not for the workers' benefit. Wages from the parent company have been replaced by contract prices with companies. The equity considerations that helped workers before are gone. And since the workers are now hired by competitive subcontractors, their wages are compared with the wages of other people doing similar work rather than with the varied employees of the firm. There is no job tenure, no pension plan, and only relentless competitive pressure from the competition of other workers.

The shift from paying wages to hiring subcontractors is a momentous change in the place of workers in a business enterprise. When workers were wage earners, there was a social component to their work. Workers saw themselves as a group, and being a member of a stable group fostered morale. Most successful firms gain from the identification of workers with the firm and the extra care and effort that produces. When workers are hired instead by a competitive service company, they have no identification with the parent firm. They have low morale and will not exert extra effort for the parent company's benefit. Intrusive monitoring replaces morale, and antagonism replaces cooperation.

The increasing role of independent contractors for the low-wage sector can be seen in the switch from consumers using taxi services to using Uber and other computer-based drivers. Uber recently settled a class-action suit by its drivers by paying them a bit more, but continuing to categorize them as independent contractors. And the bargaining power of these independent contractors will fall if Uber replaces them with driverless cars. Drivers now find their way with the aid of Uber maps on their smartphones; driverless cars can use the same maps once they learn how to drive in traffic.[6]

There also has been a sharp reduction in competition among large companies in America due partly to the growth of network effects and partly to a relaxation of antitrust standards for mergers. The reduction in competition is quite widespread, ranging from Apple and Microsoft in networks to agricultural businesses and wireless communication. The first effect is to raise prices to obtain monopoly rents. This reduces the value of poor people's wages. A second effect is to reduce the competition for workers between companies, which directly affects wages. And the growing monopolists may not be as innovative as many independent and rivalrous companies, affecting the long-run growth of the economy.[7]

The growth of finance is reducing competition between firms even more in an indirect way—from the growth of mutual funds. Companies hold reserves for their employees' pensions in mutual funds, and people do the same for their own reserves. Large mutual funds own shares in several firms in an industry and reduce competition between firms through this channel. Firms that are cooperating do not hire people from their fellow firms. The cooperating firms also present a united face to the companies who supply their labor, not allowing competition between them to raise wages. In addition to holding down wages, they also reduce competition in their product markets and raise prices from a competitive level. Worker's real wages suffer both from low wages and high prices.[8]

Competition from new immigrants increased the pressure on wages. A steady stream of migrants came from Latin America in recent decades in search of better jobs. American political and military intervention in Central America stimulated immigration to the United States, since this country has not hesitated to depose Central American leaders who were unfriendly to American businesses. The resulting turmoil diminished national economies in Central America, and emigration northward was an appealing alternative to limited options at home. There were better jobs available in the United States, and conditions at home often were dangerous and even deadly.[9]

As technology decreased the demand for labor within factories and finance reduced direct employment by other large firms, foreign competition reduced the number of factories. The massive inflow of Japanese and then Chinese products reduced the demand for American manufactures at the same time that computers changed the nature of factory work. Japanese cars in the 1980s and an abundance of Chinese consumer goods in the 1990s changed the composition of labor demand in the United States. Manufacturing jobs in the United States fell particularly fast after 2000 when the United States eliminated future tariff rises for Chinese goods. Curiously, this major economic adjustment had very little impact on real earnings, as shown in figure 2.[10]

These imports resulted from the policies of these Asian countries to use low exchange rates to promote exports and economic growth. Just as Britain and Germany expanded industrial exports in the late nineteenth century, these new industrial powers promoted exports to increase their growth a century later. The gyrations of the emerging FTE sector in the 1970s and 1980s described in chapter 2 changed exchange rates as well as domestic prices.

Finally, improved capital mobility coming from the removal of Bretton Woods capital controls allowed American firms to expand production in industrializing countries. These firms used their offshore production in bargaining with their workers. American workers were told they had to accept lower wages in order to maintain their jobs. These threats produced labor unrest, and the government increasingly favored employers as deregulation spread. Unions declined in membership and power.

As a result of improving technology, changing business organizations, imports, immigration, and threats of offshore investments, American wages today are kept down as shown in figure 2. The members of the low-wage sector find themselves in a global labor market, competing for jobs with workers who live on the other side of the world. The effects often are indirect, but they are no less potent for being distant. The cost of transportation is decreasing; even perishable products like flowers and fish are brought from far away. And the decline of tariffs and other barriers to trade mean that governments increasingly open up their economies—and therefore national labor markets—to world influences.[11]

The constancy of real wages since 1970 has had effects in other measures of well-being as well. As wages did not rise with national income, the share of labor income in national income fell. The "labor share," as it is often known, was widely assumed to be a constant of economic growth before 1970. Now we know it can change, and we know that it has decreased as a result of continuing low wages.[12]

In addition, mortality among members of the low-wage sector increased relative to mortality in the FTE sector. The result is that members of the FTE sector now live longer than those in the low-wage sector. This has implications for the social programs discussed further in chapter 12. But even with this basic information, it is clear that the argument that retirement should come later since people live longer is incorrect. Members of the FTE sector live longer, but people who need Social Security or other forms of retirement income are not living longer.[13]

The costs of international trade described here appear to undercut the theory that assures us that trade benefits all countries. The problem is that increased trade has uneven effects in each country; there are winners and losers. The theory of international trade tells us that winners gain more than losers lose, and that winners can compensate losers for their losses and still come out ahead. The theory is fine, but compensation needs to be paid in order for the losers—low-wage workers in this case—to be happy with increased trade. The failure of public policy to take account of the full theory undermines the popularity of globalization.

For example, under competition from foreign auto manufacturers and "transplants" (domestic producers of foreign-owned companies), GM implemented wage cuts in its 2009 bailout and bankruptcy: "Under agreement with the United Autoworkers union, the two-tier wage system was expanded, with wages for new hires cut to about half of the $29 per hour that longtime union members earned (although these wages were then raised to $17 an hour in 2011). Defined benefit pensions were eliminated for new hires and replaced with 401(k) plans. Overall wage and benefit costs at Chrysler and GM were brought down to be roughly in line with those at Honda and Toyota plants operating in the United States."[14]

The union was not broken, but it clearly was unable to resist the pressures put upon it. It was not able to resist having new auto workers paid only as much as those at the mostly Southern and nonunion Honda and Toyota plants. Workers earning $17 an hour earn only about $35,000 a year. In addition, these jobs are being replaced by computers and robots as shown in figure 4, and there will not be many new ones. The few new auto workers will find themselves in the low-wage sector. Their earnings are small. Yet they are expected to set aside some of these inadequate earnings to save for their retirement in their new 401(k) plans. The incomes of low-wage sector members simply are not large enough for them to do so. A recent report on the economic well-being of households found that 40 percent of nonretirees "have given little or no thought to financial planning for retirement."[15]

The decline of manufacturing noted in the FTE sector also had strong geographic effects on the low-wage sector. The growth of Japan and China accelerated the decline of American manufacturing and the demand for unskilled labor in and around factories. Industrial cities found that people were less mobile than jobs, and urban prosperity was replaced by urban joblessness. Black workers moved to Northern cities to find jobs in the Great Migration, only to find that the jobs had disappeared.

The Great Migration, which as noted earlier ended in 1970, did not lead to integrated housing in the North. As soon as Southern black workers appeared in Northern cities, white families began to move out of the cities. White flight was responsible for one-half of the increase in segregation in the 1930s. Prosperous white urban residents continued to leave cities for the suburbs after the Second World War, avoiding newly integrated schools. They were encouraged by the GI Bill and other federal policies that provided generous mortgages for suburban houses and highways for suburbanites to drive to work. Pervasive redlining that denied loans to people in urban areas restricted a comparable mortgage stimulus in the cities, and funding for aging urban transportation systems declined. Home ownership and access to jobs became harder in the city. There is clear evidence of neighborhood tipping, that is, a rapid transition to a very high minority share in a census tract once the minority share reached a threshold varying from 5 percent to 20 percent minority.[16]

White urban workers were replaced by black migrants from the South, aggravating the competition for scarce jobs in the cities. Wages for less-skilled workers declined, and urban unemployment grew. William J.

Wilson observed twenty years ago, "Concentrated poverty is positively associated with joblessness." And the public face of the low-wage sector is black. This merging of class and race fed into political decisions that expanded the Southern Strategy into a national one.[17]

Andrew Cherlin describes urban life in the low-wage sector even for working families as the result of casualization. Work is casual, short-term, not contractual, and unregulated. Family life is similarly casual with low marriage rates even among couples living together and having children. "Casualization, disengagement, rootlessness: these are the descriptors that seem apt" when describing the lives of less-educated young adults. "This situation stands in sharp contrast to the greater stability of the lives of the highly educated" in the FTE sector.[18]

Black Americans are a minority of the population and of the low-wage sector, but the desire to preserve the inferior status of blacks has motivated policies against all members of the low-wage sector. Sometimes "black" is a metaphor for "others." Since the FTE sector includes only the upper 20 percent of the population, blacks—even if they all were members of the low-wage sector—account for less than 20 percent of this sector. Hispanic immigration has brought in so many Latinos that they are now about as numerous as African Americans. Blacks and Latinos make up less than half of the low-wage sector, but not by much.[19]

President Reagan reversed fifty years of American domestic policy as he cut back federal grants to local and state governments that the federal government used to help poor people. Some benefits to individuals increased in the 1980s, but grants to governments declined or even—like general revenue sharing—disappeared. Public service jobs and job training were cut back sharply. The share of federal funding for large cities fell from 22 percent to 6 percent of their budgets. The decline of both private and public sources of employment in inner cities greatly reduced employment opportunities for white and black urban residents alike.[20]

The Reagan and Bush administrations reduced city funding, causing federal funding to drop sharply in the 1980s. Nixon's New Federalism converted federal programs into block grants to states in order to give states more choice in how to spend the money. Reagan then revealed the underlying aim of the New Federalism by reducing and eliminating block grants.[21]

The effects of the New Federalism can be seen in the 2015 crisis of lead in the public water supply to Flint, Michigan. Flint was an auto manufacturing center, but that kind of employment ended soon after the Great Migration brought blacks to Michigan for good jobs. Blacks arrived to find reduced employment, and the city of Flint was unable to pay its bills. Governor Rick Snyder was elected in 2011 and supported a controversial law that allowed him to appoint emergency managers of cities in financial trouble. He put Flint into receivership and appointed an emergency manager in 2012. There were four different managers in the next three years, not an arrangement that was likely to yield comprehensive plans.

An emergency manager took Flint off the Detroit water system to save money in April 2014. He decided to take Flint's water from a local river instead. The immediate result was brown water pouring out of the taps in people's homes, and lots of complaints from residents about the new water supply. Detroit offered to reconnect Flint to its water system in January 2015, and to forego a substantial connection fee. A different emergency manager refused.

The complaints became sharper when high levels of lead were found in Flint's water in February and March of 2015. This was known in the governor's office, but no action was taken. In September of that same year, several doctors made a public statement that many Flint children had elevated levels of lead in their blood. Soon after the doctors' news conference and a year and a half after the switch to river water, the state began to take action. Flint was reconnected to the Detroit water system in October.

But what about the residents of Flint who by then had high levels of lead in their blood and pipes into their homes that were damaged by the river water? The state government brought fresh bottled water to Flint for emergency help, but that was all it did. State funds were blocked by political objections, and federal emergency funds were blocked as well. It is unclear as this book goes to press whether the needed investment in Flint's water pipes will be made. The residents of Flint are unable to move, locked in by home ownership and other constraints. But one of Flint's emergency managers was rewarded by being put in charge of Detroit's schools—of which more discussion will follow later—a position he resigned from after the Flint scandal broke.[22]

The governor and the managers, all from the FTE sector, did not consider the health of the black low-wage residents of Flint in making decisions about public services. The FTE sector representatives wanted to limit their taxes instead of preserving the infrastructure of Flint and guaranteeing good water quality. The Lewis model asserts that the FTE sector wants to keep incomes low in the low-wage sector, and that includes lowering the quality of public services in the low-wage sector.

All of these changes in employment, public financing, and private reorganization of labor produced frustration among unemployed and troubled people that came out in the use of cocaine. Federal penalties are heavier for crack cocaine (favored by low-wage African Americans) than for powder cocaine (favored by the FTE sector), and many black users of cocaine received heavy sentences as a result. This fed into Nixon's War on Drugs, and state governments rushed to pass punitive laws such as the infamous three-strikes law that spread over the country in the 1990s, supported by ALEC and its draft laws. The prison population in the United States mushroomed from less than half a million to over two million inmates today, with drug convictions accounting for over half of the increase. Federal funding that formerly supported jobs in large cities now finances prisons in rural communities. There are now seven million people under the supervision of adult correctional systems, counting those in jail, on parole, or waiting for a court appearance. And although blacks are less than 15 percent of the population, they are 40 percent of the prison population.[23]

If incarceration rates stay the same, one in three black males will go to prison during his lifetime.[24] This shocking estimate, based on data from life tables and prison records, implies that every black family knows someone who is in jail or has been in jail. Those released from jail are denied access to social programs in most states, preventing many male former prisoners from advancing in their lives to become good role models. Training prisoners for jobs is not a high priority, and most men released from prison have trouble finding work. They often see no way to earn money other than criminal activity, and recidivism is high. The proportion of black men in the prison population makes it likely that most black families have a male family member who is in jail or recently out of jail. Young men growing up in the shadow of the incarcerated men of their families find it hard to plan for the future, to gain skills that might help them in the future, or perhaps even to think of the future or education at all.

The War on Drugs has been directed primarily toward urban black males, and it has made it harder for them to advance from the low-wage sector. The process of incarceration takes black men out of society where they might accumulate skills. After they get out of jail, their past convictions preclude their participation in any of the government programs that help poor people get jobs, training, and food assistance. And the threat of prison in the black population—everyone knows someone in jail or under adult correctional system supervision—indicates to everyone that personal effort probably will not be rewarded. The prevalence of mass incarceration has become a form of social control.[25]

The assertion that mass incarceration is for social control more than crime control is supported by the continuing rise in incarceration rates over the 1990s while the crime rate fell. The causes of declining crime are not fully understood, but the evidence indicates that increasing incarceration had little if any effect. A recent survey concluded, "There is little evidence to believe that the higher [incarceration] rates have caused the reduction in crime in the last two decades." Only budget shortfalls in the aftermath of the financial crisis of 2008 have produced a halt in the rise in prisoners, and long-time prisoners are not provided any help or services to reenter society when they are released.[26]

This repression falls most heavily on blacks, but it affects whites and Latinos in the low-wage sector as well. After all, the majority of prison inmates are white. But while poor whites are numerous, they are less visible than blacks in public discussions of programs to help the poor. Reagan's famous invocation of "Welfare Queens" in his campaign to restrict government funding for the poor was a clear racial reference.[27] The War on Drugs appears to be a law-and-order program, but its administration focuses on black men. And the resulting conditions of black men are used as examples to discourage other government funding. Even though people generally avoid racial language today, the persistence of race prejudice can be seen in the birther movement that attacked President Barack Obama's legitimacy and the hateful responses to his debut on Twitter.[28]

Attempts to deal with one part of this complex of policies run afoul of racial discrimination and expose the strength of this underlying social construction. For example, recent efforts to reintegrate freed prison inmates into society by Ban the Box campaigns have tried to encourage employers to hire ex-felons by not forcing ex-prisoners to reveal their status in job applicants. A test of this policy in the New York area found that banning the box did not help black ex-felons get a job. Employers, prevented from gaining individual information, relied on general information that blacks were more likely to be ex-felons and refused to hire them. Ban the Box policies expose the underlying racism of our society and show how hard it is to help low-wage African Americans get ahead.[29]

The growing problems of white members of the low-wage sector are equally serious. White flight to the suburbs was by class as well as by race; it stranded poor whites in the inner cities, where they are subject to economic and social pressures similar to those of poor blacks. As noted earlier, there are many more whites than blacks and Latinos in the low-wage sector. The inability to earn an income sufficient to support a family increased among whites in poor urban neighborhoods after 1970. The urban white marriage rate dropped; the rate of urban white single-family households rose. The imprisonment rate among whites in poor urban neighborhoods rose along with the rising rate for blacks. And the decay of social capital in the form of trust among these whites was as severe as among blacks. The American dual economy would exist if there were no American blacks, but the political discussion would be different.[30]

The loss of social capital in urban parts of the low-wage sector has been chronicled separately for blacks and whites. As chance would have it, two studies were done in different neighborhoods of Philadelphia. They are similar as they describe the decline of social capital, but only the one about a black neighborhood focuses on the role of police in this decline.[31] And national data reveal that over 40 percent of people living in families with female householders with no husband present now are impoverished, that is, below the American poverty limit.[32]

The similarity of social capital losses in poor urban neighborhoods, whether white, black, or Latino, supports Wilson's assertion that the pathology of black neighborhoods was due to the economic circumstances they found in these cities. He asked if each characteristic of the lives of urban blacks in the 1990s—such as growing incarceration, declining marriage rate, and increasing single-parented families—were due to black culture or what he called institutional factors. He concluded that each was due to institutional factors. This conclusion can be generalized to both white and black members of the low-wage sector; they are characteristic of people trapped in unfortunate economic conditions with little ability to escape. Putnam also found losses of social capital in the low-wage sector through his interviews. He did not emphasize the role of race and incarceration, possibly because of the selection process for interviewees, and his results only show part of the story. They do however vividly illustrate and strengthen the evidence for the effects of our urban policies on the entire low-wage sector.[33]

There are differences between black and white communities in the low-wage sector in the form that social capital breaks down. For the black community, continued pressure from the police represents a constant threat to the acquisition of social capital. For the white community, the sense of being forgotten has resulted in self-destructive behavior that increased mortality from alcohol and drugs enough to cause the mortality of poorly educated white men to rise while the mortality of other demographic groups in America was falling. The recent political arousal of poorly-educated white men may be healthy for them, although the appeal to their superiority over similar black men is troubling for the future.[34]

The trap has become more restrictive as the welfare system has been criminalized. "The public desire to deter and punish welfare cheating has overwhelmed the will to provide economic security to members of society. While welfare use has always borne the stigma of poverty, it now also bears the stigma of criminality."[35] The welfare system increasingly is being used to catch people with outstanding warrants. It is easy to have an outstanding warrant if you are on parole and miss a meeting with your parole officer or violate some other restriction on your actions. Drug felons are not only barred from voting in many states, but also from the welfare system—marginalizing them more fully from society.

Welfare payments have eroded so that they no longer provide enough funds to live on. Most welfare recipients consequently have to rely on other sources of income to make ends meet. They have to engage in some income-generating activity that needs to be hidden from the welfare office to maintain benefits. This concealment is deemed a fraud, even though it is encouraged by the welfare system itself. Drug programs similarly are discouraged as drug use is not permitted on welfare, and again fraud is encouraged. The system creates incentives that maintain poor members of the low-wage sector in a marginal existence.[36]

Stories of people caught in the repressive legal system show its extent. On one hand, urban workers who are arrested find they cannot pay the bail required to stay out of jail until their case is heard. They are under great pressure to confess to a crime to avoid jail while waiting months and sometimes many months for trials—although this decision often makes them more vulnerable in the future. On the other hand, the system extends to small towns with only two or three policemen. In one such Vermont town, when the police found drugs, they only indicted whites 12 percent of the time, but they indicted blacks 87 percent of the time, seven times as often.[37]

4

Transition

As in more traditional dual economies, some members of the American low-wage sector aspire to transition into the FTE sector. The mechanism is education, which is hard for members of the low-wage sector for two reasons. First, education requires expenditure over a long period of time and resources that most members of the low-wage sector lack. Second, the FTE sector has made this transition increasingly costly over time. I discuss these barriers in turn.

It may appear that education is far more difficult than the tradition of moving to the city in developing economies. But moving to the city was only the start of a long and uncertain process of finding gainful employment in the industrial economy. Moving to a city to find a good job started later and did not last as long as current education does, but the older process still created a formidable barrier to the initial change in location. Economists described the possibility of getting an urban job as random, while aptitude for learning is also important today. Nonetheless, even if a member of the low-wage sector does well in school, he or she faces uncertainty similar to that in developing economies when seeking a high-paying job.[1]

In our modern dual economy, the student needs to start the transition process as a young child and continue for sixteen years or more to get a college education. Recalling from chapter 3 that if current trends continue, one in three black males will go to jail, it must be hard for many black male children to make such long-range plans. Clearly, some urban black families do not have any members in jail, and this obviously helps a small child imagine more possibilities. But when that child gets to junior high, the level when male black students tend to fall behind, he knows the odds are against him in the wider world. It becomes harder and harder for his parents to keep him motivated in school.[2]

These problems continue into college. Many poor students drop out midway and do not graduate with a college degree—an entry ticket to the FTE sector. Only one-third of college students from the bottom quarter of households graduate, while two-thirds of students from the top quarter do. Both ability and class matter, and math tests show that ability matters more at low income levels. The probability of graduating from college for students who scored low on the math test was four times as high for rich students as poor ones. This gap decreases as scores improve, but graduation is still about twice as likely for rich kids than poor kids.[3]

If a student manages to complete college, what are his or her chances to find a job that will lift him or her out of the low-wage sector? White students have a leg up on black students. Most recent graduates who are white find jobs through a social network of relatives, peers from college, and friends who inform them about and recommend them for jobs. Black urban college graduates are not likely to know many people with jobs in the FTE sector or have many school mates who are moving into it. Their chances of finding good jobs are correspondingly lower than for comparable whites, and they have to find jobs in education, social work, or government. The only jobs they find in mainstream businesses are those directed at or concerned with African Americans.[4]

Most white people are unaware of this difference in social capital. They describe their own careers as the results of their own efforts, not recognizing the contributions of families, friends, and even the government. They therefore find it difficult to realize that a poor student in a poor urban neighborhood with poor schools and poor neighbors does not have the same social capital they do. Members of the FTE sector, having little personal contact with members of the low-wage sector, are particularly subject to this kind of blindness. Fish do not know they are living in water, and members of the FTE sector are not aware of the social capital that surrounds and sustains them.[5]

The problems of K–12 education will be discussed more fully in part III. I now discuss changes in the availability of college education to aspiring members of the low-wage sector, because a college degree is a ticket into the FTE sector. Public universities have been subject to the same starvation diet for funding as other state spending that benefits members of the low-wage sector. State appropriations for higher education in real dollars have fallen 40 percent since 1980. State funding for the 100 top public research universities fell from 38 percent of their budgets in 1992 to 23 percent in 2010. State and local spending on higher education fell from 60 percent of total spending on higher education in 1975 to 35 percent in 2010.[6]

Declining state support for higher education leads directly to higher tuition charges to students. Inflation-adjusted tuition and fee charges rose by 250 percent at flagship state universities from 1980 to 2012, by 230 percent for all state university state universities and colleges, and by 165 percent for community colleges. These tuition increases are another barrier in the education link between the low-wage and the FTE sector.[7]

Students' tuition increased as the dual economy destroyed the mechanism that used to finance education. Parents traditionally paid for kids' education, both directly and through property taxes for education. In the dual economy, low-wage workers cannot pay for their children's college, and the FTE sector is unwilling to help them. There is a need for inter-sector as well as inter-generational transfer, and it is not forthcoming.

Tuition increases are a major source of the student-loan crisis that holds back so many young people today. The debts are mainly to for-profit colleges and secondarily to community colleges. Most of these debtors did not finish college or get skills to move them into the FTE sector; they are still in the low-wage sector—but now with large (especially for them) debts.[8]

Since states support public universities and colleges has decreased, federal help for poor students turned to providing Pell Grants, GI Bills, and other forms of financial aid to individual students. Private for-profit schools like the University of Phoenix began to accept these forms of government support. They were accredited to receive federal student support in 1972, and their focus is to increase the number of students in the short run—to keep up their stock prices—rather than to help students and preserve knowledge in the long run. The private universities have been very profitable, but they typically have not educated students sufficiently to make it into the FTE sector.[9]

The federal government has found it impossible to control the for-profit colleges that have sprung up to profit off the individual subsidies. For-profit colleges enroll only 12 percent of college students, but they account for almost half of student loan defaults. The government is trying to contain the growing problem of for-profit colleges, but regulators are caught between an industry that complains of victimization and critics who say not enough is being done to prevent fraud and the abuse of students from the low-wage sector.[10]

The combination of students who do not complete college and private colleges that do not deliver degrees that help their graduates gain employment in the FTE sector has left many poor students still in the low-wage sector but now burdened with student debts. These debts cannot be discharged unless the former student can demonstrate "undue hardship" from the loan. The statute does not define "undue hardship," and many courts use the Brunner test, derived from a 1987 opinion. This standard includes persistent poverty and a good-faith effort to pay the loan. In the view of some more recent opinions, this standard further requires hopelessness that conditions will improve. In other words, the student faces a double bind: if she tries to transition to the FTE sector, she is hampered by her student loans. Only if she foregoes this ambition can the student loan be discharged. In New Jersey, even death may not bring a reprieve from student loans.[11]

Lewis argued more than fifty years ago that the capitalist sector had an incentive to keep earnings in the subsistence sector low. The FTE sector illustrates this aspect of the dual economy in a web of policies that now combine to keep earnings in the low-wage sector low. The New Federalism of Nixon and Reagan reduced federal aid to the states, which in turn reduced public support for state universities. Students were forced to pay more for their college education than the postwar generation, and they borrowed to fund their education. The FTE policies of deregulation and privatization allowed student loans to grow rapidly without government oversight or regulation, leading to widespread abuses of borrowers by the business firms that administer these loans. The FTE sector enlarged the effect of student loans by making them hard to reduce even in bankruptcy. And the FTE policy of privatization allowed for-profit colleges to receive student loans from the government and grow without providing students with the education to move into the FTE sector. The for-profit colleges advertise widely to attract students and government loans while lobbying the government to preserve their status.

Student loans are now held by more than forty million people who owe more than $1.2 trillion in student-loan debt. This debt is now the second largest class of consumer debt, behind mortgages, and it has a depressing effect on spending. Lower spending in turn reduces the demand for labor in the low-wage sector, helping to keep wages flat as shown in figure 2. And the growth of student debt makes the transition from the low-wage sector to the FTE sector ever more difficult.[12]

This was not inevitable. Other countries do not have this debt problem. Even if public policies force students to borrow for their college education, loans can be structured differently than they are in the United States. Since education builds human capital that lasts for most of a lifetime, it is more like investing in a house than in a car. Students could be asked to pay their loans back over thirty years, the modal length of home mortgages today. This would reduce the monthly payment and burden on the student. Alternatively, repayments could be keyed to earnings, starting a threshold near the entry to the FTE sector and taking a very low percentage of earnings above that.[13]

The problems of American student loans can be seen in the experience of one unlucky borrower, Liz Kelley. She enrolled in a private college when she was already married and had children. She was a nontraditional student, but a reasonably typical low-wage worker trying to make a transition to the FTE sector. Kelley borrowed to pay for college and graduated with a degree in English in 1994. Her debt at graduation was about $42,000 in 2015 dollars. This is close to the debt of a typical college graduate, who borrows about $32,000 to attend a private college. Despite her degree in English, Kelley did not find a job, and opted to go to law school. This delayed the obligation to repay her college loan and added $37,000 to her debt in the first three semesters.

Kelley then became seriously ill and required extensive hospitalization. She dropped out of law school and decided that her best bet was to be a teacher. To be able to earn a good salary, she needed more schooling. Her husband was working, and she had to borrow for both child care and her added schooling. She stayed in grad school from 1999 to 2004, postponing repayment of her educational loans. The interest on her loans kept accumulating at 8.25 percent, adding $60,000 to her debt. That debt, including both the loan and the accumulated interest, totaled just under $200,000.

Kelley's husband lost his job in the 2008 financial crash. The couple lost their house and divorced. She consolidated all her loans at 7 percent interest; the total had grown to $260,000. She tried to help one of her children in college and enrolled briefly in another graduate program. Kelley's loan servicer told her that her loan forbearance would expire in sixteen months. She now owed just over $400,000. If she could not pay, the loan servicer would garnish her wages and Social Security.

Kelley, now 48, would like to save for her retirement, but she is obligated to pay $2,750 a month for the next thirty years. She would like to declare bankruptcy, but federal law does not allow this solution for student loans. She is not bitter, saying, "I am not a victim, I made choices."

That is true, but it shows how hard it is for someone to make the transition from the low-wage sector to the FTE sector through education. In previous generations, parents paid for much of college education through direct help and education taxes. Public universities offered degree programs either without or with only modest tuition fees. This is all gone now, and aspiring students have to finance their own education. Kelley has come far, but still has a way to go at almost fifty years of age.[14]

The decline in mobility between the two sectors is apparent in aggregate data. There is an inverse relation between inequality and income mobility, which the chair of the President's Council of Economic Advisers dubbed "The Great Gatsby Curve." This association appears in comparisons between countries and also within areas of the United States. It is harder for people in unequal societies to move up into a higher income. There are many mechanisms that produce this relation, and the difficulty of making a transition from the low-wage sector to the FTE sector is one of them. Lack of FTE support for public education is why a fine teacher like John-David Bowman, introduced in chapter 2, is stuck in the low-wage sector despite his college degrees.[15]

II

Politics in a Dual Economy

5

Race and Gender

Not only was W. Arthur Lewis a Nobel Laureate, he also was the first black Nobel Laureate in a field other than peace or literature. It is interesting that he was treated as an African American, even though he was neither African nor American; he was born in the British Caribbean and became a British citizen. Lewis taught at Princeton University in later years, and he resented being incorporated into the American racial system.

Lewis did not want to be caught in the Jim Crow movement, and the New Jim Crow is not much better. As Ta-Nehisi Coates wrote, "A society that protects some people through a safety net of schools, government-backed home loans, and ancestral wealth but can only protect you [my black son] with the club of criminal justice has either failed at enforcing its good intentions or has succeeded at something much darker."[1]

I discuss the history of race in America at the outset of the political analysis in part II because race plays an important part in discussions of policies related to inequality in the United States. The FTE sector includes the top 20 percent of earners, and the low-wage sector has the other 80 percent. Blacks make up less than 15 percent of the American population. Even if they were all in the low-wage sector, they would still be less than one-fifth of the low-wage sector members, as I keep emphasizing. It seems odd that much of the public discussion of public policies designed to help the poor is directed to blacks, but the power of the American racial system dictates that it is so. Gender discrimination enters this story as well, providing a useful comparison with racism and revealing an important problem of American education.

Attitudes toward race in the United States have become divorced from scientific and historic evidence that races do not exist. Even though people from different areas may look different from one another and have other different characteristics, there is too much diversity within groups and too much similarity between groups to provide the basis for any biological definition of race. In America, racism has become *racecraft*, analogous to witchcraft. We no longer believe that witches ride on brooms, but we continue to believe that races have powers that we should fear. "Racecraft is a ready-made propaganda weapon for use against the aspirations of the great majority of working Americans. Sooner or later, tacitly or openly, any move to tackle inequality brings racecraft into play."[2]

Witchcraft made its last appearance in the future United States in the Salem witch trials of 1692. Accusations against the presumed witches were made in the context of Puritan religion, but there was a curious geography to the process. The individuals accused of witchcraft came from the eastern part of Salem, near the Atlantic coast that offered mercantile possibilities; the accusers came from the western part of Salem where fertile land encouraged traditional farming. Perhaps the furor over witchcraft and the dark arts even then was only the means to express the social conflict between the lure of commercial activity and the resistance to change among back-country farmers.[3]

We no longer use the criminalization of witchcraft to express the differences in the community, but racecraft has endured. The reasons for this persistence are connected with American history, starting at the same time as the Salem witch trials. When Southern farmers first began to expand farming in the seventeenth century, they employed white and black workers equally, subject to restrictions held over from medieval practices. The farmers' problem was not Africans, it was lack of labor to work their abundant land. They encouraged European immigration by loaning immigrants the money to get to America with their farm labor obligations as security. That is, the European workers would be indentured servants, who would regain their freedom of action when they had paid back their loan and their indentures were over. The farmers could not apply this approach to African immigrants because the Africans did not come to America voluntarily. Most English and Dutch migrants came because they wanted to come, while African migrants were purchased and brought to America against their will. As Oscar and Mary Handlin stated in a classic article, "To raise the status of Europeans by shortening their terms would ultimately increase the available hands by inducing their compatriots to emigrate; to reduce the Negro's term would produce an immediate loss and no ultimate gain."

The expansion of the African slave trade at the end of the seventeenth century provided Southern planters with abundant labor in a framework that had developed to differentiate between whites and blacks. The difference that had opened up between European and African immigrants led to fears of "plots and conspiracies" among the black immigrants and restrictions on black workers. "At the opening of the eighteenth century, the Black was not only set off by economic and legal status; he was 'abominable,' another order of man." The increasing need to get the consent of European workers during the eighteenth century contrasted sharply with decline in the independence of African workers—who went from villeins to chattels. "When, therefore, Southerners in the eighteenth century came to think of the nature of the rights of man they found it inconceivable that Negroes should participate in those rights. It was more in accord with the whole social setting to argue that the slaves could not share those rights because they were not fully men, or at least different kinds of men. In fact, to the extent that Southerners ... thought of liberty as whole, natural, and inalienable, they were forced to conclude that the slave was wholly unfree, wholly lacking in personality, wholly a chattel."[4]

The statement in the Declaration of Independence that "all men are created equal" meant that all *white* men were created equal. Black slaves were not included. And when slavery was abolished after the Civil War, the presumption that blacks were abominable and lacking in personality endured. Reconstruction faltered after the assassination of President Lincoln and ended finally in 1877. It was followed by Jim Crow laws and social controls that were created to reproduce something close to the antebellum relations between whites and blacks.[5]

The continuation of discrimination against African Americans has been described as white rage by some historians. It seems hard to explain the long reach of old quarrels between the North and South without some such emotion. White rage is the other side of racecraft. This rage could be seen in the 2016 presidential campaign. The Democratic National Convention contained many kinds of people: white, black, and brown. And the *National Review* responded with a blast of white rage, identifying this diversity as anti-white, "a celebration of lawlessness and racial mythology that has led to violence."[6]

The federal government did little to disturb Southern discrimination in the first half of the twentieth century since Southern Democrats had ample power to block any federal intervention. Southern congressmen represented only white Southerners as few blacks were able to vote. Jim Crow laws and violence kept black Southerners from exercising the rights given to them in the Fourteenth Amendment. Congressional representatives and senators were selected by the local elites since there was no opposition in the general election. And, once in Congress, they gained leadership positions and political power by the long tenure provided by this system.[7]

Southern lawmakers exercised their power by leaving African Americans out of the federal programs of the New Deal. Instead of excluding them directly, they excluded occupations in which blacks were highly engaged, like farming and domestic service. They insisted that all federal social welfare programs be administered by state officials so that Southern officials were free to perpetuate Jim Crow standards. And they prevented Congress from including any antidiscrimination clauses into federal social welfare programs that distributed money to the South.

This system meant that poor Southerners, white and black, were left out of the relief offered to Northern workers during the Great Depression. Their living conditions were described vividly in *Let Us Now Praise Famous Men*, which united James Agee's powerful prose with Walker Evans's vivid photographs.[8]

Social Security did not extend to blacks for the first quarter-century of its existence. The GI Bill provided educational benefits for veterans of the Second World War, but it did not guarantee admission to colleges. Few blacks were admitted to Northern colleges and universities due to bad Southern schooling. Blacks therefore applied to Southern black colleges—being excluded from Southern white colleges—which did not have capacity to take them. States refused to expand the facilities of black colleges, particularly dormitories, and much of the black demand for college education went nowhere. Black veterans also were not helped to get good jobs by the GI Bill. Local employment agencies funded by the bill directed them to traditional black jobs, ignoring learning that had occurred in the army, and often refused loans to black veterans because they lacked capital or credit ratings and lived in undesirable neighborhoods.

African Americans responded to the pressure on them in Southern states by moving north and west in the Great Migration. As described in chapter 2, black workers moved out of the oppressive South to better their lives and employment opportunities. But this move was not always successful, and blacks lost ground relative to whites after the Second World War. The national unemployment rate for blacks and whites was the same in 1930; the black rate was double that of whites in 1965. The unemployment rate for black teenage boys went from being slightly less than whites in 1948 to being almost twice as high in 1965. And the median income of black men declined to 53 percent of the income of white men in 1965.[9]

The lower incomes and employment rate of blacks reduced their accumulation of wealth. Senator Elizabeth Warren recently gave an impassioned summary of black exclusions: "Entire legal structures were created to prevent African Americans from building economic security through home ownership. Legally enforced segregation. Restrictive deeds. Redlining. Land contracts. Coming out of the Great Depression, America built a middle class, but systematic discrimination kept most African-American families from being part of it."[10]

The oppression of blacks, increasing rapidly after the war, began to meet opposition in the 1960s. The Civil Rights Movement that Johnson supported led to legislation that granted blacks legal rights to equal citizenship, but these laws were followed by the War on Drugs that generated a new system of mass incarceration that continued the Jim Crow tradition. By 2000, one out of three black men was spending time in jail. The rise of mass imprisonment put great pressure on many black families, and led to social as well as economic problems.[11]

Nixon proclaimed the War on Drugs just as the Great Migration ended. Reagan and state governments expanded the war in the 1980s as the crack epidemic grew. Blacks were (and are) far more likely to be arrested for drug offenses than whites. At the same time, industry began to decline in the American Midwest, in what is now called the Rust Bowl, and the jobs that blacks came north to find began to disappear. They found conditions in the North better than in the South, but not as good as they had hoped.

The enduring reach of racecraft can be seen in the treatment of immigrants, even though biologists have not been able to provide a satisfactory definition of race that includes all members of a given race and excludes all others. The reach of racecraft was limited in the colonial period as white Americans came mostly from the most advanced countries of Western Europe and Africans were not permitted to express cultural differences between themselves. Attitudes were stretched in the nineteenth century as varied immigrants came to the United States and are being stretched again now as Latino immigrants have become more common.

New immigrants typically were poor, and they were grouped with African Americans in the binary world of racecraft. Some immigrants fared so well in America that they graduated from being "black" to being "white." Other immigrants did not fare so well, whether because of cultural attributes or the American context when they came. But the enduring influence of racecraft meant that the record of their American success was calibrated by racecraft.

A great many Irish came to America in the nineteenth century in response to the Irish famine at mid-century. They were grouped initially with blacks as despised manual workers. The new Irish immigrants joined with abolitionists to oppose slavery out of sympathy with their attempts to free Ireland from English rule. Only when many Irish Americans had abandoned this stance were they considered whites, who then joined other whites and adopted their racecraft. This racial identification was still valid almost a century later. A boy growing up poor and Irish American in South Boston in the 1970s tried to figure out where he fit into this scheme: "Of course no one considered himself a nigger. It was always something you called someone who could be considered anything less than you."[12]

Jews followed a similar immigrant path when they began to arrive at the end of the nineteenth century in response to pogroms in Eastern Europe. They were discriminated against, and restricted in where they could live, work, and sometimes simply stay during the first half of the twentieth century—from the age of mass immigration from Eastern Europe to the end of the Second World War. There were a few rich Jews—the heirs of earlier court Jews—but they were the exception to the general rule. Most Jews were lumped in with blacks even though they were not black. After the tragic effects of the Second World War and in postwar prosperity, Jews began to be accepted everywhere; they had become white. But while they had made the transition, their movement did not affect the structure of race relations in America. Being white in America meant being superior to blacks, and many Jews adopted racecraft with their newly white status. Those who did shared its conventions of exclusion, while others remembered past discrimination and tried to help people who had not made it into the American mainstream.[13]

As the dual economy developed in the late twentieth century, large numbers of Latinos began immigrating to the United States in response to chaos in their homelands. There has been what might be called a second Great Migration of Latinos from Mexico and other Central American countries that followed the Great Migration of African Americans before 1970. The number of Latinos in the United States has grown from around 5 percent in 1970 to 17 percent today. The Latino population now exceeds the black population in the United States.

As with the Great Migration, Latinos moved north to escape repressive political regimes that denied them a path to economic advancement and security. American interventions in Central America to dislodge governments we did not approve of were followed by the North American Free Trade Agreement (NAFTA) in 1994. NAFTA exposed Mexico to the effects of globalization that had affected United States workers by then. But Mexican workers had an option that American workers lacked: they could move north to better their position.

This movement was international, not like the interstate movement of the Great Migration of African Americans. Just as the changing immigration laws of the 1920s led employers to look to the American South for workers, the end of internal U.S. migration led employers to look south of the American border for workers. The influx of Latinos, however, became entangled with the War on Drugs as Central America became a prime source for drugs. Attempts to stem the inflow of drugs led to stiffening of the Mexican border, leading in turn to an increasing number of unauthorized immigrants who have become a political football. The tension between American employers who want a new source of labor and American workers who are suffering already from the ills of globalization has kept the United States from updating its immigration policy for these new conditions.

Latinos now are overwhelmingly in the low-wage sector of the dual economy. They are concentrated in cities that lack resources for education; they are facing the same kind of social dysfunction of African American communities. There is the same perception in the white population that anyone in a Latino neighborhood is up to no good. Latinos are on the wrong side of racecraft.

Economic conditions in the United States are less hospitable than they were in the nineteenth century. This is a recent development, dating back only a few decades, unlike the far longer history of European immigration to the United States. But at this moment, Latinos are about the same proportion of the population as African Americans and occupy similar positions in the economy and the perceptions of the FTE sector.[14]

The effect of racecraft on redistributive politics has been described in many recent publications. A comparison of the United States with Europe concluded: "Racial discord plays a critical role in determining beliefs about the poor. ... Opponents of redistribution in the United States have regularly used race-based rhetoric to resist left-wing politics."[15]

A recent econometric analysis of American counties is worth quoting in detail: "Whites who currently live in counties that had high concentrations of slaves in 1860 are on average more conservative and express colder feelings toward African-Americans than whites who live elsewhere in the South. That is, the larger the number of slaves per capita in his or her county of residence in 1860, the greater the probability that a white Southerner today will identify as a Republican, oppose affirmative action, and express positions that indicate some level of 'racial resentment.'"[16]

A vivid sense of what it means to be black in America today is expressed well in a prose poem by Claudia Rankine that describes a professional man who is taken out of his car by the police, brought to the police station in handcuffs, stripped, and then released to walk home, with the refrain: "And you are not the guy and still you fit the description because there is only one guy who is always the guy fitting the description."[17]

The treatment of women is similar in some bodily aspects to current divisions about race. Women were citizens in a way that even free African Americans were not until very recently, but women's relationship to the government has long been substantially different than that of men. Slaves were freed well before women were assured of a right to vote; the Nineteenth Amendment saying women were entitled to vote was fifty years after the Fifteenth Amendment tried to do the same for African Americans.

The early United States adopted English family law without much thought or change. Men understood how much they benefitted from the old law of domestic relations, and they did not choose to change it. Married women owed their obligations to their husbands, and husbands controlled much of what their wives could do. This system of *coverture* transferred a woman's civic identity to her husband at marriage. Coverture denied that married women could have their own property and views independent of their husbands. They were denied bodily integrity and the ability to vote and to serve on juries.

Bodily integrity is a basic civil right underlying the right to vote and serve on juries, it is at risk for both blacks and women. The origins of the problems are different, as noted previously, coming from slavery and coverture, respectively. But the persistence of race and gender discrimination highlights the common risk to the bodies of blacks and women. For African American men it is the danger of being killed, while for many women of all colors it is the fear of being raped and of not having access to appropriate health care.

Across the country a number of police officers have killed many black people in recent years. Trayvon Martin in Florida, who was killed by a community watch captain, and Michael Brown in Missouri are only two of the most famous cases of young black men to be shot.[18]

Women have not been shot as often, but the bodily integrity of married women has been unstable over the years. Although husbands were expected to defend their wives from other men's violence, their property right in their wife's body was unfettered; rape was long defined as sexual assault on a woman "not his wife." Some of these laws were changed in the 1970s, but marital rape was not a crime in all fifty states until the early 1990s.

Unmarried women are still at risk, as shown by decisions in two different rape cases. One was in Puerto Rico, where a student in a program run by Worcester Polytechnic Institute was raped by the security guard of their dorm. The rapist was sentenced to twenty years in prison, but Worcester College refused to take any responsibility for the rape, accusing the victim of making risky decisions. But if you cannot trust the security guard, who can you trust? The guard was hired by a subcontractor, a practice that has become common as described in chapter 3, and the parent company was unwilling to acknowledge that responsibility went up this ladder.

The other rape took place at Stanford University. A visitor to a fraternity party drank too much and passed out. She then was raped, with the charge lowered later to sexually assaulted, by a drunken Stanford student who was detained by other students for the police. Unlike the dormitory guard, the Stanford student was sentenced to six months. He received a slap on his wrist while the dorm guard was imprisoned for many years. The student's father wrote a letter saying his son's life had been ruined by his remorse for acting badly, and incarceration was unnecessary for his "20 minutes of action." What is the message here? Is it any safer to go to a Stanford party than a Worcester mini-course?[19]

Women's right to bodily integrity also is being threatened in the early twenty-first century as politicians turn against organizations like Planned Parenthood. Women's bodily integrity seems to be threatened by denial of access to reproductive care resulting from inflammatory speech about abortion and women's health care. Half the states have refused the provision in the Affordable Health Care Act that state health care plans cover abortion, and some employers are now exempted from covering expenses for contraception under the Affordable Care Act, increasing risks for many women.[20]

The U.S. Supreme Court declared a Texas law that had sharply restricted access to abortions to be unconstitutional in June 2016. It found that Texas's restrictions requiring doctors to have admitting privileges at nearby hospitals and clinics—purportedly to meet the standards of ambulatory surgical centers—violated the Court's previous prohibition on placing an "undue burden" on a woman's ability to obtain an abortion. The decision was the Court's most sweeping statement on abortion since 1992 and a strong reaffirmation of the constitutional right to abortion established in 1973 in *Roe v. Wade*. It took the anti-abortionists only a few weeks to respond that they would not retire from the field; they would continue their attack on the rights of women to maintain bodily integrity.[21]

But the law appears to have had strong effects while in force. Death rates for pregnant women in Texas doubled after the state defunded Planned Parenthood. It is now comparable to death rates in Russia and Ukraine. Clear cause and effect has not been proven, but the timing is highly suggestive. As black men and boys are being shot in the United States by government officials, pregnant women are dying from governmental actions.[22]

Suffragettes and abolitionists were quite distinct in the nineteenth century, but their concerns were combined in the Fourteenth Amendment by its reference to "persons." While the application of the equal protection clause of the amendment was intended to reduce discrimination for African Americans, women successfully claimed its protection in the latter third of the twentieth century. It took the Nineteenth Amendment to ensure women the vote, but "the alliance of race and sex formed by the Civil Rights Act of 1964 ... relocated disparate treatment because of sex from the venue of tradition to that of discrimination."[23]

Voting for blacks was supposed to be secured in law by the Fifteenth Amendment and then the Voting Rights Act of 1965, but it is still under attack today. The Supreme Court invalidated parts of the Voting Rights Act in 2013, and Southern states have rushed to reinstate rules reminiscent of Jim Crow laws. Since the Fifteenth Amendment barred the use of race in voting regulation, poll taxes were used in its place, depriving poor whites—men and women alike—of the vote as well. Poll taxes were outlawed by the Twenty-fourth Amendment in 1964, when five states were still using them. New restrictions like identity cards now are being used to keep poor people from the polls, and the federal courts have approved many of the restrictions.[24]

The attempts to allow more people to vote had important political effects. Before 1963, racially conservative racial views among Southern white voters strongly predicted Democratic identification. But when

Presidents Kennedy and Johnson supported civil rights for African Americans, these racially conservative voters became Republicans. The shift of these voters explains three-fourths of the decline in white Southern Democratic identification. In 1960, all the Southern senators were Democrats. Now only three out of twenty-two are Democrats, and Northern Democrats struggle to accommodate to these changes.[25]

While men got the right to hold public office when they obtained the vote, women had to wait for subsequent court actions to hold public office. Both women and blacks traditionally were excluded from juries. Legislation gave both blacks and women the right to be on jury lists, but also gave prosecutors great discretion in excluding jurors they did not want. Women jurors become common as a result of changing state statutes and attorney practices only in the 1960s and 1970s; and not until 1992 did the Supreme Court rule that peremptory challenges, which do not need to be explained, could not be used on the basis of sex.

Despite the Supreme Court's ruling in 1986 that peremptory challenges may not be used on the basis of race, the practice has continued, and black jurors are still rare in the South and some other parts of the country even though Supreme Court opinions have said they may not be excluded because of their race. The Supreme Court ruled in 2016 that Georgia attorneys illegally struck potential jurors from the jury in 1987 because they were black. The prosecutor's notes showed that black prospective jurors were highlighted in green and labeled "B." Timothy Foster, an innocent African American, was sentenced to death and imprisoned for thirty years as a result.[26]

The work that women could do was limited up until the 1930s to work around the house and a few outside activities like teaching, nursing and cotton-textile production. Women were largely barred from law, medicine, and many other professional fields by formal and informal quotas. They were barred from many well-paying jobs by the practice of naming job advertisements as "men wanted" and "women wanted," which reserved best-paying jobs for men. They were limited in the work force by "protective" laws that reflected stereotypes of women's character and social roles, restricting them from work that they actually were competent to do and often—by excluding whole job categories from coverage—exposing women of color to exploitation.

Women's work only begun to change in the last generation. Slowly and after severe and often risky struggle, "the complementary practices of substituting family duties for civic obligations slowly crumbled." And in an odd interaction between race and gender, female police officers—part of the new freedom of women to choose varied occupations—are significantly less likely to fire their weapons, probably saving black lives.[27]

Women still face prejudice at work, however. Women's median earnings remain about 20 percent lower than men's. Education is not the reason—women now have education equal to those of men in similar occupations. Yet women doctors and lawyers earn less than their male counterparts. And when women achieve prominence in a field, the wage goes down. Scholars are actively seeking to understand the source of this wage gap, but it shows up even after correcting for observable differences.[28]

6

The Investment Theory of Politics

I now have shown how America is split in various ways. The first split, discussed in part I, is economically. Income inequality has progressed far enough to think of the United States as a dual economy. The second, described in chapter 5, is racially. The relations between blacks and whites originated in early times in the New World, and they have taken many strange paths since then. Despite electing a black president twice in recent years, racism—that is to say, racecraft—has not disappeared. The third split is along gender lines, discussed also in chapter 5. Despite a lot of progress in recent years, women are still not fully equal to men.

How does all this affect American politics? This is a difficult question and will take some effort to answer. I start with the Median Voter Theorem and work toward other approaches that are more illuminating.

The Median Voter Theorem is used widely in both professional and popular discussions. The theorem starts from a simple example. Assume there is to be a vote on a single issue, and everyone voting has a view ranging from absolutely yes to absolutely no with room for various positions in between. If everyone voting is selected for reasons other than their views on the issue in question, then it is likely that voters are spread out along a bell curve or one-humped camel. Technically, the distribution is very likely to follow a normal distribution, with more people in the center than at the extremes.

The Median Voter Theorem predicts that political candidates facing preferences like this gravitate to the center, to the median voter, the central figure in the distribution of voters. This view of politics is quite common and has spread from academia to public discussions. For example, Edward Luce, a journalist forecasting events in 2016 for the *Financial Times*, predicted the Republican presidential candidate in 2016 "will be too far to the right of the median voter to make it to the White House."[1]

This theorem appears to have strong predictions for politics in a dual economy. But it has serious problems. If the median person counted, American public policy would favor the low-wage sector. Since the low-wage sector contains over half the population, the median voter, if everyone voted, clearly is in the low-wage sector. But while the median voter would support, say, a higher minimum wage, it has not been raised in many years. Jamie Dimon, chairman of JPMorgan Chase, announced in mid-2016 that he was responding to the stagnation of wages by raising wages at JPMorgan Chase. This is laudable, but it is hardly the same as a raise in the national minimum wage.[2]

This paradox shows that the Median Voter Theorem is inconsistent with the dual economy. Lewis assumed that the lower sector of the dual economy had no influence over policy. Economic policy served the interest of the capitalist class; subsistence farmers had no political power. Lewis emphasized this point in the passages quoted in part I of this book to introduce his model by referring to the capitalists as imperialists, people who had little or no contact with the rest of society.

Many expositions of the Median Voter Theorem talk of people and voters as if they are the same people. But this approach is not appropriate in the United States. We have to go back to the origins of our Constitution to see why this is true and examine the history since then to understand how the Constitution was amended and reinterpreted.

The Constitutional Convention was convened in 1787 because the Articles of Confederation—the first written constitution of the United States, in effect from 1781—were not working. They had constructed a confederation of states that had no power to tax people; it could only bill states. It consequently lacked power to do much of anything else. The Convention was to propose a better alternative that would transfer some power to the federal government, but it had no power to enforce this change. Only if nine states of the Confederation ratified the Constitution would it go into effect. The Constitution therefore contained a series of compromises to persuade enough states to ratify it. Two differences among the states are relevant here: The states were (and are) of different sizes, and they were (and are) spread out from north to south.

The framers of the Constitution dealt with the different size of states by introducing a bicameral legislature. Representation in the House of Representatives was to be according to population, but each state was to have two senators, independent of the state's size. In addition, senators were to be elected by state legislatures rather than popular votes. This arrangement, adapted from England, both restricted the reach of democracy in the new country and helped convince small states like Rhode Island to ratify the Constitution.[3]

This arrangement helped the United States to come into being, but it restricted democracy in the new country. The Senate would temper the decisions of the House of Representatives, and the people's will was not directly linked to policy. The role of the Senate changed over time as the United States expanded westward and as agriculture was replaced by industrialization. People increasingly lived in cities, and cities were concentrated around ports. Atlantic ports were joined by ports on the Great Lakes and then on the Pacific Ocean. But while residents congregated in states with big ports and cities, senators came from states as they had been defined earlier. Democracy was limited by the contrast between the location of voters and the location of senators.

State legislatures had increasing difficulty appointing senators as the nineteenth century progressed. There were many gaps in the Senate in the late nineteenth century because the state legislatures could not agree who to appoint. The solution was to amend the Constitution to let the people elect senators. This was done in the Seventeenth Amendment, which took effect in 1913.

To the unequal counting of votes in the Senate, we must add the problems of redistricting the districts that elect U.S. representatives. This process has become politicized in the past several decades, and both parties have created safe districts for their members. As a result, ninety percent of representatives are in safe seats. The person wishing to influence public policy has the double burden of needing to live in a small state, for the Senate, with a competitive race for a representative. Very few American voters live in such locations.[4]

Despite this attention to the method of choosing senators, the Constitution makes no mention of eligibility to vote, instead turning the regulation of voting to the states. This was an odd way to write a constitution for a new democracy, but it was a result of the racial history of the American colonies told in chapter 5. The Constitution needed to be ratified by both Northern and Southern states to take effect.

The assumption that voters are the entire adult population may be more or less accurate for Europe, where voting rates hover around 80 percent of the appropriate population for legislative elections, but the picture is very different for the United States. The mean voter turnout in presidential elections was 56 percent from 1976 through 2008. The mean turnout for off-year elections for the House of Representatives was only 38 percent.

An analysis of voter turnout by socioeconomic status in 1980 reveals who actually votes in the United States. Over half of the middle class, as it was then known, turned out to vote, while only 16 percent of the working class and unemployed voted. As can be seen in figure 1, the middle and upper groups comprised much of the population in 1980, and the lower group did not vote. Classification by location reveals the source of this result. Voter turnout in the North and West in off-year legislative elections was above 50 percent until 1970, falling to 40 percent since then. Voter turnout in the South, however, was only about 10 percent from 1918 to 1950, rising to around 30 percent more recently.[5]

The proposed new constitution of 1787 contained compromises to attract colonies that stretched up and down the Atlantic seaboard of the newly independent union. The most important of these concerned slavery. Southern colonies wanted their slaves to count in the allocation of representatives in the House of Representatives. As slaves were then considered property, not people, they clearly were not voters. The demand for representation therefore conflicted with the idea of a democratic union. Northern colonies were reluctant to agree to this inconsistent demand, but they could not insist on excluding slaves entirely and have the Southern colonies agree to ratify. The compromise, as every schoolchild knows, was to count slaves as three-fifths of a person and ban restrictions of the slave trade for twenty years.

Given this compromise on representation, it was impossible for the Constitutional Convention to define conditions for voting. In fact, most planners of the early republic did not think that universal suffrage was a healthy part of the government. They thought property owners would have a stake in the new constitution and would preserve it well. How much property would qualify a voter? Could free blacks vote? Could women vote? These questions were too difficult and too distracting for the Convention, which passed voting arrangements to the states.

The result was that voting was never a right of all Americans; it was a privilege of a prosperous portion of the population. States experimented with allowing free blacks and women to vote, but these outliers did not last. Free black men were excluded from militias in New York, but they voted if they met property requirements. Single women who met property requirements could vote in early New Jersey, where voting laws were generic. But when women's votes were thought to have affected the outcome of an election, the New Jersey legislature inserted gender specification in the voting law. During the Jacksonian period when property requirements for voting were lifted, race specification was inserted, and votes were reserved for white men. Keyssar calls it "partial" democracy, but it was an oligarchy in the South. Participation remained low as a result of these exclusions.[6]

The Civil War made surprising small alterations in this pattern. Voting in the South was more democratic during Reconstruction, but low turn-out returned to the South due to Jim Crow laws and practices. Despite the Fourteenth and Fifteen Amendments, blacks were kept from register-ing to vote. The candidates in the general elections were chosen in prima-ries where far fewer people voted. These small gatherings of white people nominated sitting representatives and senators for reelection, and they were easily elected over and over. Their long tenure in Congress gave them enormous power because committee chairs were awarded by length of service. Due to the influence of these Southern lawmakers, the New Deal and the GI Bill delegated administration of benefits to the states. These benefits were confined to whites in the South, perpetuating this system.[7]

This pattern continues today. The Voting Rights Act of 1965 incorpo-rated provisions to deal with the legacy of Jim Crow laws in the South. The Supreme Court ruled that its most effective provision was unconsti-tutional in *Shelby County v. Holder* in 2013. This provision required selected states and regions to preclear proposed voting arrangements with the federal government. In other words, the federal government would decide whether voting arrangements would violate the Voting Rights Act before they went into effect. The provision was ruled uncon-stitutional because the coverage formula was based on data over forty years old, making it no longer responsive to current needs and therefore an impermissible burden on the constitutional principles of federalism and equal sovereignty of the states.[8]

Despite the Supreme Court's assertion that all states are alike, the states that had been listed in the original bill immediately rushed to impose voting restrictions that otherwise would not have passed pre-clearance. While it seems clear that these restrictions are racially moti-vated, they can no longer be phrased in that way. The difficulties of voting therefore affect low-wage whites and blacks.

Southern states turned to poll taxes to keep blacks from voting when the Voting Rights Act prevented the South from legally restricting blacks from voting. When poll taxes were made illegal in 1964, the states turned to literacy tests and voter ID cards instead. These measures avoided the opprobrium of singling out blacks, but they also prevented low-wage whites from voting. What began as a race issue turned into a class discrimination. And politicians in 2016 were concerned about the effect of these new requirements on voting; voter IDs appeared to be a large barrier to voting by poor people.[9]

The old Southern practice has been transferred to the North by mass incarceration. As noted already, the number of imprisoned grew rapidly after 1970, making the United States an outlier in the proportion of its population in prison. Prisoners often come from center cities and are disproportionally black. Prisons typically are built in rural areas where private employment has decreased as government revenues increasingly are distributed to rural rather than urban areas. The Supreme Court ruled that prisoners should be counted as part of the population, although prisoners cannot vote. White Northerners in some rural areas now find themselves in the same voting position as white Southerners under Jim Crow rules.[10]

Another problem with translating the Median Voter Theorem into practice is that voters typically face two or more issues in a political choice. For example, racecraft and economics might figure in a single vote. Donald Trump, Republican candidate for president in 2016, said that federal district court judge Gonzalo P. Curiel, in charge of the lawsuit filed against him by people who had lost money at Trump University should not oversee the case because the judge "was a Mexican." When people noted that the judge hailed from Indiana, Trump still claimed he was unable to judge him because of his Mexican background. Paul Ryan, the Speaker of the House of Representatives, said that Trump's attack on the judge was racist, but that he supported him nonetheless. In this situation, therefore, a citizen's single vote ties together two issues: textbook racism and economics. The Median Voter Theorem does not tell the voter how to weigh this choice.[11]

Yet another way voting practices privilege the elites comes from the timing of votes. Tuesday voting restricts voting by low-wage workers who cannot get time off from their jobs. But there is no push to change this outdated practice. Tuesday voting began in the nineteenth century when most Americans were farmers and traveled by horse and buggy. They needed a day to get to the county seat, a day to vote, and a day to get home, without interfering with the three days of worship prevalent at that time. That left Tuesday and Wednesday, but Wednesday was market day. So, Tuesday it was. In 1875 Congress extended the Tuesday date for U.S. House of Representative elections and in 1914 for U.S. Senate elections.

Most Americans now live in cities, and it is hard to commute to jobs, take care of children, and get work done, let alone stand on lines to vote. This affects voters in the low-wage sector more than those in the FTE sector who typically have more control over their time. Census data indicate that the inconvenience of voting is the primary reason Americans are not participating in our elections. Some states have closed polling places in addition, leading to long lines and waits for potential voters. Early and absentee voting makes life easier for some voters, but states trying to limit poor voters cut funds for these activities, requiring more time and effort from voters. Columbus Day, Presidents Day, and Martin Luther King Jr. Day are all scheduled on a Monday for the convenience of shoppers and travelers, but we have not adjusted to modern conditions to make voting more convenient for the sake of low-wage workers. There is little discussion of the timing of elections today, but one way to increase voting participation would be to change Election Day from Tuesday.[12]

Morgan Kausser and Alexander Keyssar remind us that the history of voting rights is not smooth and unidirectional. African Americans acquired voting rights in Reconstruction, but swiftly lost them again due to congressional and judicial decisions. They regained these rights in the Civil Rights era, but they are losing them again in "radical reinterpretations of the Voting Rights Act … and the revolutionary reading of the equal protection clause introduced by the 'conservative' Supreme Court majority." This revolutionary reading became law in *Shaw v. Reno*, 509 US 630 (1993), when the Supreme Court subjected redistricting by race to strict scrutiny.[13]

Supporters of the Median Voter Theorem do not seem to notice these historical roots of voter participation variation. Perhaps they were reassured when women got the vote in the Nineteenth Amendment and nothing changed. The expansion of the vote came after the First World War when voting restrictions were lifted in several countries. The national organization of suffragettes distanced itself from black suffragettes, but "the South remained opposed, with the full-throated cry of states' rights giving tortured voice to the region's deep anxieties about race."[14]

Nevertheless, giving women the vote seemed not to affect national elections. Class rather than race had become central—at least outside the South—and women came from the same classes as men. They voted with men, and political scientists saw vindication of the Median Voter Theorem.

In addition to the problem of a partial democracy that restricts voting, the cost of getting information in order to vote does not play much part in the Median Voter Theorem. The theorem assumes that voters are spread out on a single line, caring only for one issue in any election, and that they all know their own preferences. Those assumptions go along with the way competition is taught, where consumers choose what kind of bread or tea to buy at the supermarket on the basis of freely available information. There is little mystery to consumer choices like these, and political theory here followed the economic presumption.

Within economics, the assumption of abundant free information has eroded in recent years. In our complex civilization, people need to take time and sometimes spend money to get information to choose which product to buy. No one buys a smartphone, car, or house without getting some knowledge about what they intend to pay for. Workers seeking jobs often have to search to find one that fits their skills and needs. And it's a necessity for most adults to gather information about medical care, from finding a good doctor to choosing among various medications. Many economists have analyzed costs of information in diverse markets.

Information has costs, even if they are only the cost of time spent finding and absorbing the information. People with higher incomes can make more exhaustive searches for information about the goods and services they need. And the sellers of these goods and services invest vast amounts of resources in making information about their products available and accessible to potential customers. Advertising is the most obvious expenditure; consumers are surrounded with ads all around and in all forms, from the ads that line the subways to the ads on TV and the Internet. There are questions about the quality of information received through ads. The benefits of an advertised product often are exaggerated, and drawbacks or even dangers may be omitted. There are regulations for some kinds of ads, but there is a lot of room for unscrupulous businesses to take advantage of people.

Brand names provide one way to lower the cost of information to consumers. Many people rely on a familiar brand name as a signal to them that their purchase will provide the quality they seek. This lowers the cost of information to customers greatly. It is, however, costly for a company to establish and maintain a good brand name. Companies need to provide quality products for long enough for potential customers to know about and use and begin to trust their brands. And companies need to maintain the quality of their brand-name goods and services; even a temporary lapse can cause damage to the brand and subsequent sales.

Elections pose complex questions that rival the biggest purchases we make. For example, some candidates in recent political campaigns have made the claim that the Social Security program is about to run out of money. What does that mean? Is Social Security like your mortgage, so that running out of money means that you cease to get your pension— you are evicted from the system? Or that keeping people covered will mean benefits must fall across the board? It is hard to know from the many speeches that anticipate some kind of disaster what actually is going on.

There are problems with the current financing of Social Security that should be addressed in a calm fashion, but the strident tone of political rhetoric tends to obscure rather than explain them. A brief review of how Social Security works demonstrates how much information is needed to make an intelligent choice about the future of this program.

Social Security is not a pension plan where you pay in while young and collect when you reach a certain age. It is funded each year by taxes that workers pay to finance the expenditures due to current Social Security recipients. Since taxes in any year do not exactly equal the amounts needed for Social Security payments at that time, there is a buffer called the Social Security Trust Fund between the taxes and payments. This trust fund was built up in the last few decades to prepare for the enormous number of Baby Boomers born after the Second World War who would be collecting benefits.

Baby Boomers are now aging and have increased the number of Social Security recipients. The trust fund is now decreasing as the population ages. The Social Security administration is required to plan for seventy-five years in the future, which involves predictions about the changes in the relevant population. Current population projections indicate that the trust fund will be depleted within seventy-five years under current rules. The trust fund will be exhausted soon, and legislation is needed to deal with the problems this will raise.

Social Security is not about to collapse. It is the Social Security Trust Fund, not the whole system, which is running out of money. If the trust fund is exhausted and nothing is done, then benefits will be reduced. This will cause hardships for many Social Security recipients, but it does not mean the end of Social Security. The trust fund was close to being exhausted in 1982, and Congress took action to revise the system.

Social Security taxes are collected on wages only up to $118,500; the limit could be raised or even eliminated to balance the system. This cap on earnings subject to Social Security tax was set before inequality rose, and it now stands close to the boundary between the FTE and low-wage sectors. Raising the limit of wages subject to tax therefore would extend the funding of Social Security into the FTE sector. But the FTE sector is not interested in helping the low-wage sector, and nothing has been done.[15]

There are problems with Social Security, but people need information to understand the choices on how to address them. There is no imminent disaster. Instead there are problems that come up as conditions change and have been dealt with periodically. The latest major revision was instituted thirty years ago when inequality was not as severe as it is now, and there is a need to revise the taxes or benefits for the longer run again. These measures normally were taken by bipartisan actions and commissions set up for the long-run plans. If nothing is done at the moment, Social Security benefits will fall, and there will be administrative problems with intergovernmental payments.

How are voters to understand all this? Unfunded benefits like Social Security have almost disappeared for most workers. The history of Social Security also is unfamiliar. The choices have only appeared as occasional talking points; they have not been calmly compared to alternatives. The cost of information is high, as ordinary people need to find out where to get the relevant information and then how to access and understand it. Without that information, voter attitudes will be based more on emotion than reason.

Social Security is a relatively simple issue. Questions of government deficits or debt are far more complex. There are no simple rules or simple corrections that are needed. There are instead many separate parts that go into both the causes and the effects of these aggregate measures. Voters have very little access to this information and very little background in the reasoning used to produce plans. It is extremely hard if not impossible at times for them to have enough information to make reasonable voting choices.

Many voters in the low-wage sector want to know why their wages have not grown in the past thirty years, as shown in figure 2. Why are their wages disconnected from their productivity? Why has the American dream been denied to them? As explained in chapter 3, this is a complex problem with many parts. It is inconceivable that many members of the low-wage sector could find the information needed to put this picture together. Voters therefore have to rely on others to give them help. But who will provide the information?

As with complex goods for sale in our economy, people with money are advertising solutions to these problems. Just as large businesses dominate the information for consumer choices, large political organizations dominate the information for political choices. And brand names—party names in this case—summarize the information for voters. The problem is that there are only a few brand names in the political sphere, and there is no separate information available on the many issues voters need to take into account when voting. Voters need to know not only what they think about a variety of issues, but also how important these disparate choices are in casting a single vote.

The absence of political knowledge makes the Median Voter Theorem problematical. For example, Larry Bartels, a prominent political scientist working with the Median Voter Theorem, considered voters' opinions about the Bush tax cuts in 2001 and 2003. Finding that many ordinary people favored them, he asked incredulously: "How did ordinary people, ignorant and uncertain as they were in this domain, formulate any views at all about such a complex matter of public policy?"[16]

Similar questions arise in considering the invasion of Iraq in 2003. This invasion may have been a logical consequence of Nixon's Project Independence. It also was the consequence of George H. W. Bush's advisers: "Washington developed an Ahab-like mania regarding Saddam [Hussein]" in the 1990s. The invasion of Iraq was decided on by the Bush administration and then sold to the country, mostly by Secretary of State Condoleezza Rice and Vice President Dick Cheney. Not only was the military exempt from the desire for small government favored by the new conservatives, the war also was to be sold to the American public, not decided by them.[17]

There is no consideration of the barriers preventing some people from voting, and no consideration of the costs of information required to make choices in the Median Voter Theorem. These important aspects of the electoral process need to be brought from the periphery to the center of analysis.

An alternate approach starts from the cost of information discussed here. Just as business firms invest in providing information to consumers, political groups invest in providing information to voters. They make investments to convince people to vote just as business people make investments to convince others to buy. And large political organizations have the resources to make big investments in political education, just as large businesses have the resources to produce many ads and maintain many brands. This theory is known as the Investment Theory of Politics.[18]

This theory argues that the effects of voting are determined by entities—businesses, rich individuals, PACs—that are able to make large investments in political contests by various means. One way is to control who can vote, allowing only those people who will vote the way the investing entity wants. Another way is to advertise these entities' views heavily—on TV and on electronic billboards—and with powerful impact because voters have trouble getting other information about the effects of their votes. Voters typically need costly information for any single issue. Lacking the time or energy to get this information, they rely on advertising and party identification. They also have to vote on a small number of candidates. Each candidate represents positions on a bundle of decisions, and voters have to choose between these packages.

In the Investment Theory of Politics, in contrast to the Median Voter Theorem, voters are spread around a multi-dimensional space with scarce information needed to determine their position in each dimension. Faced with a small number of candidates, voters rely on the signals they receive from rich and powerful entities that invest in making their bundle of preferences attractive. Who can doubt the Investment Theory of Politics when politicians spend so much of their time and effort raising money? The result is that voters have less influence on political outcomes than the investing entities.

Elections become contests between several oligarchic parties whose major public policy proposals reflect the interests of large investors. The Investment Theory of Politics focuses attention on investors' interests, rather than those of candidates or voters. The expectation is that investors will not be responsive to public desires, particularly if they conflict with their interests, and they will be responsive to their own concerns. They will try to adjust the public to their views, rather than altering their views to accommodate voters. In other words, the Bush administration's policy of selling the Iraq War to the American people was the norm, not the exception.[19]

Bartels analyzed roll-call votes on the minimum wage, civil rights, budget waiver, and cloture. He found that "senators attached no weight at all to the views of constituents in the bottom third of the income distribution. ... The views of middle-income constituents seem to have been only slightly more influential." He found in an analysis of social issues that "even on abortion—a social issue with little or no specifically economic content—economic inequality produced substantial inequality in political representation." Bartels concluded from the analysis of many examples "that the specific policy views of citizens, whether rich or poor, have less impact on the policy-making process than the ideological convictions of elected officials." This is what the Investment Theory of

Politics predicts. Bartels's amazement confirms both the power of the Median Voter Theorem among academics and its great limitations in the analysis of American policy formation.[20]

The public appears more aware than political scientists of what is going on. Two-thirds of people interviewed in a recent Gallup Poll thought that major donors had a lot of influence over congressional votes. When Gallup arranged survey results by the extent to which respondents knew about the structure of the American government, the more knowledgeable people were more likely to say that major donors had a lot of influence—while people in the district electing Congress members had almost no influence.[21]

The source of these findings can be seen in the 2012 congressional elections. The proportion of votes cast for Democratic representatives was closely related to the amount of money spent on their behalf as shown in figure 5. In fact, the observations are so tightly clustered

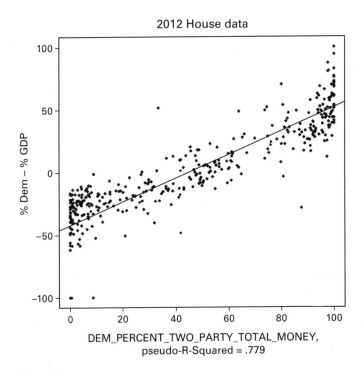

Figure 5
Money and congressional elections, 2012
Source: Ferguson, Jorgensen, and Chen 2013

around a straight line that the figure suggests that the expenditure of political funds is the most important determinant of party votes. The figure also reveals that the relation is linear: more money yields more votes. Personalities, issues, and campaign events are the focus of newspaper stories, but money is the prime determinant of the electoral outcome. Voter views captured by interviews may appear decisive, but they are in fact the mechanism by which the money spent affects votes. A more dramatic confirmation of the Investment Theory of Politics is hard to imagine.[22]

A new working paper by the same authors extends figure 5 to congressional elections since 1980. With the exception of one or two elections at the beginning, all the graphs—for both senators and representatives—look exactly like figure 5. The Investment Theory of Politics explains congressional votes well for the past thirty-five years. While there is more money in politics now and the role of dark money has mushroomed in recent years, money has been driving American congressional elections for many years.[23]

Anecdotal information suggests that figure 5 applies to local elections also, but the information is not available to make a formal test. The problem is the growth of dark money, that is, money from unidentified sources. The Brennan Center for Justice studied local elections in several states after 2010 and found that almost forty times as much dark money was in use in 2014 as in 2006. Three-quarters of outside spending in 2006 was fully identifiable, but only about a quarter was transparent in 2014. This growth of political spending without oversight facilitates corruption, and it is best understood through the Investment Theory of Politics.[24]

A study of almost two thousand policy decisions made in the past twenty years extends this result on voting to policy decisions. The authors distinguished two kinds of interests: majoritarian interests reflecting the views of median voters and elite preferences typified by the 90th percentile of income distribution, that is, by the top half of the FTE sector. They found that the interests of the elites were very different and sometimes opposed to those of the median voters. The policy outcomes did not reflect the median voters' views, seen as the majoritarian views. When the interests of the majority opposed those of the elites, they almost always lost out in political contests. The strong status quo bias built into American politics also made it hard for the majority to change policies they disagreed with. In short, the Investment Theory of Politics is a far better predictor of political contests than the Median Voter Theorem.[25]

The Investment Theory of Politics reveals how politics works in a dual economy. The FTE sector dominates decision making, and the low-wage sector is shut out of this process. This exclusion is preserved in a supposedly democratic society by maintaining that voting is a privilege, not a right, restricting access to voting by the low-wage sector, and by the promulgation of information by the businesses and rich individuals who want to steer policy toward the FTE sector. In short, we are living by "the Golden Rule—whoever has the gold rules."[26]

Preferences of the Very Rich

Figure 3 shows how the top 1 percent of the population became very rich in the past thirty years. This chapter integrates this growing share of national income into a discussion of politics in a dual economy. The Investment Theory of Politics is the connection between the income distribution in the United States and political decisions. A comparison of the percentages of the population represented in the various groups and sectors that have been described so far will help us understand the role of various groups in the dual economy. Table 1 contains the relevant data. The first and third rows contain observed information; the other rows show calculated percentages of the total population.

The United States has 320 million people in it at this time. The top 20 percent of them make up the FTE sector in our dual economy. Doing the multiplication shows there are about 64 million people in the FTE sector, as shown in the second row of table 1. This is only slightly larger than the number of blacks in our economy, shown in the third row of table 1. There is overlap in these two groups, as black managers and professionals are in the FTE sector, but they are largely distinct.

Below those rows are various proportions of the total population. The fourth row shows the top 1 percent of the population, whose increasing share of total income is graphed in figure 3. The next row shows the top 1 percent of the top 1 percent of the population, which we should think of as leading financial and business managers. There are roughly thirty thousand people in this category. The final row shows the top 1 percent of the top 1 percent of the top 1 percent of the population. They are members of the Forbes 400, a list published annually of the richest people in America.[1]

They also are the people who have tried for many years to transform their ideas about the role of government into public policy. The 1971 Powell Memorandum was a call to arms to business leaders that began a

Table 1
U.S. population and its parts

Category	Population
Total U.S. population	320,000,000
FTE sector (20%)	64,000,000
Black population	46,000,000
1% of the total population	3,200,000
1% of the 1%	32,000
1% of the 1% of the 1%	320

Source: https://www.census.gov/topics/population/data.html for the first and third rows.

complex dance between these groups of rich people that can be clarified by describing the politics of people in the last three rows of table 1 in turn. The Investment Theory of Politics asserts that people invest in policies that benefit them. This survey supports that argument.

It is of course hard to find information about the rich. They are busy and private; they set up gatekeepers to fend off social scientists who want to study them. The "1 percent" is the most numerous group of the very rich, and a sample of this group would be useful. Page, Bartels, and Seawright with great effort gathered such a sample in 2011. They started with a list of rich people that had been collected for high-end businesses to reach their desired customers. They refined this list by selecting those people with expensive houses and income-producing assets and then selecting again those who also appeared in a list of high-level executives. They tried to interview people on the resulting list, ending up with a sample of just over eighty rich people.

The average income of the respondents was about a million dollars; their average wealth was about fourteen million dollars. The mean was considerably higher than the median, indicating that the sample contained some considerably richer individuals. The sample reported constant political activity, including personal contacts with government officials. When asked what the most important problem was facing the United States, almost all of them said budget deficits.

The one-percenters said that unemployment and education were important issues, but these problems seldom were listed as the most important issue facing America. Less wealthy people also are worried about government deficits, but the one-percenters differ by favoring spending cuts rather than tax increases to eliminate the deficits. They generally favor government spending for infrastructure and scientific research, but not any of the social welfare programs of the government like Social Security and food stamps. Page, Bartels, and Seawright say, "We speculate that the striking contrast concerning core social welfare programs between our wealthy respondents and the general public may reveal something important about the current state of American politics."[2]

Even though the respondents said they were concerned about unemployment, they rejected federal programs to help the unemployed find jobs. This view contrasts sharply with that of the general public, which widely supports job help. There was a similar difference of opinion about the minimum wage and the Earned Income Tax Credit, which help low-wage workers. The one-percenters were far more negative about them than the general public. Similarly, the one-percenters were far less likely to approve of government spending to ensure that all children have good schools if taxes are needed for this purpose. And they also were less willing to pay more taxes to provide universal health coverage.

The one-percenters favor private spending to improve education. They also want to reduce regulation. The sample of rich people was not constructed to show difference within the sample, but wealthier individuals were significantly more likely to want reduced regulation than the poorer members of the one percent. This study provides a window into the attitudes and preferences of the one-percent group, which wants to reduce government activities in order to reduce government deficits. They do not want their taxes raised to lower government deficits, and they favor tax cuts when they can get them.[3]

The one-percenters were introduced by Chrystia Freeland as follows in *Plutocrats*: "They are becoming a trans global community of peers who have more in common with one another than with their countrymen back home." And she concluded with the comment of a businessman: "the per capita consumption of the Western middle class would have to decline as the developed and developing worlds 'meet somewhere in the middle.'"[4]

Moving upward in the income distribution—and downward in table 7.1—the 1 percent of the 1 percent are more intensely focused on lower taxes than the 1 percent group as a whole. They also are more politically active than the 1 percent group as a whole. They provided over one quarter of all political contributions in the 2012 election. Every U.S.

representative and senator elected in that year received financial support from the 1 percent of the 1 percent. And over four-fifths of these elected officials received more money from this select rich group than from all of the donors who gave $200 or less.

The political contributions of the very rich went to both parties. It is comforting to think of differences between the two major parties, but they draw support from the same narrow band of the income distribution. Nancy Pelosi and John Boehner, successive Democratic and Republican former Speakers of the House of Representatives, were among the representatives whose support from the 1 percent of the 1 percent was the strongest. The Investment Theory of Politics implies that their policy stances are not that different. They belong to different parties and differ on many specific policies. But they are both attentive to the FTE sector and are not eager to rock the boats of the very rich.[5]

The Investment Theory also asks what industries are behind this political support. The industry sector by far most frequently behind these gifts is what economists call the FIRE sector: finance, insurance, and real estate. This simple observation clarifies one of the important political decisions of the last decade. After the financial crisis of 2008, the financial institutions that were hurt in the crash were bailed out, but the householders whose mortgages went bad were not. As will be described in chapter 12, this failure to bail out members of the low-wage sector retarded the nation's recovery from the financial crisis. The Investment Theory of Politics leads us to important questions about the political process and indicates how the FTE sector ignores the needs of the low-wage sector.

A good summary of the policy desires of the 1 percent of the 1 percent is that they want to undo the New Deal. Roosevelt faced forceful opposition from business in the 1930s as he tried to alleviate the effects of the Great Depression. That opposition continued after the Second World War and was combined with the Southern interest in maintaining segregation by Senator Jesse Helms from North Carolina and others. Helms opposed the welfare state and labor unions as well as integration. He argued that it was better to close down public schools than to integrate them. And he considered it important to group all these policy decisions together as an opposition to socialism, keeping his opposition to integration in the background.[6]

The epicenter of this conservative business movement was Dallas, Texas. Dallas was an oil town, and it was given a great boost in the Second World War as the federal government relocated war production away from the coasts. Dallas became the "War Capital of the Southwest." Oil producers linked their conservative ideas to Ayn Rand and Friedrich Hayek after the war. They anchored their ideology in American history by arguing that the U.S. Constitution was not designed to protect rights, but instead to restrict them. In their view, the Constitution's role was to protect property rights, safeguard states' power from the federal government, and curtail democracy to preserve privilege.[7]

This view of a limited federal government appears to be at variance with the support that oil production and the owners of oil companies have continued to get from the federal government. Congress approved an oil depletion allowance in 1926, allowing oil producers to deduct more than a quarter of their gross revenues from their taxable income. The Texas senator who sponsored this tax break admitted later that oil producers would have been happy with a lower depletion allowance, but they thought that the figure of 27.5 percent gave the allowance the appearance of scientific reasoning. And of course they were happier with the bigger deduction. Roosevelt wanted to close this tax loophole in the 1930s, but nothing was done. Truman tried as well and similarly failed. Kennedy and Nixon debated the depletion allowance. Kennedy opposed it, and Nixon supported it in keeping with his Southern Strategy. The oil depletion allowance was altered and sometimes restricted in various ways since then, but when Obama tried to repeal it in 2007, his bill died in the Senate Finance Committee, which was under Democratic control.[8]

The belief in small government does not conflict with the readiness of business leaders to profit from the effects of government. The way to understand this apparent contradiction is that "small government" does not have a simple meaning. It means partly a government that does not try to help the low-wage sector of the economy. The New Deal should be repealed; extensions in the postwar years should be eliminated as well. Unions should be broken. But transfers through the tax system from the low-wage sector to the FTE sector are fine.

The Constitution empowered Congress to extend bankruptcy policies to promote business. Business operations regularly use this provision today to shift their expenses to the low-wage sector. Coal companies despoiled the countryside in Appalachia, and regulators estimate that it will cost a billion dollars to clean up after them. The coal companies, however, are going bankrupt, and the cost will fall on the low-wage sector. Donald Trump similarly used bankruptcy to make others pay for his speculative activity in Atlantic City while walking away with profits.[9]

Trump took advantage of tax loopholes that apply to real estate to the tune of about a billion dollars; likewise New Jersey suffered a loss when David Tepper, a hedge-fund billionaire, moved to Florida to be subject to lower taxes. Many companies also dodge taxes by moving their profits around. Apple, the most profitable American company, holds its profits abroad to avoid taxes. Pfizer, a leader of the profitable pharmaceutical industry, sought a tax inversion that would shift its corporate tax burden abroad where corporate tax rates are lower. States compete among themselves for rich residents by shielding their wealth.[10]

And although they work hard to reduce their taxes, the 1 percent of the 1 percent also do not hesitate to avoid taxes altogether if they can. Gabriel Zucman estimated that 8 percent of household financial wealth was in tax havens in 2014. This is almost eight trillion dollars, which is a lot of money to be hidden away from tax collectors. The exposure of a Panama bank that arranged for money to be hidden—a controversy that has come to be called the Panama Papers—has revealed some of the details of how all this tax reduction takes place. And the effective tax on U.S. businesses is falling fast as profit is hidden in tax havens. The hidden wealth of American corporations has lowered the effective corporate profit rate to half its nominal rate.[11]

Turning to the last row of table 7.1, the 1 percent of the 1 percent of the 1 percent of the population consists of about three hundred people. They are three-quarters of the Forbes list of the 400 wealthiest people in the United States. Their names are clear, and their political activities are legion. Just as their wealth is extreme, their politics are extreme. They agree with the lower members of the financial hierarchy that their taxes should be low and government activities reduced. They believe this very strongly and have become politically active to achieve their ends.

There are almost no African Americans in the Forbes 400. There are a very few who have made enough money to be in this list of unbelievably wealthy individuals. Extraordinary people of African descent have made it to the top of this field as they have made it to the top of other fields. W. Arthur Lewis, who formulated the model used here, was a top economist; President Obama is a top politician. But racecraft has kept the number of African Americans in the Forbes 400 far below the fifty or so black faces we would see if American society and economy were completely integrated.

When African Americans get elected to public office, they face daunting challenges. They typically want to correct some of the ills that have befallen minorities in the United States, but they cannot be seen as being too obviously in favor of the disadvantaged to remain in office. President Obama seemed, as the first African-American president, to be uniquely in this position, but other African Americans who have been mayors, governors, and senators have faced similar conflicts of interest. And of course, they have all experienced disappointments as whatever they were able to do was limited in the face of the forces of racecraft.[12]

Unlike the 1 percent as a whole who give money and talk to government officials, some members of the Forbes 400 formed a secret organization in the 1970s to promote their ends. Charles Koch, who with his brother, David, is in fifth place in the 2015 Forbes 400, was energized by Powell's secret memo of 1971. He started ALEC, the American Legislative Exchange Council, in 1973. This state lobbying organization operates under the radar of most people interested in national politics because even interested observers cannot keep all states in view. But, as explained in chapter 2, ALEC is most successful when state legislators lack resources of their own to investigate proposed laws. States are increasingly strapped for money given that Nixon's New Federalism as implemented by Reagan and succeeding administrations deprives state government of resources. The combination of policies leads to increasing effectiveness of ALEC.

Koch also formed a secret organization to advance the interests of large businesses and rich executives by following the model of the John Birch Society—a conservative, small-government and anti-communist organization founded around 1960—on a vastly expanded scale. Although this organization was designed to bring down much of our government, its aim was not to be called anarchism in order to avoid association with terrorists. As Charles wrote in 1976, "In order to avoid undesirable criticism, how the organization is controlled and directed should not be widely advertised." This dissembling echoes Jesse Helms's indirection.[13]

We know about this secret organization primarily from Jane Mayer's book, *Dark Money*. This remarkable book sheds light on the dark Koch enterprise, which she calls the "Kochtopus." Mayer wrote a *New Yorker* article on the Koch brothers in 2010 as she began her publications on political dark money. The Koch brothers responded by hiring a private detective to dig up dirt on Mayer. They wanted to accuse her of plagiarism, one of the most damaging practices of irresponsible reporters. They tried to kill the messenger and preserve the secrecy of their organization. Mayer is a responsible journalist, and the Koch brothers did not succeed in shutting her up. Much of the following detail comes from her book.[14]

Koch Industries is not in Dallas, but its primary business is refining oil. It owned the Pine Bend Refinery in Minnesota, which refined low-grade oil from Canada to sell widely in Minnesota and Wisconsin. It was profitable to refine this poor oil into good gasoline, but the refinery used massive amounts of energy and polluted its environs. Koch Industries management did not warn employees about the dangers of working there and was resistant to both internal whistle blowers and external government challenges, particularly from the Environmental Protection Agency. As Charles Koch wrote in the *Libertarian Review* in 1978, "We should *not* cave in the moment a regulator sets foot on our doorstep. ... Do not cooperate voluntarily; instead, resist wherever and to whatever extent you legally can. And do so in the name of *justice.*" [15]

Like the Dallas oil producers, Koch aspired to shift the costs of production to the low-wage economy. The mechanism, however, was different. While the Dallas crowd was happy with a subsidy in the form of the oil depletion allowance, Koch imposed costs directly on his employees and the people around his refinery who were affected by the pollution it generated. His opposition to government regulation was both ideological and profitable. Koch Industries was accused in a Senate investigation in 1989 of stealing from Native Americans, a minority population at the opposite end of the income distribution. The investigation of this theft led to lawsuits and a large judgment against Koch in 1999. The company also was listed as one of the top ten air polluters in the United States in 2010. [16]

Early in 2010, the Supreme Court decided the landmark case *Citizens United*, ruling that the government could not restrict independent political expenditures by nonprofit companies, greatly easing the flow of campaign contributions from companies. Koch and his secret organization were quick to seize the opportunity. Reasoning that their money would have more impact in smaller markets, they poured money into state races for governors and representatives in the 2010 midterm elections. Democrats were slow to take advantage of this opportunity. They were neither disciplined nor under centralized control; even if they had realized the opportunity, they would not have agreed on how to allocate their resources. And of course they had far fewer liquid resources at their disposal than the Kochtopus.

The Democrats lost control of Congress and many conservative governors were elected in 2010. President Obama and the Democratic Party did not know what hit them. They discussed ideas and tactics in retrospect, but they did not follow the path outlined in the Investment Theory of Politics that the money and industries supplying the money are the key actors in political competitions. And the secrecy of the Koch political organization, now augmented by the secrecy allowed by *Citizens United*, made it hard to find the source of political money.[17]

This story is only about the effects of one very rich family. There are other politically active people in the Forbes 400, but we can only give a few pointers to what be many relevant stories. The Kochtopus gets funds from rich people in financial industries. We do not know who they are because of the secrecy that surrounds this secret Koch organization, but the concentration of financial people interested in deregulating finance cannot be surprising. Looking only a little way down the list from the richest people in the country we find Sheldon Adelson, who is active in politics along the same lines as the Koch brothers.

Roughly equal in wealth at around $25 billion, George Soros expresses his views by funding quite different activities that range from promoting democracy in Eastern Europe to encouraging varied approaches to economics through the Institute for New Economic Thinking. While most rich people appear to be conservative to one degree or other, there is some variety among the very richest Americans. But the presence of a few highly visible philanthropists should not blind us to the conservative views of most of the top 1 percent and especially the very rich. The Investment Theory of Politics tells us how important these views are for the future of the United States.[18]

8

Concepts of Government

It is helpful to step back from this account of political pressures and think about the concepts of government being used by the various parts of the dual economy. This can be seen very simply by distinguishing three types of government: democratic, oligarchic, and autocratic. A *democratic* government is one that is controlled by all or almost all of the people. Lincoln's immortal words, "a government of the people, by the people, for the people," describe it well. It may take the form of a republic if the numbers in the democracy are too large for unified meetings and actions. An *oligarchic* government is one controlled by only part of the population. It may be a large or small part of the population, and it may behave differently depending on how large the oligarchy is. It is called an aristocratic government when membership in the oligarchy is bestowed by birth and a plutocracy when membership is by income and wealth. An *autocratic* government is one ruled by an individual, a family, or another very small group.

A dual economy is a plutocracy, since the FTE sector determines policy for the whole economy. Most Americans refer to their country as a democracy, but this is not accurate. The growing inequality of income has generated politics that are oligarchic and even at risk of becoming autocratic.

Autocratic governments have been the rule during most of recorded history. From Roman emperors to Western European kings, single men (almost always men) have ruled over other people. Only a few cases of democracy and oligarchy are known before the Industrial Revolution. Greek cities and the Roman Republic are famous for recording the dealings of these more complex forms of government. Some medieval cities also were republics. But the general pattern was that democracies did not last; they were succeeded by one or another form of autocracy.

Modern democracies only made their appearance about two hundred years ago. The United States was the first modern democracy. The conventional story is that the American colonies broke away from the autocratic English government to form an independent democratic country. But it is clear from the history in chapters 5 and 7 that this is a misleading story. Slavery was very important to the Southern colonies, and they were determined to continue owning slaves in the new government. As they saw it, black people were not fit to be considered in forming this government. They thought of themselves as democrats, but only of and by white people. Their attitude toward slaves may have been shared by some in the North, but after a bloody Civil War and various constitutional amendments and laws, racecraft is no longer part of our legal framework, although its residue is still in our society and economy.[1]

From the point of view of the people involved, the framers of the U.S. Constitution were democrats. Southerners insisted on a series of compromises to preserve both their representation in the new government and the institution of slavery. The resulting document can only be seen in the twenty-first century as a deal between the democratic Northern states and the oligarchic Southern states.

This deal broke down as the United States spread west, and it finally erupted into the Civil War. Even though the North won the war, it did not succeed in destroying the oligarchic organization of the South. As described in chapter 5, the long tradition of viewing voting as a privilege rather than a right has combined with a growing inequality of income to make our current government more oligarchic than democratic. We have gone in the last generation from an aristocracy—when Southern political control was vested in the descendants of slave-owning families—to a plutocracy. We had something close to democracy in the interval between these different oligarchies in the middle-class economic growth after the Second World War, but it did not last very long.

Democracy appears to be unstable in the United States because of the legacy of slavery. Voting was conceptualized in the new country as a privilege, not a right. Until we shake that conception, we will have trouble sustaining a durable democracy. Change will come slowly because of the federalized nature of our government. The federal government delegated voting regulation to the states to implement the constitutional compromise. This practice was sustained by whites who wanted to maintain blacks in subservient positions, a view supported by racecraft. States delegate the administration of voting to localities, where the privilege concept is still expressed. In order to change the fundamental nature of American voting, we need to restructure many levels of government.

This can be seen in major developments of the past few decades. The close presidential election of 2000 was decided by the Supreme Court, which took the unusual step of banning further recounts of votes. The Court stated that *Bush v. Gore* (531 US 98 [2000]) should set no precedent. Perhaps that was true for court decisions; the impact of this decision on the lives of low-wage workers and the future composition of the Supreme Court were immense. President George W. Bush appointed two conservative justices to the Supreme Court. The Supreme Court weighed in again in *Shelby County v. Holder* in 2013, in which they ruled the most important part of Johnson's Voting Rights Act of 1965 unconstitutional. This part of the act allowed the federal government to ban restrictive state voting rules before they went into effect. The Voting Rights Act had been renewed by several sessions of the Congress with lopsided votes, but the Supreme Court, with conservative Bush appointees, differed. The result was a spate of new voting restrictions in the states. Ironically, even though the Supreme Court stated that the old Confederacy was gone and should not be discriminated against, most of the new voting restrictions appeared in the states that had been part of the Confederacy.[2]

This history is very important, as it is only in a democracy that public policies will be made for all the people. This is the implication both of the Lewis model and the Investment Theory of Politics. It also is common sense. We can expect gifts from others for many reasons: family occasions, reciprocity for past favors, and high spirits. But if we want sustained policies to alter conditions created by past political decisions, we need universal voting and governance. An oligarchy will not willingly provide social insurance for all. Only a functioning democracy will do that.

What would such a policy for all the people look like? One way to summarize the role of a democracy is as a promoter of security, which can be seen also as a reducer of risk. Living is a process that involves many risks, ranging from bankruptcy to illness and beyond. The government is in the best position to offer people insurance because it can compel people to join in the insurance process, it has a perfect credit rating since it can tax and print money, and it can monitor people at risk. The government has to want to offer security and insurance, and a democratic government responsive to its citizens will want to do so.

The American government can be thought of as offering insurance in three stages. The first stage in the nineteenth century was to provide security for business. The second phase in the first half of the twentieth century provided insurance for workers. And the current phase since then provides security for all. This progression is due partly to the increasing incomes of Americans and partly to the expansion of the franchise to bring the United States closer and closer to being a democracy.[3]

One of the first ways the United States helped reduce risk was by allowing limited liability for businesses. In this process, an investor could limit his or her liability if the company failed. Another way to improve the security of businesses is to keep prices stable. The United States had an enviable run of stable prices in the nineteenth century, and the government has been active since then in trying to deal with the price effects of wars, depressions, and financial crises.

Bankruptcy is both a business and a personal risk. It is a way to socialize the risks, that is, to make others share in the risks facing a business or person. If a company or person borrows heavily, there is a risk that the debts may be too many or too large to pay off. This problem arises for individuals all the time, and this risk spreads around the economy in times of crises. Since every loan has a lender and a borrower, how can we know who is at fault? Bankruptcy makes the lenders and borrowers share the cost of excessive loans, reducing the size of loans in bankruptcy proceedings.[4]

Insurance for workers applies the same principles to workers' risk of injury on the job. The worker obviously suffers from an injury. Workers' compensation eases the burden by compensating the injured worker for lost wages. As in bankruptcy, the cost of the accident is shared between the company and the worker. Government is needed here to compel all companies to carry workers' compensation. If it were voluntary to offer this insurance, companies would try to compel workers to take jobs without compensation. Workers' compensation was initiated in the early twentieth century and has been augmented by regulations from the Occupational Safety and Health Administration, known everywhere as OSHA, a century later.[5]

Social Security protects people in their old age. Many workers do not earn enough for them to provide for a retirement by themselves. Social Security allows workers to retire and maintain something close to their prior standard of living. As described in chapter 6, the system is not set up as an investment made by individuals for their own retirement, but by an intergenerational bargain in which current workers pay for the retirement of the last generation in the expectation that future workers will pay for their retirement. Like workers' compensation, Social Security is done best by the federal government, which can assure workers both that all eligible workers will pay into the system and that these funds will be used to pay their benefits.

Product liability law developed to provide purchasers of goods a way to share the loss they may incur from poorly designed or fabricated goods. This branch of law is like workers' compensation for consumers. As the economy increasingly moves to technical, financial, and electronic products, the link between the maker and the consumer of products has become increasing opaque. The new Consumer Financial Protection Bureau extends product liability from manufactured goods to financial products.

Medicare and Medicaid provide medical care to individuals who qualify for these programs. As in the previous examples, the cost of illness is socialized, so that the cost is not borne entirely by the sick person. These programs are set up as insurance systems, and the government allows every eligible person to ask for help. This help is financed by taxation, and the cost is borne by everyone who pays taxes. Medicare for older people is run by the federal government; Medicaid for poor people is run by states. As noted earlier, state control often is a way to deny benefits for disadvantaged people. African Americans and recent Latino immigrants have been denied Medicaid benefits by lack of funds after the 2008 financial crisis and by state politicians objecting to the Affordable Care Act.

The Affordable Care Act that President Obama signed into law in 2009 was approved by the Supreme Court in 2012 with the caveat that states could opt out of the part that was run through an expansion of Medicaid. Many states chose to deny the expansion of Medicaid to their residents even though the federal government would pay all the costs for the first few years and most of the costs thereafter. The states that opted out of the free extension of Medicaid were clustered in the South, reflecting again the racecraft involved in such decisions on compensation of care.

Part of the anger against the Affordable Care Act, popularly known as "Obamacare," is because its benefits are seen in racist terms by some critics as gifts from one black man—who happens to be the president—to the black population. This factor may be most important to less educated whites. Another reason for the anger is that Obamacare raised taxes on the very rich. In fact, the Obama administration raised taxes in two ways: by letting some tax breaks for people earning over half a million dollars to expire, and by the Affordable Care Act provisions raising taxes on the rich to support healthcare for the poor. Some among the very rich, as noted in chapter 7, do not take well to having their taxes increase.[6]

Falling ill is something that happens after being born, but there are additional risks in being born. Perhaps the biggest birth risk we take is in the identity of our parents. We do not choose our parents, and John Rawls, the author of *A Theory of Justice*, suggested that we think of a random process assigning children to parents. If we turn that around, we can say that the largest risk that a person faces in America is of being born into the "wrong" part of society, in the low-wage sector with a black or brown skin. Rawls argued that we should agree to organize a democratic society to reduce the risk of a disadvantaged birth. Such a society would be a just society, and Rawls urged us to minimize the effects of the risk inherent in the family-matching process. This summons provides a framework for the role of a democratic society in minimizing risks to its members.[7]

Democracy has waxed and waned in American history, and the federal government expanded over time its efforts to provide security for all citizens. In good times, like the equitable growth that followed the Second World War, the government increased its role of reducing risks. In times when our democracy looks more like an oligopoly than a democracy, the care has been restricted in one dimension or another.

The opposite pole from democracy is autocracy. The actions of the very rich suggest that we should try to visualize what autocracy might look like. Start by considering 1 percent of the Forbes 400. That yields four people. Consider a government dominated by the four most politically active of the Forbes 400—or any smaller group drawn from these four: Charles Koch, David Koch, Sheldon Adelson, and Donald Trump. That would be an autocratic government, and we know from their actions what the policies of this government might be.

It would make policies without anyone but a few advisers knowing why. Secrecy would be the watchword, and information about the reasoning behind policies would be managed by the autocratic leadership. Recall the invasion of Iraq in 2003, which anticipated autocratic operations.

An autocratic government would reduce taxes greatly. More precisely, it would greatly reduce or even eliminate taxes on rich people and large business firms. Tax relief might extend throughout the FTE sector, although it might not get down the income ladder very far. It would not extend to the low-wage sector. Essentially all government revenue would be raised from the low-wage sector.

Since the autocratic government would try to balance its budget, government services would be cut back significantly. The regulatory state that has been constructed since the Great Depression would be starved into impotence or eliminated outright. There would be a free market in the anarchist sense, although not in the sense used by most economists. The Securities and Exchange Commission, the Dodd-Frank Wall Street Reform and Consumer Protection Act, the Environmental Protection Agency, and other checks on autocratic decisions in governance and finance would disappear. There would be no government agency devoted to preserving level playing fields between companies. Social Security and Medicare would be phased out; Medicaid would be funded entirely at the state level.[8]

Education also would be financed and controlled entirely at the state level. No federal funds would flow to the states, and no centralized direction would come to the states. Given the inability of states to raise enough money to support a good educational system without federal funds, education in American would continue to decline.[9]

The federal government would restrict itself to a few functions: national defense (interpreted broadly), federal prisons, the Federal Reserve System. Within that minimal framework, life would be anarchic. It might look more like a current kleptocracy such as Putin's Russia than a preindustrial kingship. Corruption is the key to operating any activity in a kleptocracy. Businesses operate corruptly in that system, and the autocrats reward their friends by direct support and the elimination of competitors. The organization of a corrupt economy is stable because any attempt to oppose it by operating a noncorrupt business that did not pay bribes or engage in other underhand actions would likely fail. In this dog-eat-dog environment, corrupt business firms with ties to the government would be able to eliminate honest businesses one way or another.[10]

Autocracy needs prisons to control the population. I discuss prisons as social control in chapter 9, but they can also serve the function of keeping the peace when dissenters threaten an autocratic government. The United States is an outlier in the size of its prison population, which grew rapidly since 1970. Its prison system now differs from the prison systems in other more or less democratic countries and resembles the prison systems in autocratic ones. There would be little capital cost in modifying our judicial system to accommodate a political change.

Between democracy and autocracy lies oligarchy. Oligarchies are where materially endowed actors defend their wealth. They defend both their wealth and the flow of services from their property in the form of income. The extremes can be described more easily than oligarchies because there are many varieties of oligarchies. In other words, oligarchies take different forms in the space between the extremes of democracy and autocracy. There can be an oligarchy like the early Northern United States and Britain in the early nineteenth century, where the right to vote was defined by gender and a property requirement. If the property requirement was low, then the government was almost a democracy. If, by contrast, one-third of the population was excluded from voting, as slaves were in the antebellum United States, then the oligarchy seems closer to autocracy. The dual economy that we live in today is governed largely by the FTE sector, one-fifth of the population. That is an oligarchic government we know from our own experience.[11]

The political history of the United States can be summarized in these terms as follows: From the signing of the Constitution to the Civil War, the country was divided by slavery into two parts. There were experiments with democracy in the North, but oligarchy was maintained in the South where slaves could not vote—or even get an education. From the Civil War to the First World War this condition more or less continued. African Americans voted in some states, but the experiments with opening the vote to women in the North had ceased. The inequality of income at the end of the nineteenth century meant that rich people dominated politics by the various avenues open then.

After the war, women got the vote, and the franchise opened up somewhat. African Americans, however, still were denied the ability to vote until the Civil Rights Movement of the 1960s. With that stimulus, the United States came close to being a democracy for half a century until the Supreme Court gutted the 1965 Voting Rights Act in 2013. Inequality increased between those dates, and the Investment Theory of Politics teaches us that the effectiveness of the ordinary voters decreased as rich people and large businesses began to influence elections. It may not be misleading to say that the effectiveness of democracy has been decreasing over time since the initiation of the American dual economy in 1971, and democracy has now given way to a new oligarchy or, to be more specific, a plutocracy.[12]

The process became visible in the 1990s when Congress, dominated by the adolescent FTE sector, shut down the government over a dispute with President Clinton and then voted to impeach him. It was even more dramatic in the resolution of the 2000 election to choose Clinton's successor. The election was close, but it did not end up in the House of Representatives as the Constitution anticipated. Instead it ended in disputed votes in the state of Florida, whose governor was the brother of the Republican candidate George W. Bush. Governor Jeb Bush did not recuse himself, as a judge would have done, but instead worked to certify his brother's election. Then the Supreme Court, in *Bush v. Gore*, 531 US 98 (2000), ruled that there should be no recounts and therefore George W. Bush would be president. The chief justice was William Rehnquist, appointed to the Supreme Court by Richard Nixon in 1971 (confirmed in 1972). The memory of democracy assured that this political decision by the Court was accepted peacefully, but the excesses of the process stimulated a literature on how to make sure that people could vote and their votes would count. This literature assumed that public policy would work to restore democracy, while public policy increasingly has worked to restrict influence to an ever richer and more select plutocracy.[13]

How much difference did this controversial conclusion to *Bush v. Gore* make? It is hard to conjecture what might have been, since we know only what was and have to guess about possible alternatives. Parts of domestic policy might have been more or less similar, as Clinton had approved the 1994 crime bill that confirmed and may have encouraged mass incarceration. But Bush reduced taxes while invading Iraq, creating federal budget deficits similar to those run by Reagan. The invasion of Iraq and the ideological handling of the aftermath was one of the causes for the formation of ISIS that plagues Europe and America today. According to a recent history of this organization, "ISIS's command-and-control tier emerged with 'made-in-US-run-prisons' tags. ... Seventeen of the twenty-five most important leaders [two-thirds of the leaders] running the war in Iraq and Syria spent time in US-run detention facilities between 2004 and 2011." Exporting incarceration for social control to Iraq backfired mightily.[14]

The Republican State Leadership Committee (RSLC), founded in 2002, was considerably more successful in its effort to take over Congress. With a budget of more than $30 million from the U.S. Chamber of Commerce, an organization close to ALEC, and many large companies, the RSLC focused in on a variety of state races in 2010. The Democrats were discouraged after the fight for the Affordable Care Act and the slow recovery from the financial crisis of 2008, and they did not understand how quickly *Citizens United*, decided in January, was changing the political landscape.

As a result of this lopsided spending, Republicans emerged from the 2010 election with just shy of thirty Republican state governors and almost as many Republican-controlled state legislatures. The RSLC then put into operation its REDMAP, a plan to redistrict in favor of Republicans. Gerrymandering is a traditional American practice, but REDMAP was the first set of state actions orchestrated in a national effort. The first step was to jam voters likely to favor your opponents into a few throwaway districts where the other side could win lopsided victories, a strategy known as "packing." The second step was to arrange other boundaries to win close victories, "cracking" opposition groups into many districts.

As a result of REDMAP, Democrats received 1.4 million more votes for the House of Representatives in 2012, yet Republicans won control of the House by a 234 to 201 margin. Democrats would have had to win the popular vote by 7 percentage points to take control of the House given the newly manipulated boundaries of REDMAP districts (assuming that votes shifted by a similar percentage across all districts), a margin that happens in only about one-third of congressional elections. The ability of democratic voters to change the leadership of the House of Representatives is very limited; plutocrats—the 1 percent—have sharply hampered their access.[15]

As the middle class shrinks, the FTE sector increasingly directs public policy. Democratic preferences no longer dominate policy decisions. Given the free use of dark money in politics, the oligarchy has gotten smaller. The oligarchy is moving further away from a democratic state and closer to an autocratic one. In that sense, the extreme cases are useful to characterize the tendencies, if not the actual operations, of different oligarchies.

President Obama nominated Merrick Garland, a federal appeals court judge, to the Supreme Court in March 2016, a month after the sudden death of Justice Antonin Scalia, who was personally connected with many rich and conservative people and the leader of five conservative justices who often voted together to make conservative decisions. The refusal of the Senate to process Obama's nomination of federal judges and particularly a Supreme Court justice nominee in 2016 indicates that we are moving in the direction of an autocratic government. The Constitution is perfectly clear. The president nominates judges, and the Senate is directed to provide advice and consent for the president's nominee. The Senate also had held back confirming many of Obama's candidates for federal district court judges, a breach of its constitutional duty that only came to light in the Garland stonewall.[16]

There were over one hundred prior cases where an elected president faced a vacancy on the Supreme Court and began an appointment process. In all of these cases, the president was able to both nominate and appoint a replacement justice. There were only six cases in which the Senate sought to transfer a sitting president's appointment power to a successor. These exceptions were confined to cases where the president was appointed rather than elected or where the nomination came after the election of his successor. Neither of these conditions was present in 2016; the Senate's actions were without historical precedent and risk politicizing the Supreme Court in a way that threatens the very foundation of our government.[17]

Senator Ron Johnson stated, "We absolutely will not allow the Supreme Court to flip." The Majority Leader of the Senate, Senator Mitch McConnell said, "I can't imagine that a Republican majority in the United States Senate would want to confirm, in a lame duck session, a nominee opposed by the National Rifle Association, the National Federation of Independent Business that represents small businesses." This refusal to follow the Constitution is an extension of the 2010 redistricting coup that moved our oligarchic society closer to an autocratic one. If it succeeds in politicizing the court system and restricting the Executive Branch, it will distort greatly or even destroy the division of political power set by the Constitution into three independent branches.[18]

The Kochtopus spent more than $40 million on state races in the 2016 elections, and, as the regression shown in figure 5 predicted, its candidates generally won. This kept conservative state governors in power and conservatives in Congress still powerful. We are on the way to an autocratic government.[19]

"Whoever has the gold rules." And nothing is new under the sun. Augustus, the first Roman emperor, kept the form of the Roman Republic intact while wielding autocratic power; the Koch brothers and their friends could do the same.[20]

III

Government in a Dual Economy

9

Mass Incarceration

Part I focused on economics. Part II focused on politics. Part III applies these disciplines to explain how the preceding political economy of a dual economy affects government activities in the United States.

The Lewis model predicts that the FTE sector will not do anything to help members of the low-wage sector because its members want wages in the low-wage sector to remain low. Racecraft and white rage give rise to fears of revolt by minorities of different races and lead to active repression of black and brown members of the low-wage sector. The oxymoron "majority minority" expresses white people's fear that they will become outnumbered in the United States. Everyone else is a minority by definition, since the founding fathers were white, even if by 2030 or so the minorities will be the majority.

These strands combine in a political plan to lower taxes, the prime aim of the very rich. The FTE sector as a whole does not want to increase wages and well-being in the low-wage sector. The result is to starve or even destroy the welfare state built up during the twentieth century. Only the very rich want to destroy the New Deal and its 1960s extensions; the FTE as a whole seems willing to keep these programs functioning at a low cost. The connection between race and incarceration rates has been noted by sociologists, but the connection of both to the worsening distribution of income often has not been drawn.

As this plan has developed, it has taken the form of reducing the resources allocated to various government welfare programs. These programs need to scrimp and save; the quality of their services goes down. Then the FTE sector argues that the programs are working badly and should be privatized. This is expressed in the oxymoron of "private public" schools, colleges, jails, and so on. Academics debate how well these private substitutes work, while the very rich see privatization as an end in itself.

The single government activity approved by the FTE sector is the military. The FTE sector is eager to enlarge military spending and they support militarization of government services that they cannot do without. Police in the United States have become paramilitary organizations. The Pentagon gives them surplus military equipment, and the police use the same equipment in the United States that the military used in Iraq.

This can be seen in the reaction to the tragic events in Ferguson, Missouri, when a policeman shot and killed Michael Brown, an unarmed black teenager who was about to start college, in the late summer of 2014. The community was outraged by this apparently random killing of a black teenager, and there were massive public demonstrations in the following evenings. The police showed up for one of the evening demonstrations in a fortified military personnel carrier. This was a dramatic sign that the police were at war with the black residents of Ferguson.[1]

Another sign was the killing of a sniper who shot at police officers in Dallas while they were protecting a peaceful protest in 2016. The police used a "bomb robot" to carry a bomb near the shooter and then detonated it. In doing so, they repurposed a remote-controlled bomb-disposal vehicle normally used to inspect dangerous crime scenes or pick up suspected explosive devices for detonation or dismantling. The decision to deliver a bomb by robot stunned some law-enforcement officials, who said they believed the new tactic blurred the line between policing and warfare. The objective in war is to kill your opponent; police should have a different and more nuanced function. But the further you reduce a police officer from the effects of using force, the easier it is for him or her to use it, and some officers said they would use a bomb in similar circumstances. Observers compared this military escalation with the armored personnel carrier used in Ferguson.[2]

The aftermath of the Ferguson shooting also is revealing. The local prosecutor presented evidence to a grand jury investigating the shooting and declined to indict the police officer. The federal government then investigated the Ferguson police department for violating equal-protection laws. They found that the police department violated these laws in several ways. The most prominent way was to finance itself by imposing fines on black residents of Ferguson for trivial events like traffic violations and failing to show up for legal procedures.

The city and the federal government reached agreement on a plan to reform the actions of the Ferguson police force in accordance with the law. When the city reneged on the agreement, the Department of Justice sued. The town needed to raise taxes to substitute for the revenue previously obtained from fines on black residents and avoid a court case. But voters rejected part of a tax package the city leaders had described as essential for carrying out the legal settlement with the Department of Justice. Voters approved an increase in the sales tax, and they rejected a proposed property tax increase.

This outcome illustrates how the Lewis model applies to the United States today. Blacks in Ferguson are almost entirely in the low-wage sector. The Ferguson negotiators with Washington agreed on taxes to replace the fines on black drivers and arrested men and women. The voters rejected an increase in property taxes because the FTE sector does not want to pay taxes to help the low-wage sector. Sales taxes were fine, in contrast, since they are mostly paid by members of the low-wage sector. The fate of legal policing in Ferguson is up in the air.[3]

The United States has a dual judicial system where the FTE sector pays taxes and occasionally fines, and the low-wage sector is subject to frequent fines and imprisonment for failure to pay fines. This pattern has been repeated in many other cities large and small, including police shooting of unarmed black youngsters, racist policing, taxation through police fines, and federal government attempts to deal with the resulting legal violations. The federal government is limited in its power to protect poor black communities. The resulting destruction of social capital often does not emerge clearly in the legal and economic problems of the militarized police and city administrations, but it is an important part of the dual economy in the United States.

Speed traps levied primarily on black drivers are a source of income in other governments around St. Louis, and lawsuits are pending in some of them. Chicago black residents also have been experiencing disproportionate traffic and street stops; they account for three-quarters of the four hundred people shot by the Chicago police between 2008 and 2015. Militarization and racism make a destructive and often lethal combination.[4]

Immigration similarly has become militarized. The immigration issue is reduced to border control, and the tensions between the businesses that want Latino workers and the white workers opposed to black and brown competition are not resolved. Militarization of the border can't resolve this complex issue. Continuing debate focuses on military solutions, and Latino immigrants suffer and sometimes die as a result. They are at risk of winding up like Nelson Fernandez, the father of a United States citizen and a legal permanent resident for twenty-six years. He had been arrested and served probation in 1992 and is now facing deportation for that offense. He is incarcerated in a county jail where he cannot not get the medical care he needs.[5]

These programs are supported by the FTE sector's efforts to repress anticipated opposition by African Americans and Latinos. Militarization in the form of incarceration brings this need in line with the aims of destroying the welfare state. The War on Drugs is the center of the push to destroy black and brown communities through mass incarceration. The unique American combination of race and class affects both the structure and operation of the government, and the effort to keep African Americans and their more recent Latino neighbors in their place imposes large costs on the great majority of Americans today.

Mass incarceration began in 1973, shortly after Nixon's introduction of the War on Drugs. The economic disturbances of the 1970s were described in chapter 2; they led to an apparent rise in crime, although the reports may have only shown better crime measurement. Urbanization was increasing, the Great Migration had brought many African Americans into the North, and baby boomers born in the years after the Second World War were becoming young adults—the prime age to commit crimes.

The response to these economic and social disturbances was determined by Nixon's New Federalism and Reagan's reduction of funding for social programs. The alternative was to get tough with crime, to punish rather than prevent crime, to incriminate instead of educate. This approach was started in New York with the Rockefeller Drug Laws of 1973. It was followed by Nancy Reagan's appeal to "Just say no" to drugs and by Clinton's 1994 drug law that increased incarceration at the same time it gave funds for prevention. This toughness appeared justified in the face of the heroin, cocaine, and crack cocaine epidemics in succeeding decades of the late twentieth century. And it focused the anger of working whites at their economic troubles and social disruptions on African Americans in the form of white rage.[6]

African Americans are far more likely to be incarcerated than other population groups, and the New Jim Crow is an important part of the complex of measures designed to keep African Americans poor and politically marginalized in America. Bruce Western concluded from a careful analysis of the causes of mass incarceration that "law-and-order politics grew out of reaction to the gains of the civil rights movement and anxieties about rising crime rates among white voters." Incarceration grew fastest in those states where jobless rates were highest. And while political parties were hardly identical, their actions were not so different that changing the results of some elections would have changed the outcome of mass incarceration very much.[7]

The costs of mass incarceration are not confined to the black community. It takes resources to process and house so many prisoners. States pay about $50 billion a year to support prisons. They pay about $75 billion for higher education. If the cost of prisons were cut in half, leaving the cost of incarceration still above the cost in almost all other countries, states could spend far more on state colleges and universities. Tuition costs are about $40 billion a year; they could be reduced by two-thirds. This change would sharply reduce the growth of student debt chronicled in chapter 4.[8]

The costs also are far higher than conventionally measured due to the need for several agencies of the government to spend money on prisoners. Prisoners held for bail in local jails probably cost half again as much as directly measured. A comparison of costs in two counties in Kansas and New Mexico found that the average cost per inmate was twice as expensive in one than in the other. The low-cost county had been reducing jail overcrowding for the last few years, providing substantial savings for taxpayers. The county pays less for out-of-county jail beds, and it is closing housing units with all their associated personnel costs. There are ways to reduce the cost of incarceration that do not pose significant dangers for the community.[9]

Massachusetts presents a strange picture in this regard. Regarded as a liberal state with many universities and lots of FTE activities, Massachusetts nevertheless spends as much on incarceration as it does for higher education. The apparent disconnect is explained by the Lewis model. The strong FTE sector is involved in its own activities and tacitly approves incarceration policies that affect the low-wage sector.

One aspect of Massachusetts incarceration practice that has been observed is for prisoners waiting for trial. Bail to ensure the accused shows up for trial should be set according to the probability of that person showing up for trial, but decisions whether to release an accused person with bail are influenced by factors unrelated to this risk. The rate of African Americans in jail awaiting trial varies widely among counties, suggesting the process is discriminatory, and bail amounts for African Americans on Cape Cod are four times as high as for whites. These practices suggest discrimination at work, although this suggestion has not been tested. It is clear, however that the use of bail to hold people for a trial imposes large costs on poor people who cannot raise even small bail and have to spend time in jail. Their incarceration frequently means losing a job and causing other hardships for friends and family.

This is particularly true when women are incarcerated. The number of women in jail awaiting trial has gone from 150,000 in 1970 to 750,000 in 2014. The increase is largest in small counties, where total incarceration has grown to exceed the rate in cities. The jailed women are largely poor and black or brown, and the effect on their families is large. Attorney General Loretta Lynch said, "Put simply, we know that when we incarcerate a woman we often are truly incarcerating a family, in terms of the far-reaching effect on her children, her community, and her entire family network."[10]

If counties reduced pretrial confinement, they could save in many ways. Food and laundry expenses are reduced. Labor costs fall as fewer guards and other service people are needed. And even more savings accrue when housing units can be closed. Massachusetts could save large amounts of money by gathering a data bank to track pretrial prisoners and find out how best to deal with them. That would be easy for an interested FTE sector to do. A more complex plan would be to provide pretrial assessment of prisoners with the aid of professional nonprofit agencies. Some states have taken advantage of new possibilities, but many have an FTE sector that cannot be bothered.[11]

One in three black men can expect to go to jail in America today, as noted in chapter 3. As explained there, it is very hard for ex-convicts to enter the labor force on a par with others who have not been in jail. The effect on black incomes is strong. With one-third of black men out of the effective labor force, the other two-thirds of black workers would have to be more productive by one-half than white workers to make the incomes of blacks and whites the same. This imposes a huge cost on the African American community.

Comparison with the rate of Latino incarceration shows that this policy affects other minority groups as well. While one in three black men goes to jail, one in six Latino men also goes to jail. The rate for white males is one in seventeen, and the incarceration rate for Latino males is closer to the rate for black males than to the rate for white males. One in six is still high, and Latino communities suffer some of the same costs to their social structure as do blacks. The War on Drugs represses Latino communities, making it harder for Latinos to integrate completely into American society.[12]

Whites and blacks use drugs at the same rate, but blacks are far more likely to be charged and convicted on drug charges than whites. Blacks are more than three times as likely to be arrested for marijuana possession, although whites and black use marijuana at the same rate. Marijuana arrests increased during the decade before 2010 and now account for over half of all drug arrests. Given the number of blacks in the United States, blacks are a minority of people in prison today even though they are arrested more often. Blacks are about 15 percent of the national population and 40 percent of the total number of prison inmates, making blacks three times as likely as whites to end up in prison. As noted in chapter 3, whites in the low-wage sector have as low levels of social capital as blacks. They are the majority of inmates, and our judicial system keeps low-wage whites down as well as operating as a new form of Jim Crow.[13]

Three-quarters of today's imprisoned drug offenders did not have any serious history of violence before their drug conviction. Half of them are in very low criminal history categories, but the average expected time served for drug offenses is close to ten years. Mandatory minimum jail stays markedly increase the length of sentences. And almost all drug offenders are held in state prisons, making it hard to reduce our bloated prison population by, say, cutting drug jail sentences in half. A bill to reduce mandatory minimum sentences with bipartisan backing failed in the Senate as 2016 election posturing got in the way.[14]

The United States now has far more of its population in jail than any other industrial country, and prisons cost a lot of money at a time when government resources are tight. The prison population has gone down slightly in recent years, but this has been accomplished by freeing inmates who have been in jail a long time rather than reducing the inflow into jails. To change arrest and conviction rates, a major change has to be made in laws and behavior. Since most incarceration happens at the state level, change would have to come there as well; it will be a long process even if it is eventually successful.

The United States treated insane people who acted badly as criminals early in our history. Many people became disenchanted with this process before the Civil War, arguing that ill people should not be subject to the same poor conditions and harsh prisons as criminals. Led by Dorothea Dix, reformers persuaded states to open insane asylums for these mentally ill people. By the 1950s, however, insane asylums had become bloated and inefficient. Reformers induced states to close asylums in favor of outpatient treatment. Lawmakers closed insane asylums, but they refused to fund outpatient clinics to help the patients take the newly introduced antipsychotic drugs. The Supreme Court ruled in 1975 that it was unconstitutional to hold anyone in jail who was not dangerous to others against his or her will.[15]

This decision changed the judicial question of insanity to a question of danger to others. Judges are hampered in trying to rule on this question by the failure of states to fund either outpatient mental-health clinics or other mental health diagnostic facilities. We have returned to the antebellum conditions of throwing insane people into prison with the mass of drug users and other criminals without much thought.

One sad result of these policies was the rape and murder of a young white woman in 2009 by a black man who had been in and out of the judicial system for many years and ended up incarcerated for the rest of his life. The financial and social costs of mass incarceration are apparent; this example reveals a painful and expensive human cost. The rape and murder were committed by Isaiah Kalebu, the son of an African immigrant and an African American woman, who grew up in a violent household where disputes and disagreements were expressed physically. Isaiah was bright and did well in school when he could focus on his studies, but he became steadily more distracted from his studies as he advanced and dropped out of college.

Isaiah spent the next few years living and fighting with his family, landing frequently in front of judges and sometimes in jail. The judges who let the young man go had limited time and information to make these decisions. His mother and sister, who had borne the brunt of dealing with him, obtained restraining orders to keep him away, and his aunt became the main caretaker. When it became too much for her, she also got a restraining order. Isaiah's aunt died in a fire almost immediately, which may have been caused by the increasingly troubled young man. He was on the street without the support of his family—who clearly could not cope with him.

Shortly thereafter, Isaiah raped and murdered a young woman living in a poorer part of Seattle who was engaged to be married. He was tried for murder and sentenced to life imprisonment without parole. The total cost of his many contacts with the judicial system and his expected life in prison exceeds $3 million. This is far more than treatment of his problems would have cost if a suitable way to provide appropriate treatment had been operational. The long history of the criminal insane suggests that it is hard to construct and maintain such a system in our political structure.[16]

There are two ways to see this story. It can be seen as a rerun of the famous Willie Horton ad that was run in the 1988 presidential election and may have cost Michael Dukakis the presidency. This ad featured a black prisoner out of jail on a furlough program who raped a white woman and stoked the fears of white Americans against their presumed angry and dangerous black neighbors.[17] Or it could be seen as a warning sign that our system of mass incarceration is blinding us to the real needs of society. We want dangerous people to be removed from harming us, but we lack a good method of distinguishing who is dangerous. Given the 1975 legal standard and inadequate funding for mental treatment in the United States, judges are likely to err on the side of leniency. Their decisions are good for many ill people, but increase the probability of dramatic and tragic stories like this one.

Public defenders are supposed to help the judicial system deal fairly with accused people, as indicated by the Supreme Court in 1963. But spending on indigent defense amounts to barely 1 percent of total government spending on criminal justice and has not risen in the past decade even though felony cases have risen by almost 50 percent Almost 90 percent of states require indigent defendants to pay a portion of their lawyers' fees. The defendant can be acquitted of his or her drug offense only to be convicted for being unable to pay for the legal services the state is required to provide. Funding for public defenders in Louisiana is so low that the waiting list for an attorney is over two thousand people long—and in jail—and growing.[18]

At the other end of the income distribution, rich people in the FTE sector accused of crimes are asking judges to lock them up in gilded cages. Since the rich are separated from low-income travelers on cruises to keep them from being disturbed by the hoi polloi, they do not understand why their stay in jail should be any different from a luxurious cruise.[19]

The FTE sector is not interested in heeding this warning. It treats mental health and the judicial system the same way it treats education, as described in chapter 4 and the next chapter. Incarceration and education are complex and have long-term effects; they do not affect conditions in the short run. When states are short of money, these services are cut. Then we deal with the resulting problems by militarized means. And support for that sequence of events is increased by repeating alarmist stories, like the one about Willie Horton.

Scare stories are persuasive due to the view that can be traced back to Nixon—like so much in this book. According to this view, crime is a breakdown in social order best combatted by tough measures usually associated with wars. Criminals are not regarded as people who have done bad things, but rather as bad people. Just as racecraft condemns people with dark skins to punishment, the belief in criminal mentalities condemns people to jail and continued punishment after they are released. While the United States was vastly imprisoning more people after 1971, other advanced democracies were systematically reducing incarceration rates.[20]

Prison reform is made more difficult by the growing influence of private prisons as the majority minority oxymoron interacts with the private public oxymoron. The American government has turned to competition for incarceration to solve society's problems without added cost to the government, just as for-profit colleges were approved to solve problems of higher education at low cost. Two prison firms dominate the expanding business of private prisons. Both firms were started in the 1980s, perhaps by entrepreneurs who realized that the decline in state revenues from the New Federalism and the rise in prison expenses from the War on Drugs would create an opening for privatization. The private prison firms have rapidly increased the penal population in their prisons, although they still account for only a small part of the county's mass incarceration. Their interest is getting more—not fewer—people into prison.

The growth of private prisons illustrates many themes. It is a clear example of the private public oxymoron, with the problems just described. It also is an example of the willingness to support military action over cooperative efforts. Activities to rehabilitate prisoners for life outside prison and educate them for future jobs will not be found in these private prisons. Criminalization of ordinary activities has extended the militarization of police into a conception of prisons that are more like prisoner-of-war camps than what we hoped prisons could be. The shadowy trail of prisons for immigrants provides glimpses of what goes on in the varied jails and prisons around our country.[21]

The private prison firms communicate their interest in more prisoners to state legislators in various ways: by campaign contributions, personal relations, and lobbying. The Corrections Corporation of America has spent over $20 million on political campaigns and lobbying and is continuing these efforts today. They also lobby through the American Legislative Exchange Council (ALEC), the conservative, nonprofit organization founded and funded by the Koch brothers in 1973 and described in chapter 2. ALEC promoted model bills on mandatory minimum sentencing and three-strikes legislation that helped promote the growth of mass incarceration in the 1990s. The influence of the private prison firms and ALEC impedes efforts to reduce American incarceration. Lobbyists from the private prison industry actively campaigned for three-strikes laws.[22]

ALEC is one of the ways that the Koch brothers and their supporters affect political outcomes. Started soon after Powell's secret memo of 1971, it is the only lasting national legislative organization, and it has enough money to treat state legislators in a princely manner. Its success shows that there are other ways to affect public policy than to elect favorable representatives and provides evidence in support of the Investment Theory of Politics.

For example, private enterprise has entered parts of the judicial system we do not ordinarily think are open to the private public oxymoron. When you dial 911, you typically get an outsourced answering service. Private equity firms, the "corporate raiders" of an earlier era, increasingly have taken over a wide array of civic and financial services that are central to American life since the 2008 financial crisis. Like private prisons, their interests do not align with the public programs for safety. Their aims are to cut costs, increase prices, lobby, and litigate to expand their reach. As might be expected, response times have grown, ambulance equipment often does not work, and people in need get short-changed. And if you are in prison and need to be transported elsewhere, chances are you will be moved by Prisoner Transportation Services of America, the nation's largest for-profit extradition company. They pack prisoners in and pay so little attention to them that they did not discover a dead prisoner until after they had driven seventy miles after the prisoner died.[23]

Martha Minow, dean of the Harvard Law School, examined the pros and cons of public-private partnerships. One argument for involving private companies in incarceration and education is frustration with the low quality of government programs. Another argument is the presumed benefits of competition where dissatisfied critics can take their business elsewhere. But, says Minow, "If information that would allow for informed choice among options is not generated, or if people are not free or able to choose among options, the promised benefits are not likely to emerge." Prisoners cannot choose their prisons or their transport mode, and legislators do not spend much time or energy comparing prisons or considering how such a comparison should be done. (The next chapter applies Minow's insights to education.)

The problem is that prisons serve several functions for society. They remove dangerous people from general circulation, punish people who have done wrong, and may even reform misguided people who engage in criminal activity. To this list, keeping minorities from achieving their full potential recently has been added. The argument that competition increases prison efficiency is not clearly defined. And for handling emergency calls and prison transport, competitive choice is not appropriate.

There are many costs in performing all these aims, and reformers have presented ways to reduce costs, most obviously by limiting the number of people incarcerated. But private prisons have a different aim. They want to maximize profits, which are increased by having more prisoners. Private prisons may be more efficient at some of the aims society has for the prison system, but this efficiency is achieved at great cost. The various aims are collapsed into warehousing prisoners, rather like prisoners of war, instead of pursuing the other societal aims, and any gains from the presumed efficiency will be captured by the prison companies rather than society as a whole.

These are academic questions for members of the FTE sector, for they mostly do not know anyone in failing schools or prison. They may have divided views on the merits of privatization and the merits of competition in social services, but they can live with the choices that politicians make. To the extent that they think of these issues, they classify the people involved from the low-wage sector as blacks, immigrants, or veterans to whom a military career was the best option. Even though there are not enough of these "others" to populate the low-wage sector, poor whites only occasionally are visible in public discussions. And since many poor whites traditionally do not vote, they have had little effect on public policies. They voted in presidential primaries in 2016, but we do not know how long this new pattern will endure.[24]

There are a few bright spots in this picture of mass incarceration as enterprising local officials try to alleviate some of the pressures in this system, although the big picture remains bleak. The police chief in Gloucester, Massachusetts, a small seaside city north of Boston, shifted his department from incarceration to treatment as the way to deal with drug addicts. As he said, "Any addict who walks into the police station with the remainder of their drug equipment or drugs and asks for help will NOT be charged. Instead we will walk them through the system toward detox and recovery" and send them for treatment "on the spot." Gloucester's population is small, but its new approach is meeting with broad acceptance in the region. Perhaps the idea of treatment instead of incarceration will catch on, although there are strong forces against it.[25]

Most reforms being proposed today seek to help former inmates rather than to reduce mass incarceration. The governor of Virginia recently restored voting rights to felons, arousing strong opposition in the legislature. The United States barred federal agencies from asking job applicants if they had been convicted. A county in Western Massachusetts started a program to prepare inmates for jobs and help them find jobs to reduce recidivism. And Robert Rubin, formerly Secretary of the Treasury, proposed educating prisoners, removing barriers to employment (as the federal government has done), and admitting former prisoners to public housing and health care.[26]

These proposed reforms may have only limited effects if adopted due to the growth of legal financial obligations that rose rapidly in the 1990s and now condemn many former prisoners to a lifetime of payments that are neither payable—because the former prisoners lack the resources— nor able to be foregone—since they are not cleared by bankruptcy. We have, according to an assessment, "a two-tiered system of punishment: one for those with financial means and one for those who are poor." Most felony defendants in state courts come from poor neighborhoods with high unemployment and failed schools; they cannot pay or escape their legal financial obligations even if they are released from prison. They cannot fully reenter society as long as their debts are outstanding and remain under court jurisdiction for payment of the principal and interest—always with a threat of reincarnation. The growth of legal financial obligations increases inequality and maintains poor people in a state of uncertainty that interferes with normal lives. In a cruel irony, the fines and obligations that were imposed initially to repay crime victims for their losses now barely serve to support the bureaucracies that collect the obligations.[27]

Sociologists have argued that incarceration is used in the United States to keep the poor quiet as politicians destroy the safety nets that used to help them. Their arguments are in sympathy with those presented here, but they do not go far enough. The middle class is vanishing at a rapid rate, as shown in figure 1, and increasing numbers of working people are living only slightly better than the poor shown in the bottom line of that figure. These workers are supporting themselves and not in need of direct assistance, but they want their children to get an education to live better than they do. But 40 percent of people living in households headed by females—resulting when men are locked away by mass incarceration— are in poverty. And they go to schools in poor areas as a result.[28]

Government policies make the transition from the low-wage to the FTE sector more difficult. It is not impossible, but fewer people can make this trip than in the decade after the Civil Rights legislation in the 1960s.

Mass incarceration increased as school quality deteriorated. The two policies may not have been designed to complement each other, but they increasingly form parts of an integrated system. As exiting from the low-wage sector becomes harder, there is more reason for the FTE sector to support mechanisms of social control. And as more people go to prison, there is less pressure on the schools to try to retain and educate them.

10

Public Education

I discussed the problems of college education in chapter 4; I now focus on K–12 education and the ongoing crisis in public education. It might be thought that schools that serve the poorest children would get the most resources in a democracy, but the opposite is the case in the United States today. This is because the FTE sector does not want to help the low-wage sector; history matters, and we live in an oligarchy rather than a democracy.

Thirty years ago, Lisbeth Schorr wrote a book on urban education with the hopeful title, *Within Our Reach*. She argued that we knew how to educate students who were growing up in poor and dysfunctional families and neighborhoods. Her primary argument was that schools in poor areas needed extra resources in the form of medical and psychological help that would enable poor children to learn in school. This book was published before the income distribution had become as unequal as it is now, and there was still the illusion that we were all working together for the good of all. Her project, however, ran afoul of racecraft and fears that the advancing integration and improving fortunes of African Americans would undermine positions of white power. Her book today stands as a memorial to a better time, and a reminder of the programs that we knew were needed then and are still needed now.[1]

The roots of our current problems in public education are entangled with gender as well as race. American industrialization in the nineteenth century led to increasing gender specialization, and the roles of men and women became more distinct as part of this process. Despite getting the vote in 1920, women were not emancipated from their traditional roles, and they continued to have restricted job choices for two-thirds of the twentieth century. Many jobs women were allowed to hold were still in cotton goods, clothing, and boots and shoes, the traditional nineteenth-century industries. Teaching remained a good job for women—considerably more interesting and more attractive than the alternatives.[2]

This changed in the 1970s as women greatly increased their college attendance and graduation rates. Oral contraceptives let women choose when to have their children. With the aid of "the pill," they could plan their education and integrate family and career plans. Women chose to get more education, and they began to spread out into a variety of professional occupations. Teaching was no longer the only interesting job that American women could find. And the wages of women with graduate education began to rise relative to the salaries of female teachers in the late 1980s, climbing from 20 percent more to 40 percent more by 2000.[3]

Teaching lost its position as one of the most interesting or the best paid jobs for bright young women as careers of doctors and lawyers became available to them. Teacher unions became more strident as women teachers lost ground in earnings. Waves of teacher strikes spread across the country in the 1970s and 1980s as teachers tried to keep up with other educated women. Despite some gains, the unions were unable to bring teachers' wages up to those of the newly opened career choices for women.[4]

Public education today is hobbled by the lack of resources to make teaching an attractive career. We can reorganize education in many ways, but we will not have a large effect on student learning if we cannot attract more skilled and creative teachers to public education. But—like the public universities described in chapter 4—public education in America has suffered from inadequate resources. School districts cannot raise teachers' wages because they do not have the resources to do so. Many urban school districts do not even have enough money to maintain school buildings as a result of government policies at many levels. Wages for both men and women teachers continued to decrease relative to wages for comparable jobs after 2000, and the erosion of relative teacher wages was sharpest for experienced teachers.[5]

An important decision by the Supreme Court in 1974 condemned urban school systems to growing poverty. Justice Lewis Powell was part of the 5–4 majority, as was Justice William Rehnquist, in *Milliken v. Bradley* (418 US 717). This case was brought by the NAACP to challenge the implementation of *Brown v. Board of Education*. That decision set out a straightforward idea of integrated schools that proved very difficult to implement in the aftermath of the Great Migration.

The case came from Detroit, which had absorbed many black families seeking work. They were excluded from white neighborhoods by restricted access to mortgages and the opposition of white neighbors. The Detroit school district was two-thirds black by the 1970s, and the NAACP filed suit against Michigan Governor William Milliken and others, charging direct discrimination against blacks in the drawing of school districts. The Supreme Court held that school districts were not obligated to desegregate unless it could be proven that the lines were drawn with racist intent. Arbitrary lines that produced segregated districts were not illegal.

Intent is a familiar concept in criminal law, where it has been used for many, many purposes. The application to public policy, however, is fraught with problems. Public decisions often are made by many people interacting in complex political processes. The records of their discussions typically are brief and often bland. It is harder to find intent in a committee's actions than in an individual's actions. The Supreme Court used a traditional indicator in a way that accepted cities' policies without inquiring into their causes or effects.

The 1974 decision in *Milliken v. Bradley* made it clear that white flight would successfully separate white suburbanites from their new dark-skinned neighbors. The decisions also ensured that black urban communities would lack an adequate fiscal base. The Supreme Court would not combine or otherwise alter existing school districts, and whites fleeing cities for suburbs would be able to separate their children from those of urban blacks. The decision also mandated poverty conditions for the urban school districts, which became poorer and more completely black over time. The tax base for urban schools decreased as urban factory jobs also decreased and fleeing whites avoided paying for urban schools. The result was segregated schools with inadequate resources for urban schools attended by the children of the Great Migration. Separated and unequal, one might say.

Powell, only two years after becoming a Supreme Court justice, had made Nixon's Southern Strategy into a national policy. The Supreme Court limited school busing across city boundaries by a rule that stalled integration efforts and encouraged rising racial segregation between inner cities and suburbs.[6]

The process of income separation has continued as the FTE sector moves to its own communities and progressively disengages with the low-wage sector. The authors of studies that revealed this extension of white flight summarize the effects as follows: "Segregation of affluence not only concentrates income and wealth in a small number of communities, but also concentrates social capital and political power. As a result, any self-interested investment the rich make in their own communities has little chance of 'spilling over' to benefit middle and low-income families. In addition, it is increasingly unlikely that high-income families interact with middle- and low-income families, eroding some of the social empathy that might lead to support of broader public investments in social programs to help the poor and middle class."[7]

American schools and particularly American urban schools have proven inadequate in recent years to fulfill the task set for them, but it will be very hard to improve school quality without attracting more highly talented teachers. There are many creative teachers like John-David Bowman, and we would attract more of them if teacher salaries were competitive with the earnings of other stimulating jobs. None of the current reforms even comes close to making that attempt. They are doomed to failure as a result. The worst schools are predominantly black, but the crisis extends to most public schools. Testing is popular as a way to evaluate schools, changing their role from informing teachers how well their students are learning to informing administrators how well their teachers are teaching. This further discourages good potential teachers from considering the field, and drives excellent but frustrated teachers into other professions, and it has not notably improved the quality of schools.[8]

And tests often preserve racial disparities. This can be seen in the activities of schools in Broward County, Florida. Like many other places, they had inflows of black and Latino students, but these students of color were far less likely than white students do be included in programs for gifted students. The county introduced a universal screening test based on a short nonverbal test for second graders in 2005. The results were startling. The proportion of black and Latino students identified as gifted tripled!

This startling result came from two sources. The nonverbal test did not favor students in families where English was not spoken, written, or pronounced as it was by mainstream Americans. In addition, teachers were not involved in the ratings. Teachers have expectations about students, and they do not see gifted students in unexpected places. This effect is pervasive, and it can be seen in symphony orchestras as well as schools. When the orchestras changed their auditions to have candidates play behind a sheet so their gender could not be seen, many more women were accepted into orchestras.

Despite these positive results, Broward County suspended its universal screening program in 2010, as the financial crisis of 2008 reduced tax revenues. Racial and ethnic disparities reemerged like those seen before 2005. A new test was adopted in 2012, but it was verbal and involved teacher judgments. It did not replicate the effects seen before 2010.[9]

The FTE sector is far from failing schools, and members of the FTE sector have options available for educating their children. They move to suburbs with good schools, paying high taxes to support them. If that is not good enough for them, they send their children to private schools. (Only a few dedicated reformers send their children to urban public schools.) At the lower end of the FTE sector, many parents are frustrated with the quality of their schools, but the FTE sector talks about improving individual schools without disturbing the current structure of American education.

Schools in the North have become as segregated as they were in the South before *Brown v. Board of Education*. The media are full of observations, analyses, and hand-wringing about schools with predominantly black students. A recent paper found that "school desegregation significantly increased educational attainment among blacks exposed to desegregation during their school-age years, with impacts found on ... attending college, graduating with a four-year college degree, and college quality." But the residential pattern of black cities and white suburbs makes this kind of gain hard to expand.[10]

American education has split into two separate educational systems, echoing the division of the population into two sectors. Children in the FTE sector go to reasonably good schools, whether public schools in wealthy suburbs or in private schools. Children in the low-wage sector go to poor urban public schools. Since one third of black men are gone due to mass incarceration, most black children live in poor urban neighborhoods where the low-wage schools are starved for resources. One of the difficulties of school reform today is to distinguish between these two educational systems because their needs are quite different. Another problem is of course the reluctance of the FTE sector to spend money helping education in the low-wage sector. We had a dual school system based on race before *Brown v. Board of Education*; now we have a new dual school system based on class.[11]

The FTE educational sector has problems obtaining adequate teachers and other resources, but it functions well along traditional lines. There are concerns that even these favored schools are not doing all they can. Average performance on math and reading tests by high school students has fallen in recent years, while the federal government argues that excessive testing is getting in the way of a good education. And various people have called for more emphasis on STEM (science, technology, engineering, and mathematics) subjects so that students can find good jobs.[12]

Schools for the low-wage sector are failing students in more severe ways. Buildings are old, students are not engaged with the instruction they are offered, and many students do not finish high school. Studies in various states confirm poor results and poor conditions of black public schools. For example, many ninth graders in neighborhood high schools in Philadelphia have been there two or more years, and many of the first-timers are over age or below grade level in reading and math.[13]

The push for privatization noted for prisons has extended to schools in the form of charter schools that use public funds, but are not subject to the control of local school boards or unions. Charter schools, although hailed widely as a key to unlock public education, are not universally effective. There is a lot of variation, and not all students or all charter schools work well, but on balance, charter schools help poor, underachieving urban students. Successful charter schools are allowed to expand in some states, but not all states control the expansions to ensure that only good schools do so. And while public schools have to accept and help all students, charter schools have not always kept to that high standard, forcing out the most difficult students and those with special needs.[14]

Charter schools as a whole have no impact on test scores and a negative impact on earnings. In other words, the average student of a charter school has test scores no better than students at public schools and earnings below them. The best charter schools increase test scores and four-year college enrollment, but they do not have a statistically significant impact on earnings. Other charter schools decrease test scores, four-year college enrollment, and earnings. The private public oxymoron is not helping public education.[15]

The dual education system in the United States does damage to the country as a whole in addition to restricting the opportunities of students from the low-wage sector. By restricting the access of most of the population to the benefits of education and professional training, we reduce full participation in the economic and social benefits of America and the possibility that truly extraordinary young people will be able to fulfil their promise to the benefit of all. The benefits of full integration are shown in the outstanding Olympic victory in women's gymnastics in 2016 with a team of gymnasts made up of two African Americans, two European Americans and a Latina. The captain was Jewish, and the big star was black.[16]

The experience of Detroit schools shows what happens when the private public oxymoron is taken to the limit. Michigan allowed unlimited charters to open in 1993. The cap on charters in the original law was abolished in 2011 at the same time that oversight by the State Department of Education was eliminated. But funding remains low for Detroit schools at about two-thirds of the spending per pupil in Denver and Milwaukee. Many charter schools were started in Michigan, and 80 percent of the new charters were in Detroit, where only 10 percent of high school seniors are college ready. The best Detroit charters are the most selective in the students they admit, and the average charter school is no better than the average public school. Detroit is awash in choice but hardly in quality.[17]

Economic analyses of both charter and public schools in New York, Houston, and Boston have found a set of best practices that help poor urban students make progress in school. These practices include close attention to traditional skills, frequent support for teachers using test feedback, and intensive tutoring for students identified by poor test results. By traditional skills, these studies mean reading, writing, and arithmetic—still the building blocks of human capital in the twenty-first century and the keys to further exploration of skills and knowledge. Best practices findings also state that teachers need to get feedback on how each student is going to direct his or her attention where it will be most useful; tests should be treated as diagnostic rather than as conclusive. Finally, students who need lots of help should get it. Teachers need to deal with whole classes; tutors are needed to pinpoint assistance to the neediest students.

Economists who have identified these effective measures have argued for their wider use. These best practices are present in some urban charters, and those are the charters that pull up the ratings of urban charter schools. The characteristics also work in public schools when they are tried. But although charter schools are privately run, they typically cannot expand freely even if they employ best practice methods. Minow's critique of privatization in chapter 6 applies here to education. Regulations and inertia have prevented these insights from making a large difference in low-wage sector schools.[18]

This discussion of teacher salaries, racial segregation, best practices, and privatization exposes how complex the problems of education are. Several members of the very rich, notably Bill Gates, the Walton family, Michael Dell, and Eli Broad, supported public education through philanthropy. They had grown rich by finding new ways to provide other services, and they thought that the key to improving public education could be found similarly. Cory Booker, then Mayor of Newark, agreed with this approach and convinced another billionaire, Mark Zuckerberg, in 2010 to provide $100 million dollars a year for five years to Newark schools to emulate the spectacular successes of Microsoft, Walmart, and Facebook.[19]

Booker used the outside funds to hire a private firm of educational consultants who eventually earned close to $300 million advising Newark. These highly paid members of the FTE sector were supposed to bring their wisdom to fix the low-wage sector's education problems in Newark. But their knowledge was of the FTE education system, not the low-wage education system, and they were woefully uninformed about the latter. The most obvious gap was in their conception of the community whose children were being educated. This was not the suburban community that supported schools to get their children into college, but low-wage people who wanted their children to be educated by the institutions they knew. Traditional schools were an important part of the community, through both employment and local politics. The community saw existing schools as their friends; the consultants saw the existing school principals and teachers as their enemies. The consultants also were white, while the community was black.

The consultants' plan was to drastically shrink the authority of the Newark school district and replace most public schools with charter schools and specialized schools for gifted and problematic kids. The children would be tracked in a central database, and the school principals would run their schools like managers in private business. Taking this analogy further, they planned to move managers (principals) and workers (teachers) around to maximize productivity (test scores). They would overcome Minow's objections to privatization by making the whole school system into a big firm with a set of competing plants. Booker argued this had to be done quickly. He and the state governor might soon be out of office. The donors needed to see speedy results. And, Booker said, "Entrenched forces are very invested in resisting choices we're making around a one-billion-dollar budget. There are jobs at stake."[20]

One casualty of the speed was the organization of the school reform itself. No one was in charge, and the integrated reform effort dissolved into a variety of different initiatives. The new charter schools were supposed to grow rapidly, providing what the reformers thought of as a good education. But this growth would denude traditional public schools of funds while leaving them with the neediest students. The traditional schools would go into a death spiral, losing support from social workers and guidance counselors while getting higher and higher proportions of problem students. Newark parents were not enthusiastic.

The consultants had no plans for this transition. They argued that once the transition was over, all children would be fine in the new charter and special schools. But what was to happen to the most vulnerable students in the meantime? Perhaps consultants hoped that Newark could stabilize like Detroit, Washington, DC, and Philadelphia with 55, 44, and 28 percent charter schools among all district schools, respectively. But the anticipated beneficial results for students did not appear immediately, and the plan collapsed. Cory Booker went from mayor to senator in 2013. Consultants left for greener pastures, and the children of Newark were abandoned.

Russakoff concluded her vivid narrative of the Newark fiasco with a statement of the problem: "It is obvious that urban public schools are being asked to overcome nothing less than the effects of poverty. ... Much more support is needed." Schorr had identified this problem thirty years earlier and described how added support could help. Nothing had been learned in the meantime, however; only the problems have grown.[21]

Poor urban public schools do not appear to have the ability to adopt best practices on their own. But there are exceptions to this rule. The schools in Union City, not very far from Newark in northern New Jersey, seemed about to collapse around 1990 when enrollments rose sharply due to a large inflow of Latino immigrants. The schools were saved by a combination of interrelated actions. The Union City school department leaders decided to work with gifted teachers already in the school system and launched a plan to redesign the curriculum. Emphasis was concentrated on early education. The school system instituted pre-kindergarten programs to introduce poor families and children into the educational system. These were full-day preschools with curricula built around stories in both English and Spanish that would appeal to the students. This beginning helped families support the changes underway and prepared students who came from poor houses with no books to focus on reading.

This early education can be seen as the starting point for a serious approach to the education of poor children. A first step would be prenatal help to the mother so the baby will be born with a normal birth weight. Then talking to and playing with young infants has large impacts on children's future development. Every mother would like to do this, but not every mother has the time and energy to read and interact with her child. Children of the low-wage sector typically have disadvantages dating from their preschool years that are not overcome once school has started.[22]

James Heckman, a Nobel laureate in economics who has studied the effects of early education, states this point forcefully: "The accident of birth is a principal source of inequality in America today. American society is dividing into skilled and unskilled, and the roots of this division lie in early childhood experiences. ... While we celebrate equality of opportunity, we live in a society in which birth is becoming fate." Heckman goes on to say that success in life depends on more than cognitive skills, that is, human capital. It depends also on noncognitive characteristics, that is, social capital, including "perseverance, attentiveness, motivation, self-confidence, and other socio-emotional qualities." These aspects of social capital are best acquired in children's early years. When families cannot teach, public policy is needed to make up for the problems of low-wage families.[23]

The second action, following the Union City school leaders, is to increase the education budget. Taxes in Union City were raised to aid the schools, and the Supreme Court of New Jersey decided a case in its *Abbott* series of school-funding decisions by asserting that hugely unequal funding of schools in different school districts was unconstitutional. The court monitored compliance to its rulings over the next decade and made sure that the schools in Union City received more funds. Starting in 1990, at the same time as Schorr's book, *Within Our Reach*, the experience of Union City shows that public schools, with the aid of dedicated teachers and adequate funds, can deal with the problems that poverty creates for education.[24]

The preschool program supported by the New Jersey Supreme Court's *Abbott* decisions has been shown to have such substantial effects on children in fifth grade that the evaluators have promoted it as a national model. The effects from two years of preschool are more than twice those from one year and close from 20 to 40 percent of the achievement gap between minority and white students. The continuous improvement was promoted by teacher self-assessments, collection of data on individual children's progress, and coaching by master teachers.[25]

Instead of expanding the emerging progress of the second-generation majority minority, Chris Christie, Governor of New Jersey, demonstrated the force of the Lewis model by trying to destroy the *Abbott* school funding system and replace it with a flat allocation of funds to school districts similar to the flat tax plans of conservative political candidates. A flat allocation would transfer state money from under-served minority urban schools to prosperous white suburban ones. As the *New York Times* Editorial Board said: "This toxic plan does nothing less than pit rich against poor, black against white and city dwellers against suburbanites, and it could well poison state politics for years to come, even if Democrats succeed in fending it off."[26]

The third step in school reform is to commit to slow and steady progress, as the leaders of the Union City school department did. These leaders were drawn from the community, and they were determined to help their families and friends and neighbors. They were not investors from Silicon Valley or politicians on their way to Congress; they were educators who were dedicated to their profession. They thought in terms of decades rather than years, and—like the proverbial tortoise—they won the race.

The sequence of white flight and poor urban schools is most apparent in Northern cities and suburbs, but not all African Americans left the South in the Great Migration. Many African Americans still live in Southern states, where they often are living in abandoned rural communities, as opposed to the inner cities of Northern cities. Rural schools in the South face the twin problems of inadequate funding and poor job prospects for graduates in the local area. It is as hard to keep these Southern rural black students as it is to keep Northern urban black students engaged in learning. Educators have proposed varied solutions for dealing with these combined problems. One that complements the idea of best practices in urban schools is to reverse the order of instruction. Instead of starting with skills in reading and math and then applying the tools to problems that could interest students, educators have proposed starting with local stories and problems that the students can identify with and then teach reading and math through the stories the students are investigating. This is the same kind of approach used in Union City. There have not been systematic comparisons of schools run along these lines with traditional approaches because poor Southern students are scattered throughout the countryside, but Union City's track record is promising.[27]

There are no quick fixes or miracle cures for urban education. The success of schools in Union City shows how sustained effort can upgrade low-wage sector schools over time. These schools used many of the best practices identified by economists, supplemented by preschool for all children age three and older, attention to the absorption of immigrants, and the active involvement of parents. Instead of the rapid coming and going of venture capitalists, the slow and steady growth of trust between the community and schools, and between teachers and students, has been a necessary part of school success. Social capital is needed for successful investments in human capital.[28]

The pressures on families in the low-wage sector make the need for investments in social capital very important. Suburban schools can think about social and emotional intelligence within their schools, but they do not have to build social capital in their communities. Progress in towns and cities like Union City requires active investment in the community as well as in the schools. The severity of this need can be seen in a few New York City schools where half the students are from homeless households.[29]

The contrast between the two school systems now operating in the United States can be seen in the contrast between Head Start and NCAA basketball. Head Start was started by President Lyndon B. Johnson as part of his War on Poverty to provide the kind of preschool preparation that the Union City reformers supported. Head Start began giving grants to school districts in 1965; it was received well and still operates today. But while enrollment doubled in the fifteen years after 1970, the funding (adjusted for inflation) only rose by one fifth.[30]

Many scholars have found that Head Start improved the education and lives of students who went through the program. The results have been controversial because the teaching in Head Start was multifaceted, supporting social as well as intellectual skills, and some observers accused the program of wasting money. In the terms used here, the critics looked only at human capital, while the supporters of Head Start look also at social capital. As argued here, acquiring social capital is a big hurdle for education in the low-wage sector, particularly in communities ravaged by mass incarceration.

Evidence shows that graduates of Head Start are more likely to graduate from high school and attend college; they are less likely to be charged with committing a crime. Detailed studies of the allocation of resources used in Head Start show that higher spending on child-specific activities reduced behavior problems and grade repetition while increasing reading and vocabulary. Head Start also diminishes child mortality, which allows these effects to be seen.[31]

Some critics have asserted that the effects of Head Start rapidly dissipate when students enter grade school. This effect is stronger for black than for white children, and this fading out comes from the inferior, low-wage sector schools that most black students attend. In other words,

Head Start is not an education in itself; it is only a good start to a longer process of education. To get the full effect of Head Start and other pre-school support, children need to continue to get a good education in the schools they attend—as was achieved in Union City.[32]

Nevertheless, when George W. Bush renewed funding of Head Start in 2007, he said, "I am pleased that this bill addresses several longstanding Administration priorities, such as increased competition among Head Start providers, improved coordination of early childhood delivery systems, and stronger educational performance standards." "Competition" is code for the private public oxymoron, looking for charter Head Start programs. "Coordination" is code for reducing the multidimensional focus in very young children, and "performance standards" means tests for short-run impact on human capital rather than the important impact on social capital. President Bush was trying to reform the low-wage educational system along the lines tried in Newark, appropriate perhaps to the FTE schools, not to low-wage schools. President Obama reversed this direction in subsequent years, looking to evaluate Head Start teachers on their relationships with the students rather than focusing on multiple-choice tests for the students.[33]

It is a long way from Head Start to college basketball, but the value of social capital is illustrated well in a story of success in the NCAA basketball tournament in 2016. Ryan Arcidiacono was a star scorer on the Villanova Wildcats that made it into the Final Four; he was looking forward to scoring at the end of the game to the cheering of the crowd. But when he got the ball with less than five seconds to play in a tied championship game, he passed the ball to an open teammate. The resulting shot was successful, and the fans erupted. The news reporter said, "The game was ... classic and wondrous, because the Wildcats didn't win it with superstars. ... Those players were selfless, and trusted that their teamwork would give them the edge." This is social capital: the trust that people who have mutually agreed what to do actually follow through. Teamwork is a form of social capital—which is the key to preschool education for low-wage communities.[34]

Good education, improving both human and social capital, is a tall order for the low-wage sector, and it goes against the grain of politics in a dual economy. The threat of mass incarceration hangs over black and Latino communities, and the presence of hostile militarized police makes investments in social capital even harder. Far more resources need to be allocated to urban education to make progress, but none will be forthcoming soon. Instead, poor education will keep black and brown communities down, providing more opportunities for mass incarceration. And mass incarceration will contain the people operating without social capital in prison. The money that should go to schools will go to prisons instead.

The abandonment of urban public schools has produced a growing education gap between rich and poor. Comparison of reading and math skills between the richest and poorest 10 percent of the population reveals a gap that has grown dramatically in the last few decades to be equivalent to several years of education. For children born in the postwar boom, educational results were more equal than the incomes that blacks could earn. For children born later, the education gap between rich and poor has grown due to the low funding extended to urban, predominantly black schools. The education gap now exceeds the racial gap in income.[35]

Some political scientists claimed that integration has decreased trust among students, implying that separate schooling is preferable to integrated schooling. But causation goes the other way. Social capital—that is, trust between people—is lower in low-wage sector communities. When white students from the FTE sector are integrated with black students from the low-wage sector, the level of trust goes down. But it is not because everyone mistrusts everyone else, but rather that the new average is the average of the high social capital of the white students and the low social capital of the black students. Inequality, not diversity, causes distrust.[36]

And diversity is healthy, and not just in schools. Sociologists have found through market simulations that diverse market participants reduce the frequency and damage of booms and busts. When everyone thinks alike, it is easy for people to convince themselves that a bubble is not taking place. Michael Lewis in *The Big Short* found that only oddballs saw the financial crisis of 2008 coming.[37]

11

American Cities

Milliken v. Bradley fit in with other government decisions that supported a massive movement of the white population into suburbs in the decades following 1974. Tax revenues were used to facilitate suburban expansion by building roads, schools, water, and sewage systems to serve the suburbs. In contrast, the maintenance of the urban infrastructure abandoned by the new suburbanites was gradually decreased.[1]

The ability of cities to finance decent schools was made even harder in the 1980s as Presidents Reagan and Bush cut back federal grants to cities; federal grants to large cities fell over the decade by 35 percent, from $5.2 to $3.4 billion. Cuts were most severe in general revenue sharing, public service jobs and job training, and other block grants that gave states freedom to choose which programs to support. The schools of both black and white urban children lost resources and effectiveness. No wonder that poor urban children who got to college did worse than rich suburban kids.[2]

One result of the cuts in funding was that school buildings were not replaced. The lead contamination in Flint, Michigan, which was described in chapter 3, raised the question whether these old school buildings were dangerous as well. Lead in water is dangerous to health, affecting the development of intelligence in children and causing disease. The unfortunate sequence of ill-informed economic choices that increased lead in our water began over a century ago. As municipal water systems were expanded and repaired before the First World War, cast-iron pipes were replaced with lead pipes because they lasted longer. This was particularly true in cities with acidic water, since cast-iron pipes eroded faster there. Acidic water is soft water; hard water contains minerals that reduce soap suds and leave deposits on sinks and bathtubs. People like soft water, but the acid in soft water erodes pipes faster.

When iron pipes corrode, people ingest iron and zinc, which are not harmful to most people. When lead pipes corrode, people ingest lead, which is harmful. Although public health authorities in the nineteenth century had noted the ill effects of lead in water, water companies were more interested in lowering their costs. They wanted more durable pipes in cities with soft, acidic water. They chose to replace worn-out iron pipes with new lead pipes.[3]

This choice became relevant to schools in the twenty-first century because underfunding led urban school systems to use older school buildings. Education reformers have argued that old and dilapidated school buildings discourage poor urban students from learning. In the aftermath of the Flint lead crisis, many urban school systems are discovering that their old buildings are not only depressing, but actually dangerous. Among the reasons for low success in urban schools may be the results of lead in the pipes of old schools.[4]

Congress has not appropriated funds to fix the pipes in Flint after the 2015 lead crisis. It is not likely to fix the problems in other urban school systems as well. Decades of neglect have left poor cities with limited budgets to face accumulated problems of underinvestment and deferred maintenance. The FTE sector will not raise taxes to help the low-wage sector's schools.

Not far from Flint, the decrepit state of Detroit school buildings emphasizes how cumulated neglect stands in the way of improving urban education. Congress passed a law to upgrade water sources containing lead in schools in 1986, but it was largely stuck down by a federal court in 1996. The only operative federal regulation is an EPA rule issued in 1991 requiring periodic tests and setting the safe limit for children at fifteen parts per billion. Schools pose the biggest problem for lead as they have old pipes, many a century old, and are occupied by children. Older urban schools serve mostly children from the low-wage sector, and the FTE sector does not have an incentive to push for their property tax dollars to be spent replacing pipes for urban schools.[5]

We have a dual residential system. Low-wage workers live in decrepit cities, and the FTE lives in ever more separated suburbs. Since the FTE sector will not support city services, urban conditions continue to deteriorate. FTE sector people do not experience many of the urban problems as they live separately and only visit cities when they want to. Many of them probably think that America's urban troubles belong to a separate, less developed country.

Some of the very rich, the plutocrats, are moving now into tall glass towers in center cities. These well-maintained apartment buildings are very different from the underfunded buildings containing subsidized urban housing. The plutocrats travel in their own cars or car services; they seldom take public transportation. They often are not raising children in the city, and they send their children to private schools if they are. They are in the city, but only partially engaged in urban activities.[6]

The disadvantages of black students extended into some new suburbs. Public policy tried through subsidized housing to bring black families into the suburbs, but political pressure from local residents convinced the government to locate the new public housing in poor parts of towns. The result was to relocate some of the conditions that formerly had been in the center of large cities to smaller suburbs.

A federal case, *U.S. v. Yonkers*, was brought in 1980 to contest this pattern in a New York City suburb. The evidence showed that Yonkers was segregated in schools and housing, and the conflicts in enforcing the eventual judgment illustrate the anger of the new white suburbanites to the blacks among them. The concentration of poverty was decreased in the 1990s by rapid economic growth, but the trend was reversed after 2000 to produce more concentrations of poverty in smaller cities and towns.[7]

Oscar Newman was a city planner hired in 1987 as a consultant to the city of Yonkers by order of the court. He created the idea of *defensible space* to explain how concentrated public housing could destroy social capital. He argued that tall public housing encourages illegal and violent behavior because it has public spaces that no one cares for. City planners in Yonkers concentrated public housing in one section of the town, and they built them tall to save space. The government did not provide enough funding to keep elevators and corridors clean and well lit. Tenants did not have jurisdiction over these public spaces, and there were too many tenants to get together informally. The result was that residents maintained nice apartments that could be reached only through disreputable and often dangerous elevators and halls.

Newman argued that space that no one controls always deteriorates in this way. Defensible space that people can and will maintain is space under their control. For families and neighborhoods, families need to own or have responsibility for the spaces around their dwellings. Residents of ground-floor apartments have responsibility for their front yards and walks. Street barriers that prevent through traffic speeding through local streets empower neighbors to keep the resultant dead-end streets clean and safe. Defensible space is the space that someone has responsibility to maintain. Large buildings with insufficient funds for maintenance have too much indefensible space.[8]

This insight has important implications. City planners in the 1950s and 1960s did not understand the idea of defensible space and unwittingly built public housing in tall buildings. They were encouraged to do so in cities where land was expensive and in suburbs where white residents who had escaped from cities did not want public—and largely black—housing near them. Public housing designed to help poor people survive in cities and suburbs may have hurt them instead by speeding the breakdown of community spirit. In the language of the Lewis model adapted to modern conditions, these families lost social capital.

Newman's insight illuminates a controversy about the lack of social capital in Northern black neighborhoods. William Wilson argued that unemployment and poverty in Northern poor black neighborhoods produced the observed lack of social capital. Charles Murray reproduced Wilson's results in Northern poor white neighborhoods. Their analysis showed that the lack of social capital in Northern cities today was due to current conditions more than the legacy of distant history.[9]

Although the causes of social dysfunction may have been similar for blacks and whites, there was still tension within public housing between the races. Affluent whites escaped from mixed neighborhoods by moving to the suburbs; poor whites did not have that option. They comforted themselves by regarding themselves as superior to people with dark skins. The resulting conflicts gave the violence caused by poverty and bad housing design a racial content.[10]

Newman's theory of defensible space explains how public policy designed to cure social ills instead worsened them. Public housing designed to create better living conditions for poor people in urban neighborhoods contributed to the breakdown of social capital in these neighborhoods. The lack of defensible space in public housing led to the breakdown of trust and the growth of antisocial behavior. The War on Drugs criminalized much of this behavior and led to steep losses of social capital. The escalation of conflict between the police and residents then further diminished social capital.[11]

Recent research has shown that when African Americans move out of the toxic buildings and neighborhoods they have been forced into, they regain some of the lost social capital. This effect has been hard to demonstrate because it is visible largely in the second generation. The children of parents who move into better neighborhoods go to better schools and live in safer and greener areas where there is little indefensible space for antisocial activity. The children are more likely to attend college and less likely to become single parents. It is not simply the legacy of slavery that destroys black families; it is the conditions in which poor African Americans are forced to live—partly because their ancestors were slaves—that erode their social capital.[12]

Policies toward cities since 1970 have starved urban schools of funds. They have created hostile environments for black families stuck in these cities and recreated the conditions of blacks—and now increasingly Latinos—before the Civil Rights Acts. African Americans were deprived of education completely when slaves and given only the semblance of an education before the First World War. They began to get good education in the 1960s and 1970s, but opposition to the Civil Rights Movement has blocked and reversed these gains.[13]

Recent policies also have eroded the mobility of urban residents as they sought work or to get out of their local neighborhoods. The neglect of American infrastructure can be seen by looking at a few specific items such as bridges and mass transit. The American Society of Civil Engineers (ASCE) provides a "report card" for American infrastructure every five years, most recently in 2013. An advisory council of ASCE members assigns grades according to eight criteria. They noted that grades have been near failing as we start the twenty-first century, averaging only Ds, due to delayed maintenance and underinvestment across most categories.[14]

ASCE gave American bridges a C+ in 2013, a low grade for one of the world's richest countries. One-third of the total bridge decking area in the country is structurally deficient, indicating that there is a long way to go to universally reliable bridges. American bridges on average are over forty years old and near their fifty-year design life—the time that bridges are expected to function without problems. ASCE concluded that preserving aging bridges while replacing deficient bridges is a significant challenge for cash-strapped state and local governments to manage.

ASCE gave American mass transit a D. Rail-based systems carry just over a third of all mass transit trips. But they have the greatest maintenance needs of all mass transit modes, with a backlog of $59 billion, compared with $18 billion for non-rail systems. Rail systems are some of the oldest infrastructure assets still in use, particularly the heavy-rail systems in cities like New York, Chicago, and Boston. Reducing the maintenance backlog is complicated as many transit agencies do not systematically monitor the conditions of their facilities. As with bridges, the funding needs are a significant challenge.[15]

Problems are particularly acute in the Northeast Corridor from Washington, D.C., to Boston. The interstate highway system was started in the 1950s and cut into railroad revenues in the following decade. While the roadbed for trucks was constructed and maintained by the government, the roadbed for trains was built and maintained by the railroads. The U.S. Postal Service switched its business from trains to trucks and airplanes in 1966. Congress combined several troubled railroads into Amtrak in 1971—that pivotal year—to preserve passenger train transport. Amtrak is a private enterprise, and it was expected to make a profit, but Amtrak is heavily regulated and prevented by Congress from dropping unprofitable routes. Amtrak makes profits on the Northeast Corridor and has large losses in less populated areas. As Minow observed, restrictions like the ones Congress imposed do not allow railroad passenger traffic to benefit from privatization.

The ridership of Amtrak and commuter trains has doubled since 1971, but its infrastructure has not been updated. Its tracks, power lines, bridges, and tunnels have begun to wear out. The result has been a series of delays and cancellations that have made passengers miserable. Passengers also are missing work, and the Northeast Corridor Infrastructure and Operations Commission established by Congress estimated that a one-day shutdown of the corridor would cost the country $100 million. The commission has a five-year plan to update the capital structure of transport in the Northeast Corridor, but it is woefully underfunded.[16]

Recent political decisions have not been productive. Chris Christie, the governor of New Jersey discussed in the last chapter, canceled the proposed third Hudson River rail tunnel that would have increased mass transit access to New York City in 2010 on the grounds that the state was unable to pay its share of anticipated cost overruns (at least too poor if the state did not increase the low New Jersey gas tax.) Every day, approximately 275,000 people commute across the Hudson River to New York. During rush hour, Amtrak and regional trains are full, and the two Hudson River automobile tunnels are near or at capacity. A third tunnel would have provided room for 70,000 more commuters to reach Manhattan each day; in its absence, Amtrak says that rail delays may become the new normal.[17]

A new tunnel would have increased the reliability of commuter trains, reduced automobile congestion, supported economic growth, and increased neighboring house values. But the direct gains would have gone mainly to members of the low-wage sector, and the members of the FTE sector are not interested. Even though the FTE sector depends in part on the services of the low-wage sector, American politics do not seem to consider indirect effects. Many members of the FTE sector would rather keep their taxes low than consider investments that may indirectly help them, much less the needs of the low-wage sector.

Boston received a wake-up call about its mass transit system in the winter of 2015 when extensive snowfall led to a protracted breakdown of the transit system. Charlie Baker, governor of Massachusetts, acknowledged the problem, but like the governor of New Jersey, he was not willing to spend money or raise taxes for mass transit. The result parallels recent educational reforms that have done their best without costing any extra money. The results have been disappointing because the reforms do not correct major problems. The same future appears to be likely in mass transit.[18]

Federal transit investigators found the Boston subway system lacks a comprehensive plan for maintaining the system. They requested quarterly reports to show how the system is complying with federal guidelines for employing disadvantaged companies in their repairs. But estimates of the needed plans amount to around $7 billion, and the subway is running a deficit in its current operations. Boston and Massachusetts leaders think more about how to fix the deficit than about how to raise funds to keep the whole system operating.[19]

The Metro in Washington, DC, is half the age of the Boston subway, opening in 1976. But the capital's once-glorious subway system is now a terrible mess. It is unreliable, complained about by everyone, and on the edge of being unsafe. It is facing a large current deficit and predicted to be nonfunctioning in a decade if not repaired. How did Congress, which oversees the capital, respond? Congress said it would not "bail out" the Metro. As in other cities, the supervising authority with access to funds will not use those funds to maintain—not bail out—the city's infrastructure. The FTE sector does not want to spend its money on infrastructure that helps the low-wage sector.[20]

The appalling state of American infrastructure has become a common story. The *Financial Times* ran a story saying the neglect of infrastructure globally is sadly in disrepair. Political arguments were mentioned that are not very different than those raised here, albeit stated differently. The *New Yorker* more recently had a column on system overload, meaning decaying infrastructure. Economists wonder why governments don't upgrade their bridges, roads, and schools when interest rates are near zero.[21]

But when the issue is presented to the electorate, the supporters of lower taxes win the day. Governments have to borrow to finance reinvestment in the absence of more tax revenue now. But the FTE sector wants to reduce the public debt. An infrastructure bill passed Congress late in 2015, but it was only for highways and to relieve congestion. This limited kind of spending was approved by both political parties because members of the FTE sector get caught in traffic and waste time. For them, but not for members of the low-wage sector, will the government authorize a plan. But since Congress appropriated only a small part of the planned spending, it is not clear how much of this limited plan will be done. Both candidates for president in 2016 campaigned on promises to repair our infrastructure, but recent history does not suggest that these promises will be kept.[22]

12

Personal and National Debts

The discussion in part III has concentrated on tangible assets used by the low-wage sector, willingly or unwillingly: prisons, schools, bridges, and public transportation. It is now time to add some intangible assets and liabilities that affect the low-wage sector. This chapter interprets the treatment of debts in a dual economy. Individual debts are concentrated in bad mortgages and education loans. Societal debts come from the efforts of a democratic government to reduce risks for its members.

Individual debts are contracted between borrowers and lenders. Borrowers are largely individuals, and lenders in our advanced economy are largely financial institutions. Often, although hardly universally, debts are contracted between borrowers from the low-wage sector and lenders from the FTE sector. In that case, the treatment of debts involves relations between the two sectors of the dual economy.

If something goes wrong with a debt and it cannot be paid, then someone will take a loss. It seems appropriate that the loser should be the party that caused the debt to go bad, who was at fault in the collapse of the debt contract. A mythology has risen recently that says that borrowers are always at fault when debts fail, perhaps because the financial part of the FTE sector has become more important in our economy. Fault sometimes is attributed explicitly to unworthy borrowers, and it also may be implicit in the allocation of costs to borrowers. Within a dual economy, banks and other financial institution do not feel obligated to articulate all the reasons why members of the low-wage sector are obligated to pay for debts that go bad.

We have a dual financial system, where the FTE sector generally has more assets than debts and the low-wage system is largely in debt. Finance is seen in the FTE sector as a way to make large purchases or deal with emergency needs. But it is seen in the low-wage sector as a burden or a form of oppression that may lead to prison. Many workers in the low-wage sector say they cannot find funds for an emergency for which they need a few hundred dollars without selling something they would otherwise want to keep.

Consider mortgages, debts that home owners secure using their houses and condos as security. The median worker did not see figure 2 as it developed in the 1980s or the developing split of the American economy that was already under way. Instead, working families had increasing trouble trying to continue the spending habits they had developed before. In terms of figure 2, they acted as if the earlier sharing of growing national production had continued unchanged.

How could these workers continue to increase their spending trends as their earnings stagnated? By relying on their largest asset, their homes. House values rose in the 1970s, and public policy encouraged home ownership for everyone. It seemed only natural to remortgage your house as its price rose to get the resources to support your previously increasing lifestyle.

As with the political decisions of 1971, the actions by individual workers took a while to affect the whole economy. The aggregate impact also was delayed for a decade as economic policies in the Clinton administration led workers' earnings to resume their rise temporarily. Only after the start of the new millennium did the increasing demand for mortgage income run up against the aggregate supply of houses. It led to a large housing boom that collapsed spectacularly in the 2008 financial crisis.[1]

The fall in house prices and collapse of the credit markets left households with massive debts—often more than the value of their houses. Mortgage default normally is considered a problem for each individual, but the accumulation of household debt, which doubled relative to income after 1980, was encouraged by government subsidies through tax deductions, guarantees from Fannie Mae and Freddy Mac for home mortgages, and the stagnation of working incomes. The accumulation of mortgage debt has impeded personal expenditures, depressing consumer expenditures after the crash. The result is that employment has remained low since the 2008 financial crisis due to low consumer spending.[2]

Mortgage relief would promote prosperity better than standard fiscal policies because it would help people most likely to increase spending. This can be seen by looking at the location of spending changes. The net worth of the poorest fifth of the population vanished in the crisis and rose to less than one-quarter of its previous value in the recovery. The net worth of the middle fifth—still in the low-wage sector—fell and rose, but still remains only three-quarters of its previous value.

Consumption fell furthest in states where housing prices decreased the most, and the consumption rebound has been much weaker in these same states.[3]

A report to Congress describes how plans to relieve mortgage problems after the 2008 financial crisis went astray. Congress included mortgage relief in the law authorizing the Troubled Asset Relief Program (TARP) in 2008. The government announced in early 2009 its housing program, entitled the Home Affordable Modification Program (HAMP). Money was allocated for the modification of home mortgages, and mortgage holders in trouble were invited to apply to HAMP for help. But only a small proportion of the money was spent and few potential homeowners were helped. The problem was that the banks involved with HAMP rejected more than seven out of every ten homeowners who applied. Citibank denied 87 percent of its HAMP requests. JPMorgan Chase rejected 84 percent, and Bank of America rejected 80. The banks holding the mortgages refused to write them down even when subsidized by the government—and the government did not enforce and impose this obligation on them.[4]

This should not have been a surprise. HAMP was designed to help banks rather than underwater debtors. Timothy Geithner, then Secretary of the Treasury, admitted, "We estimate that [banks] can handle ten million foreclosures, over time. This program will help foam the runway." Just as planes cannot take off from foamed runways, homeowners cannot get relief from their accumulated debts through HAMP.[5]

Banks and other financial institutions are owned by members of the FTE sector. They are owned by plutocrats or even smaller and richer subsets of the rich. These institutions can be highly levered to make more money, assuming that the greater risk does not harm them, and their balance sheets may be positive only in theory. Their balance sheets changed in the 2008 financial crisis to become negative when some of the assets were found to have little value. The problem of nonperforming loans affects banks and other financial institutions both in America and Europe.

The story of educational debt described in chapter 4 is similar, although these debts are concentrated in the low-wage sector. Public support for public colleges and universities has been declining since the 1980s. When states get into financial difficulty in a recession or similar cause, it is easier to cut support for higher education than to lay off police. Public funds for state colleges and universities have decreased in a series of downward steps.

Public colleges and universities have become more and more private, as the private public oxymoron expresses. Private public colleges need to charge tuition to stay in business, and students have seen the cost of college rise rapidly. The result, as described in chapter 4, is a massive growth in student debt.

Mortgage and educational debt are parts of a single problem. The accumulation of these debts was promoted by public policies, subsidizing mortgages and withdrawing public support for college education. And they have left consumers in the low-wage sector burdened with debts that inhibit their spending. Government policy to reduce this debt and increase household net worth would be more effective than traditional fiscal policy in restoring prosperity to America. But the problems of debt relief are suggested by the difficulties of HAMP. The government, run by members of the FTE sector, has been unwilling and unable to pressure organizations owned and operated by members of the FTE sector to engage in programs to help people in the low-wage sector.

People with massive debts and debt payments do not consume very much. Debt payments take the cash they would have used for consumption, and debts discourage efforts at family formation. The mortgage and education debts are large enough that they may be affecting the national income. Economists have disputed the cause of slow growth in the United States and asked if the cause was due to a shortage of supply or demand. Low consumption due to debt is an additional argument for the demand side.[6]

Interest rates are at record lows, where they have remained since the 2008 financial crisis. It is the perfect time for business firms to borrow and invest in new plants and equipment. They are accumulating cash instead of making new investments because demand is low; they fear they will not make a profit from new investments. Demand is low because people with massive debts from mortgages and education loans do not have enough money left over from servicing their debts to buy new objects or furnish a new abode. The economy may grow more slowly in the future because of problems in the supply of innovations or the low growth of population; it is growing slowly in the short run at least partly due to FTE policies that deny debt relief to members of the low-wage sector.[7]

High aggregate demand leads in turn to high demand for workers, and this leads in turn to rising wages in the low-wage sector. As President Kennedy said, a rising tide lifts all boats. It does so slowly in a dual economy, but aggregate demand is important even in a dual economy. A low unemployment rate is not a good measure of aggregate demand when demand has been low for a while because the unemployment rate only counts workers actively seeking jobs. In a long slump, workers get discouraged, cease their fruitless job searches, and are not counted. The participation rate that measures how many of the available population is at work gives a better picture. This rate has been declining since 2008.[8]

This chapter concentrated on personal debts. But we should not leave this subject before saying a bit about our national debts. I do not refer here to the stated national debt that the very rich are intent on reducing; that is not a problem, and servicing the debt requires only a tiny bit of our federal budget. Instead, it is important to recall the commitments the federal government has made to the low-wage sector. These are the products of the New Deal of the 1930s and its extensions, called the New New Deal more recently. These obligations were accepted by the federal government, that is, enacted into laws and sustained by courts. Unlike personal debts, these programs are not now a problem, but the FTE sector and particularly the very rich are working to renege on the government's obligations.[9]

The impact of a dual economy on Social Security debates illustrates this effort. The discussion of Social Security in chapter 6 revealed how hard it is for voters to understand what is going on. One part of this discussion is clear and informative. Social Security taxes are levied on wages up to $118,500 at the moment. If this cap on taxable wages were eliminated, the financial problems of Social Security would vanish. The cap was introduced in the 1930s and covered almost all wages. Now it stands near the division of the American economy into two sectors. If the cap on taxable income were removed, that would be a tax increase imposed largely on the FTE sector. People who rely on Social Security to maintain their income as they grow older in their retirement are largely in the low-wage sector.

This solution, which has ease and perhaps fairness to recommend it, is politically difficult. Members of the FTE sector oppose new taxes vigorously. Politicians supporting the FTE sector invoke a sense of impending disaster to obscure the nature of decisions to be made. Instead of a calm discussion of the best way to fix Social Security, we are likely to have highly charged political debate on whether benefits to recipients should be cut. As explained earlier, that will be the eventual effect of inaction.

The recent history of the Affordable Care Act provides another example showing how the dual economy affects government policies. The

Supreme Court stopped short of declaring the act unconstitutional, but it said that the federal government could not force states to expand Medicaid. This program is designed to help members of the low-wage sector. It also has been vilified as serving African Americans even though they are a majority of those served in only a few states. Given the Supreme Court's decision, several states opted not to expand Medicaid even though the federal government would pay the whole cost for three years and 90 percent after that. As described earlier, the geography of states that refused to expand Medicaid as a free gift reproduced the Confederacy with a few additions up the Mississippi River. And Aetna, one of the largest health care providers, reduced its participation in the Affordable Care Act when the federal government denied its attempt to increase its market power by buying one of its rivals.[10]

These economic policy measures show how the leaders of the FTE sector ignore the needs of the members of the low-wage sector. A recent political action reveals both the pervasiveness of the dual economy and how the economic division is connected firmly to race. The Voting Rights Act of 1965 was passed in order to complete the integration started by the Civil Rights Act of the previous year. Giving all Americans the vote could lead to policies that would benefit all Americans. It would help the United States to become a democracy.

The Voting Rights Act was reauthorized by a succession of administrations of both parties and wide majorities in Congress, but the Supreme Court decided in *Shelby v. Holder* that the preclearance requirements that some states—mostly Southern—needed for voting rights changes were based on old data and placed an unconstitutional burden on these states. The result was an immediate explosion of state actions to restrict voting in various ways. These actions have been contested as illegal, but the legal cases are of course subject to the dictates of the Supreme Court.[11]

Shelby County v. Holder was decided in a 5–4 vote—as was *Milliken v. Bradley*—with Chief Justice John Roberts in the majority. Roberts clerked for Nixon appointee Justice Rehnquist, worked in the Reagan administration, and was appointed to the Supreme Court by Bush in 2005. His career has been intimately connected to Nixon's Southern Strategy, and some people have seen this consistency as part of a continuing conspiracy to roll back the accomplishments of the Civil Rights revolution of the 1960s.[12]

An implication of the dual economy model is that the FTE sector operates independently of the low-wage sector. If substantial parts of the low-wage sector in addition are not able to vote, then the neglect of the interests of the low-wage sector will not be represented in the political process. Present trends will continue and perhaps accelerate. The federal nature of the United States means that if a block of states operates with restricted voting, this block can have a powerful effect on national policies, as it did a century ago.

The FTE sector and the very rich assert over and over again that we cannot afford to spend money on education and infrastructure; we must instead reduce the national debt. They idolize Reagan, but ignore the massive federal debt he created. The drumbeat goes on despite the enormous decrease in the federal deficit that has taken place since the financial crisis of 2008. Yet, as noted earlier, military expenditures are exempt from this directive. As in the eighteenth century, the function of the state is confined to defending the realm. We have been involved in wars in and around the Middle East for thirty years.

Our military involvement in the Middle East was stimulated by the OPEC action that raised the price of oil dramatically in 1973. Nixon, the initiator of so many policies that led to the dual economy, proclaimed "Project Independence" to secure cheap oil for America. George W. Bush massively increased our military involvement by invading Iraq in 2003. We have spent more than three trillion dollars on our Middle Eastern wars, and there is no end in sight. We continue to spend massive amounts of money dropping bombs in the Middle East with no apparent aim or end. And the richest part of the FTE still keeps saying we cannot afford to spend money on programs to help prisoners and urban schools, repair and improve infrastructure, or provide debt relief.[13]

The war in the Middle East will not end any time soon; its current phase was initiated by George W. Bush's willful invasion of Iraq in 2003: "ISIS can be seen as an extension of AQI [Al Qaeda in Iraq], which was itself a creature of the 2003 U.S.-led invasion of Iraq and its aftermath. ... The organization [ISIS] has tapped into the communal rift that grew after the U.S.-led invasion of Iraq in 2003."[14]

Our military activities, however, are far from the eighteenth-century pattern. They are instead a massive example of the private public oxymoron. The United States military increasingly outsources its functions to private military firms, which grew rapidly after 1990. About six thousand firms like Kellogg, Brown & Root, a division of Halliburton, employ twenty thousand private employees to perform military functions. While their main activities are in construction and transport, they suffered almost one thousand casualties in Iraq by 2005. Kellogg, Brown & Root is thought to have had an Iraq contract of $13 billion, large enough—if redirected to purposes within the United States—to have massively beneficial effects on, say, inner city schools.[15]

This military activity is supported by the American arms industry that promotes government spending on the development of new weapons and the export of arms to troubled parts of the world. The arms industry uses all the means described in chapters 6 and 7 to advance their interests. They finance think tanks that promote military action, and they donate to the campaigns of congressmen. As described earlier, these paths to political power are not visible to many people; the names of think tanks do not reveal the source of funding. Their effectiveness however provides additional evidence for the Investment Theory of Politics.[16]

The recent growth of jobs illustrates possible effects of spending on domestic rather than foreign military activities. Middle-income jobs, which have been growing slowly for years as shown in figure 4, grew faster than high- and low-paying jobs from 2013 to 2015. The job growth was "primarily in fields like education, construction, transportation and social services." Median income rose over 5 percent in 2015, and the growth was seen in black, white, Latino, and Asian families. In fact, median wages rose more rapidly from 2010 to 2015 than in the recoveries from previous recessions. If the FTE sector were to support domestic activities, the middle class would not vanish as quickly as the long-term trend suggests.[17]

IV

Comparisons and Conclusions

13

Comparisons

I argue in this book that the United States economy has developed into a dual economy in the spirit of W. Arthur Lewis. The prosperous part of the economy, known as the FTE sector, is the sector that readers of this book most likely live in and often envision as the whole American economy. The depressed economy, known as the low-wage sector, is the largest part of the American economy nonetheless. The decline of the middle class has left us with these two parts of an economy, governed by policies made by the FTE sector for the benefit of the FTE sector.

This book is about the United States, but is the United States unique? I expand the focus here to see if parts of the American dual economy model apply to other countries as well. The growth of inequality extends beyond the United States, but politics are different in other countries, and only in some countries have the politics turned the economic forces into a dual economy. Consider three propositions. First, the world income distribution has become more equal in the period discussed here, from the 1970s to the present. Second, the failure of incomes in the American low-wage sector to grow is apparent even on the world stage. Third, political decisions in the context of national histories are needed to resolve the contrast between the first two propositions.

To understand this conflict, start by distinguishing inequality within countries from inequality between countries. This book considers inequality within America, and only now places the United States in a world context. While inequality within countries has increased in many countries, inequality between countries has decreased around the world. Overall world inequality therefore has not changed much in recent decades, although the location of inequality is changing.

It also is useful to distinguish movements at the top of the distribution from those at the bottom, as argued earlier for the United States. Inequality between countries has decreased mostly due to economic growth benefitting poor people in China and India, while inequality within countries has resulted mostly due to increasing incomes among the richest people.[1]

For the richest, the growth of finance, technology, and electronics has increased their incomes both because they have done well within their own countries and because they have engaged in international commerce. Globalization increased the reach of financial and industrial activities, providing greater scope for any individual action. As American firms became active around the world, they enlisted local counterparts and established new businesses. Political decisions within countries moderated the growth of inequality in some countries, and the degree of inequality across countries is a result of both economic and political decisions.[2]

For the poorest, the forces of globalization just noted for the American low-wage sector have subjected workers to ever more international competition. Add to that the technical change that enabled machines to do the work of semi-skilled workers, and you have similar divisions of workers around industrial countries.

Figure 6 extends the analysis of varied job growth in figure 4 to European countries, where the hollowing-out effect is stronger than in the United States. If the United States were added to figure 6, it would be near the right-hand end, with a smaller effect of technology on mid-level jobs. The effect of the new technology was stronger in Europe than it was in the United States, and the share of European workers in highly paid jobs rose to slightly more than one-third in 2010. Political decisions moderated the effects of the shifting demand for labor on unskilled workers in several European countries; the results on the distribution of income were affected by both economic and political decisions.[3]

The comparison of figures 4 and 6 reveals the power of political choices in America. The change in the distribution of jobs was relatively small in the United States, but the increase in inequality was relatively large. The preceding chapters of this book showed how the peculiar history of the United States led to the American dual economy. None of the European countries has America's long history of African slavery and subsequent efforts to subordinate African Americans in other ways. Without the American attempts to divide populations into different groups—us and them—economies of rich and poor may not have separated into dual economies. The great flow of Syrian refugees to Europe in 2015–2016 may produce something like the American division if measures are not taken to avoid it. Only studies of individual countries can

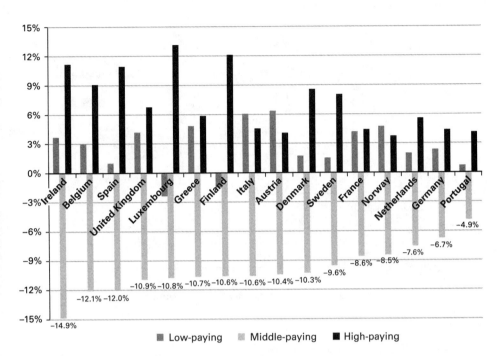

Figure 6
Change in occupational employment shares in low-, middle- and high-wage occupations
in 16 EU countries, 1993–2010
Source: Goos, Manning, and Salomons 2014

illuminate how economic and political factors have worked out within
each country.

This account shows how the United States can stand at the top of the
countries in per capita income—behind only Switzerland and Norway—
but rank sixteenth in social progress indicators. This is still high among
the 133 countries listed, but distinctly lower than other rich countries in
the index of basic human needs, foundations of well-being, and opportunity. Had we the data to see only the FTE sector, its social progress rank
undoubtedly would be close to its per capita income rank. But the
low-wage sector has a far lower score in the index and drags the national
index down. For example, the United States ranks very far down the list
of countries by the proportion of children in poverty, with a rate of child
poverty more than twice as high as the Scandinavian countries and close
to the rates in Spain and Mexico.[4]

Another graph helps us see the United States in a world context. Figure
7 shows the growth of individual incomes in the twenty years before the

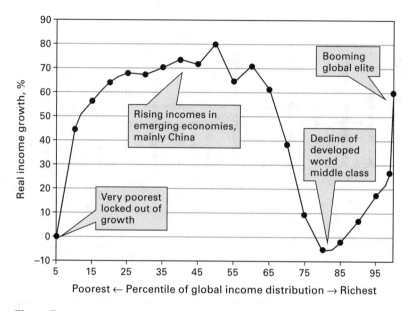

Figure 7
Global income growth from 1988 to 2008
Source: Milanović 2016 (explanatory boxes added)

global 2008 financial crisis by the relative income of different groups of people. As you can see, this is not a bell curve; it looks more like an elephant. This graph shows results of household surveys conducted in many countries and combined in the Luxembourg Income Study, World Bank studies, and regional sources. There are difficulties in comparing surveys from around the world and in different currencies, but the main outlines shown in the figure appear clear.[5]

The elephant's back shows how the growth of incomes in China, India, and smaller countries is reducing income inequality between individuals in different countries. The back feet of the elephant reveal that the poorest people, many of them in Africa, have been left out of this growth. And the elephant's trunk shows what has been happening in richer countries. The high point at the top right of figure 7 represents the growth of the very rich in the United States and elsewhere, and the low point shows the stagnation of worker's wages in the United States and other rich countries.

One way to calibrate this contrast is by comparing the experience during the last two decades of low-wage workers in the United States with the experience of highly paid workers in China. The American group had stagnant earnings, while the income of the Chinese group grew rapidly. Far apart in 1988, the two groups were very close by 2008. Branko Milanović called the losers in this comparison the "lower middle class of the developed world" and summarized the argument made here as follows, "Technological change and globalization are thus wrapped around each other."[6]

Anthony Atkinson, in a book about inequality in England and Europe, agreed, "The twin forces of technological change and globalization ... are radically reshaping the labor markets of rich and developing countries and leading to a widening gap in the distribution of wages." Atkinson went on to agree with the views expressed in chapter 3: "Technological progress is not a force of nature but reflects social and economic decisions. Choices by firms, by individuals, and by governments can influence the direction of technology and hence the distribution of income."[7]

14

Conclusions

This book has described how the vanishing middle class has left behind a dual economy as depicted by the Lewis model. The FTE sector makes political choices largely for itself, neglecting the needs of the low-wage sector in order to keep their taxes low. As Lewis observed, the "capitalists" of the FTE sector want to keep wages low in the low-wage sector to provide abundant cheap labor for their businesses.

The choices made in the United States include keeping the low-wage sector quiet by mass incarceration, housing segregation, and disenfranchisement. These oppressive policies were justified by racecraft, that is, the belief that races exist and that racial discrimination is warranted, as explained in chapter 5. The low-wage sector includes roughly 80 percent of Americans, but African Americans are only 15 percent of the population. Even if all blacks were in the low-wage sector they still would comprise only a minority. Nonetheless the policies designed to keep the low-wage sector in place are rationalized by assertions that the members of the low-wage sector are black, with racecraft providing support. It does not seem to bother political discussions that the majority of people in the low-wage sector are white. Latino immigrants have joined African Americans in the low-wage sector in recent years, reducing the white share to a slim majority.

Any member of the low-wage sector who tries to rise into the FTE sector must do so through education. Finding his or her way through the educational process to gain skills that offer a good chance of entering the FTE sector has been made difficult in several ways. The loss of social capital in the low-wage sector makes it hard for members to stay with education long enough to make this transition. And the policies of the FTE sector have crippled the fabled American educational system to the degree that very few members of the low-wage sector have access to schools that can pave the way to the FTE sector. This has been conceptualized as the failure of increasingly segregated black schools in the early twenty-first century, but the damage is much wider than the damage to this minority population. The failure of schools affects white and Latino members of the low-wage sector as much as blacks. Social mobility has decreased as inequality has increased.

Low-wage whites were largely invisible in public policy until the political turmoil of 2016, and increasing numbers of them were dying in their lives of quiet despair. The mortality of less-educated, middle-aged white men increased from drug and alcohol poisoning, suicide, and chronic liver disease and cirrhosis. The mortality of all other groups and ages continued its long-run decline, and the contrast with the increasing mortality of low-wage whites stands out sharply from this trend. Whites with less education—those who had not made the transition to the FTE sector—had the largest increases in mortality.[1]

The presidential race of 2016 revealed and fostered the anger of the low-wage sector. Donald Trump, the candidate of the Republican Party, appealed to whites in the low-wage sector to express their frustration and despair. The poor whites were unnoticed collateral damage until this campaign, but their anger dominated meetings where Trump spoke. Violence may have been stimulated when the candidate alluded to the majority minority oxymoron and assured the audience they were better than African Americans and Latino immigrants. Bernie Sanders, an insurgent Democratic candidate, appealed to another branch of the low-wage sector, those who were trying to move into the FTE sector. As described in chapter 4, they more often did not make it and had to deal with massive student debts. Only time will tell how these attempts to wake this sleeping giant will affect America.[2]

The FTE sector makes plans for itself, typically ignoring the needs of the low-wage sector. This can be seen in policies for health care, public education, mass incarceration, infrastructure investment, and debt reduction since the 2008 financial crisis. Public support has eroded since the 1970s for both health care and public education, typically on the basis that the benefits would go primarily to African Americans. Latinos entering the United States after 1970 typically started off poor and in the same schools. As public education increasingly failed to provide a transition into the FTE sector for members of the low-wage sector, mass incarceration acted as a New Jim Crow policy to keep blacks and Latinos more recently from full participation in American society. The failure to maintain and update the nation's infrastructure and to revive the economy by reducing mortgages that could not be paid after the housing bubble burst demonstrates the FTE sector's separation from the low-wage sector and its unwillingness to spend its members' money on things that do not benefit them directly, even though there might be indirect effects that benefit the whole economy.[3]

The top 1 percent of the population shown in figure 3 has disproportionate effect on economic policies. Even more than other members of the FTE sector, the top 1 percent resists tax increases and asserts that the government should cut government spending instead. One percenters say that government debts are a larger problem than any of the problems discussed here. Their remedy is to cut spending on these programs even more.[4]

The division of the economy comes in part from the hollowing out of the wage distribution and the consequent destruction of middle-class jobs. David Autor, an expert labor economist, argued that technical progress will continue and that the shape of employment will evolve. He compared the low-wage sector to Luddites who opposed the introduction of machines in the Industrial Revolution and appealed to the industrialization that eventually raised their wages. But it took a half century from the "Hungry Twenties"—the 1820s when Luddites were active—for British wages to begin their ascent, with many political changes along the way. The danger for America is that the combination of a dual economy and racecraft is leading to political decisions that freeze the dual economy in place. It will be hard for the forces of technological change and globalization to reunify the American economy in any reasonable time.[5]

We are in a time of crisis similar in many ways to the crisis of the 1930s. John Dewey, philosopher of modern education that plays a central role in the revived Lewis model, gave a set of lectures published in *Liberalism and Social Action* in 1935 that provide a clear way to close this discussion. Dewey argued that liberalism arose in the nineteenth century as a theory of individual actions to oppose and destroy the restraints on individual actions that had accumulated through centuries of European civilization. But while this ideology led to beneficial changes at the dawn of industrialization, the changes were outmoded later by the very fruits of liberal actions. Small-scale production characteristic of the first Industrial Revolution was superseded by the large business firms of the second Industrial Revolution a century ago. Scarcity as a general condition of society was replaced by abundance in America. Insecurity went from a stimulus to economic progress to a condition that leads to despair. The promotion of security has now become the mark of a successful democracy, as described in chapter 8.

In this new context, Dewey stated, "The liberal spirit is marked by its own picture of the pattern that is required: a social organization that will make possible effective liberty and opportunity for personal growth in mind and spirit in all individuals. Its present need is recognition that established material security is a prerequisite of the ends it cherishes." This view was restated more precisely by Piketty in *Capital in the Twenty-First Century* where he said that social states of the twentieth century were based on providing education, health, and retirement for all. In these passages, I believe that "all" means all, irrespective of race, gender, or income.[6]

In order to achieve these ends in today's environment, I propose a set of five actions. They will be difficult to accomplish in our current political context, but they provide a plan of action that could start now and grow. Even if we can act on only the first few recommendations, they may be sufficient to start us toward the others.

1. Restore and expand public education by focusing on preschool and early education, family involvement, and building reconstruction.

2. Shift our resources from repression of the low-wage sector by mass incarceration and bad schools to investing in the human and social capital of all Americans.

3. Repair our abandoned and aging infrastructure; forgive the mortgage and educational debts oppressing the low-wage sector.

4. Reject the private public oxymoron and move toward a truly democratic government;

5. Reject the majority minority oxymoron and embrace American diversity.

The first recommendation starts with providing high-quality preschool education available for all children in the United States. Head Start demonstrated that early education has a very high payoff. This is vitally important to start making a change in our dual economy since education benefits every individual and benefits to the country as bright students grow into innovative adults—as explained earlier.

The benefits of early education, however, only continue if the educational system continues to stimulate and teach growing children. Early education is only the start of education; we need to upgrade all of education that now serves the low-wage sector. We need to recognize that education in a dual economy is not simply a program for children. A commitment to education is easier to make if repressive policies are abandoned, and these recommendations support each other. School reforms done in a vacuum tend not to have lasting effects; urban schools need to offset the harmful effects of social disintegration caused by low wages and unemployment. Preschools are needed to introduce three- and four-year-olds to reading when they come from homes without books. This student-friendly approach can be coupled with the best practice of schools that have been discovered and with the extra resources for poor families and children recommended thirty years ago.

Public universities also need to be refinanced. The current system of low public support for state universities leads to borrowing by students and the growth of educational debts. Just as support for early and K–12 education needs to be increased, public support for state universities needs to be supported as originally designed to provide a college education to all. Only then will our educational system begin to merge into a unitary educational system.

The second recommendation is to reverse the package of policies that act together to repress both white and black poor people. Depriving men of a good education dooms many of them to unemployment and criminal activity. They land in prison, and their children grow up in single-parent families. The boys grow up to be men like their absent fathers, and the cycle repeats itself. (Women are also at risk, but men are more frequently arrested.) To eliminate this pattern, we need to work on several fronts at the same time. We need to end mass incarceration and differential rates of arrests and convictions of black men by local and state police and judges. We need also to improve education for the children of felons and allow freed felons to rejoin the workforce. And we need to rethink our urban policies to pursue the integrated housing that has so far eluded us.

The first two recommendations are two sides of the same coin. American education cannot be universal until mass incarceration is abandoned. And mass incarceration will not be an inevitable result of growing up in a poor neighborhood until urban public education equals the quality of suburban schools. These joint changes will benefit white, black, and brown Americans alike. As noted earlier, even though the political discussion focuses on African Americans; poverty affects children growing up independent of color. And since many white Americans are poor, these improvements will affect more white Americans than African Americans and Latino immigrants combined.

The third recommendation is to start upgrading our infrastructure. Both candidates for president in 2016 campaigned on promises to do this. They claimed it would help low-wage workers by providing jobs for them as well as improving our cities. The process will take a long time, and it will provide both short-term and long-term benefits. It may increase the federal debt in the short run, as the very rich fear, but this increase should be viewed as an investment in the American economy. If done well, it should help the economy to grow the way a good investment helps a business to grow.

This recommendation could provide jobs for many workers who dropped out of the labor force after the 2008 financial crisis. This improvement in the incomes of households who are suffering from the problems described earlier will spread the recovery from the 2008 financial crisis more widely among the American population. The short-run benefit will turn into a longer benefit as better roads, bridges, and public transit will enable our cities to function better. Good infrastructure is not by itself the major part of economic growth, but it is like an oil that lubricates the private economy and stimulates economic growth.

Forgiving the accumulation of debt in the low-wage sector also would stimulate economic growth. These kinds of debts have mushroomed since 1970 and 2008; they oppress the low-wage sector and reduce the power of consumption. The politics of this issue are even more difficult than infrastructure politics. There, only taxes need to be raised. Here, most debts are to private financial institutions, and these banks and other lenders need to be paid off or convinced to write down loans. This has proven to add difficulties to any resolution.

The fourth recommendation is to recognize and reverse our slide into the kind of country that Lewis described in his model of a dual economy. We need to acknowledge that a democratic government is the best tool to increase the income and security of all its citizens. We have neglected our physical and educational capital stock to an alarming degree. Privatizing them will not unify our country; private businesses have different goals than public agencies do. Using the tools of democratic governments is the only thing that will enable all citizens to achieve their potential. If the government appears laggard today; that is due to lack of political and economic support. More appropriations will strengthen government programs and morale.

It became more difficult for the government to spend money to help the economy, particularly the low-wage sector, after the Supreme Court decided in 2010 in *Citizens United v. Federal Election Commission* to regard money as speech and allow the very rich to have a dominant place in politics. The Investment Theory of Politics came into its own in this new framework. As described in chapter 7, the Kochtopus took advantage of *Citizens United* faster than the disorganized Democrats could and elected several conservative governors and many conservative members of Congress. It has become difficult to sustain existing government programs, much less initiate new ones.

The last recommendation is to revive what has been called the Second Reconstruction of the 1960s and 1970s to point the way to an integrated American society. This means overcoming three hundred years of American history, far more than the thirty or forty years that are the focus here. It should start with Congress or the Supreme Court reversing the 2013 decision to diminish the Voting Rights Act in *Shelby County v. Holder*. Making our oligarchic form of government more democratic will provide a powerful stimulus to full citizenship by all citizens.

This should help start a public conversation to understand our complicated past. The United States was based initially on slavery. We no longer approve of this subjugation of people, and we do not have slaves. Nevertheless, we still oppress the descendants of American slaves. We should instead work toward integrating African Americans, Latinos, and other immigrants into our neighborhoods and schools. We should educate these students well to allow extraordinary individuals to flower and benefit us all.

This is a tall order, and the political structure of the United States appears to be dysfunctional. As discussed in chapter 10, early education is key to starting to close the gap between the sectors of our dual economy. Education leads to mobility, and education has to start early to overcome the problems arising from poor and dysfunctional families.[7]

Even if we cannot get very far in the quest for a just society, education benefits all and is worth pursuing. One of the reasons that the United States has been at the forefront of many economic activities is that there are lots of people here who have creative ideas. There is no reason to believe that people are born smarter in the United States than elsewhere. But if everyone here gets enough education to use his or her creative abilities productively, we all can benefit. There will be more people with the opportunity to have creative and useful ideas. Even the richest person needs a secure place for financial assets; a strong United States implies a safe place to store value.[8]

We can work with and in schools as we learn more and allocate more resources into education. There is a long way to go, and this is a good way to start. As Dewey realized in 1935, liberalism must now become radical in perceiving that thoroughgoing changes are needed in the current setup of many institutions. We must aim to provide all children with a roughly equal start in life, through our schools and early educational programs if their parents are absent or incapacitated. A just society strives to give all its members a chance to participate fully in society, and early guidance and instruction for low-wage children moves us toward a just society.[9]

Making these changes means going from W. Arthur Lewis to a new, inclusive, and democratic model of our society, and it will be a long process. As described here, we have been digging ourselves into this hole for over forty years. It will take us many years to climb out. The first step when you find yourself in a hole, however, is to stop digging.

Appendix: Models of Inequality

The big book about inequality around the world is Thomas Piketty's classic, *Capital in the Twenty-First Century*. Piketty worked mainly with tax data from various countries, and his sample was restricted to those developed countries that had good records extending back into history. In terms of figure 7, he focused on the growth of the global elite. And to show that politics matter, he contrasted the experiences of France and the United States. None of the growth in inequality that happened in the United States since 1980 happened in France! This counterexample shows that the effects of technological change and globalization can be altered by political actions.[1]

This is too short a summary of the book that bought inequality into the center of political debates in the United States. It may help some economists reading this book to explain how Piketty saw the tension between economic and political fortunes and how his analysis relates to the approach used here. He summarized his main conclusion as a race between the rate of growth of the economy and the rate of interest. When the economy grows at a higher rate than the rate of interest, then inequality decreases. When the interest rate exceeds the growth rate, inequality grows. French policies opposed this economic pressure; American policies encouraged it.

The logic behind this conclusion is that the rich save much of their incomes. As Keynes said long ago, consumption rises with income, but not as fast. When the interest rate exceeds the growth rate, these savings increase the capital of rich people faster than income grows. And, of course, a large capital stock protects rich people from the risks of life described in chapter 8 and allows them to live well whether times are good or bad. Piketty went further than other writers on inequality to stress the centrality of the distribution of capital ownership in an economy's inequality, stating this importance in the title of his book.

Piketty's insight helps clarify policy choices in the United States today. As noted earlier, the richest people do not want their taxes to rise. If that objection could be overcome, it is necessary to differentiate taxes on income from taxes on capital. Increasing taxes on America's highest incomes will help fund some of the social programs that a democracy expects. However, it will not affect the capital stock of rich people, enabling them to continue their political programs. Only taxes on capital can result in durable changes in the distribution of income. Piketty supported capital taxation at very low rates as a result of these considerations and to make tax avoidance harder.

Older people today recall the years between the end of the Second World War and the start of income inequality in the 1970s and 1980s. It was a period of rapid economic growth, partly in recovery from the world war, and with a growing middle class. People living then thought of these years as normal, but Piketty asserted that these years were highly unusual in the history of the past two centuries—and even beyond. While there is no inevitable winner in the race between the interest rate and the growth rate, the interest rate normally wins.

I used the Lewis model and Piketty's data as frameworks for the analysis of income inequality in this book. Piketty appealed to "fundamental laws of economics" to structure the data in his book, and I compare the models of inequality used by Piketty and in this book to clarify my arguments.

Piketty's fundamental laws come from the model of economic growth created by Robert M. Solow about the same time as W. Arthur Lewis published his model. The Solow growth model is even more well known than the Lewis dual-economy model, and Solow—like Lewis—won a Nobel Prize for his model. It is a curious coincidence that both Piketty and I reached back half a century to get frameworks for our contributions to the study of inequality.[2]

Piketty's first law connects wealth and income through the interest rate. His second law shows how the ratio of wealth to national income changes over time—rising with the savings rate and falling with the economy's growth rate. This is a restatement of the equilibrium in the Solow model, reversed to make the main focus the ratio of capita to output instead of the growth rate of income. A third relation, not quite a law, strengthens the second law by looking at the return on savings. The ratio of wealth to income rises when the rate of interest, defined in the first law, is greater than the economy's rate of growth.[3]

I used the Lewis model to frame my account of class and race in America. I emphasized Lewis's insight that a two-sector model was the key to understanding how far inequality has progressed in the United States. I relied heavily on the part of the Lewis model showing that the upper sector will aim to keep incomes in the lower sector low. This is a darker aspect of the Lewis model than many economists remember, and it is integral to the way the model works.

The two models were formulated more than a half century ago. Lewis and Solow wrote soon after the Second World War ended when the progress of nations seemed promising. Piketty and I wrote as the growth of high incomes is threatening the stability of political structures in advanced economies. These are the countries invested with great hopes in the period when Lewis and Solow were writing.

One way to see how the world has changed is to look carefully at Piketty's use of Solow's model. Solow considered growth as his main interest; the primary economic issue in the 1950s was economic growth. He found that the ratio of capital to labor played a crucial role in the determination of the growth rate. Piketty reversed this to make the ratio of capital to income his focus. (Note the different denominators of the two ratios.) The formal treatment of capital by Solow and Piketty was similar, but the implications were far different. While Solow was determining the rate of aggregate economic growth, Piketty was chronicling the progress of the economically entitled.

This book used the Lewis model of developing countries to describe conditions in the most successful industrial country—the United States of America. This seems paradoxical as the Lewis model was designed for developing economies, not for leading ones. But as I described earlier, the United States has undergone deindustrialization that has made the economy more like that of developing countries than industrial ones. American roads and bridges are more like those in developing countries than those in Western Europe. This is not the progress implied by Lewis and Solow.

Another difference is in the treatment of economic growth. Piketty emphasized the critical role of savings as a contributor to economic growth. The growth of wealth, defined by Piketty as equivalent to capital, only happens if people save from their income. Lewis argued that the capitalist sector grows from retained earnings. He assumed that members of the capitalist sector reinvest their retained earnings. In other words, both models rely on savings, but the determinants of investment are quite different. Lewis and Solow were working within a Keynesian framework in which capital referred to the means of production: factories and machines are the prime examples.

Simon Kuznets, a third Nobel Laureate in economics, also was focused on economic growth in the 1950s. Using the data available to him, he formulated what came to be called the Kuznets Curve that asserted that income inequality would first rise and then fall during economic growth. He was reacting to the declining income inequality he observed around him and a political-economic view that richer countries would choose policies that increased equality.

Piketty argued that Kuznets was living in a very unusual economic period during the years after the Second World War. Only in that period, Piketty observed, was the growth rate of income higher than the interest rate, promoting equality. Since then, the American economy reverted to its more usual pattern where the interest rate is larger than the growth rate. I argued on different grounds that the "golden age of economic growth" was unusual, that it was a protracted recovery from the preceding thirty years of war and depression. Either way, the rapid growth of income inequality in the United States since the 1970s contradicted Kuznets' optimistic view.[4]

Piketty and I defined capital in very different ways. Piketty equated capital and wealth, including the value of both public and private financial assets in his definition of capital. He was interested in gathering data on income inequality over several centuries, and he restricted his data on wealth to assets traded on markets. He then could sum varied forms of capital at market prices to get national capital stocks by adding their prices.

Piketty drew on a literature that argued for the role of finance in economic growth. Economists collected data on the growth of financial intermediation and showed that while finance grew as a result of economic growth, there was good evidence that financial development caused economic growth. Piketty did not discuss this research directly, focusing instead on more concrete issues such as the imputed rent from owner-occupied houses.[5]

This procedure raises an important question of national income analysis. We do not have a good way of measuring the productivity of modern finance, even though all economists agree that financial activity is important for economic growth. Does that mean that the growth of financial assets in the housing boom before the financial crisis of 2008 was all productive? This question is important, but it is too complex to be pursued further here.[6]

The literature on the role of capital in economic growth and development went in other directions after Lewis and Solow published their models. Solow discovered a startling fact in the empirical work that accompanied the publication of his model. The growth of capital as defined by Lewis, while important for the dynamics of the Solow model, accounted for only a tiny part of the economic growth of the United States in the twentieth century.[7]

Economists initially reacted to this finding by denying its importance, saying the unaccounted part of growth was simply a residual. But labor economists at the same time introduced a new kind of capital—human capital. This kind of capital was embodied in people; it was increased by formal education and informal training. Jacob Mincer used the term "human capital" in the title of an article in the late 1950s, and Gary Becker published a book by that title in the 1960s.[8]

Education was hardly new in the 1950s, and many authors had noted over the years how useful it was in economic affairs. The new element lay in the formalization of its effect and insertion into economic models. The contribution of education to growth then could be compared with the contribution of other kinds of capital to provide a more detailed and complete analysis of economic growth and account for much of the economic growth not explained by the accumulation of capital in Solow's model.[9]

A third kind of capital came into general use several decades later. It was popularized by Robert Putnam, who wrote first about the differences between Northern and Southern Italy and then about the United States. He emphasized the role of social capital, defined to be the networks of relationships among people who live and work in a particular society that enable their society to function effectively. As with human capital, this was a formalization of a concept that was widely noted in previous work.[10]

A generation after Solow found that physical capital alone could not explain the progress of the United States in the twentieth century, economists found that they could explain the differences of output per worker in different countries far more completely than Solow if they used all three kinds of capital—physical, human, and social. They altered Solow's question in two ways: they expanded the kinds of capital they used, and they compared different countries at the same time instead of one country at different times. This concept has penetrated economics to the extent that when Partha Dasgupta wrote a very short introduction to economics, he wrote it entirely about the difference between social capital in developed and in undeveloped countries. Economics in this view was a tool to answer this critical question: "Under what circumstances would the parties who have reached agreement trust one another to keep their word?" Social capital has become as important as physical capital.[11]

Piketty gathered prodigious amounts of data for capital that could be "evaluated in terms of market value: for example, in the case of a corporation that issues stock, the value depends on the share price."[12] Since human and social capital are not traded on public markets, they could not be measured this way and were relegated to the sidelines.[13]

I incorporated these two new kinds of capital into my modern adaptation of the Lewis model. I compared two sectors of a single dual economy, just as others compared different countries, with the illumination provided by all three kinds of capital. Human and social capital differ sharply between the two sectors of the American dual economy, with important effects on economics and politics. Despite this different approach, Piketty seems sympathetic to the analysis presented here. Early in his massive compilation of data, he wrote, "The resurgence of inequality after 1980 is due largely to the political shifts of the past several decades, especially in regard to taxation and finance."[14]

Notes

Introduction

1. What does "median" mean and how is it determined? Consider a group of three people: the person who delivers your morning newspaper, a hedge-fund manager, and you. These three people clearly have very different incomes. Ranking them by income, the median is the person in the middle—most likely you. The median differs from the mean—or average—because the average is one-third of the sum of the incomes earned by the trio. Assume the hedge-fund manager earns about $10 million a year, a modest income for hedge managers. Then the average income of the trio is more than $3 million, far higher than your income as the median person—unless you are a hedge-fund manager. One-humped camels are dromedaries, and two-humped ones are Bactrian camels.

2. Piketty 2014.

3. Dylan 1963; Case and Deaton 2015.

4. Goldin and Katz 2008.

5. Goldin 2006.

6. Levinson 2015. This story was published as the *Boston Globe* was trying to lower its delivery costs by hiring a new delivery company. The effort failed. Arsenault 2016. See Edin and Shaefer 2015 for more examples of jobs like this.

7. Confessore 2015; Kaufman 2016; Smith 2016; Eligon 2016; Davey 2016a.

8. Bonczar 2009.

9. Alexander 2010.

10. Temin 2016.

11. Levy and Temin 2007.

1   A Dual Economy

1. Edwards 2004.

2. Freeland 2012; Piketty 2014; Reeves 2015; Reeves and Joo 2015; Goldin and Katz 2008, 300.

3. Economists can find further discussion of the Lewis model in the appendix. The Lewis model also describes initial phases of economic history described by Hicks (1969).

4. Jones 1997.

5. Lewis 1954, 49.

6. Ibid.

7. Harris and Todaro 1970.

8. Pamuk 2015 provides a vivid fictionalized description of the operation of the Lewis model in Turkey over several generations.

9. Figure 2 ends in 2007, but wage stagnation continues (DeSilver 2014; Reardon and Bischoff 2016). Piketty opened his book with an expanded figure that looks very much like figure 3, although it is for the top decile of the population (Piketty 2014, 24).

10. Pew Research Center 2015. I divided the sectors by the proportion of college graduates in the paper that turned into this book (Temin 2016). Some of the sources cited in this book divide the workforce by income, and some divide it by education. The Pew Research Center report came out after I had submitted that paper for publication, and their income numbers are closer to the definitions in the Lewis model than the education numbers I used in the paper. I accordingly reduced the proportion of people in the FTE sector from 30 to 20 percent of the population, increasing the sharp identification of the two sectors. A recent IMF working paper updates the Pew Research Study in a framework of income polarization (Alichi, Kantenga, and Solé 2016).

11. Gornick and Milanovic 2015; Komlos 2016; Schwartz 2014.

12. Saez and Zucman 2016.

13. Subsequent economists have assumed that farmers were maximizers like the capitalists, albeit of their income instead of profits (Harris and Todaro 1970). That is as far as we can take the model here; we will return to this issue in chapter 10.

14. See the appendix for references to the economics literature on human and social capital.

15. Putnam 2015, 44–45, 265–266.

16. Temin 1999.

17. Page, Bartels, and Seawright 2013.

18. Kozol 2005.

2   The FTE Sector

1. Triffin 1961; Temin and Vines 2013.

2. There may have been a more nuanced transition from Johnson to Nixon. Hinton argued that Johnson's creation of the Law Enforcement Assistance Administration (LEAA) "made national policy makers meaningful partners in

law enforcement and criminal justice at all levels." She concluded, "Johnson paradoxically paved the way for the anticrime policies of the Nixon and Ford administrations to be turned against his own antipoverty programs" (Hinton 2016, 8, 14). See also Thompson 2010.

3. The "Nixon Shock" was a combination of three policies, but the change in exchange-rate regime was the lasting and important one. The need for a new policy should have been obvious from Bagehot and Keynes, since the primary function of a central bank with a fixed exchange rate is to preserve the exchange rate. The Mundell-Fleming model that formalized this insight was only a decade old and probably not yet widely understood (Nixon 1971; Eichengreen 2011).

4. Bacevich starts his history of the Middle East wars with Nixon's proclamation. Bacevich 2016, 5.

5. Neal 2015; Zucman 2015, 22.

6. Powell 1971. See also Phillips-Fein 2009, chapter 7; Mayer 2016, 73–76. The Powell Memo is not mentioned by his biographer, who spends 600 pages arguing that Powell was a moderate judge (Jeffries 1994).

7. Doogan 2009, 34; http://www.heritage.org/about.

8. Steinfeld 1991, 2001.

9. There are still ties between white supremacist organizations and conservative politicians today (Wines and Alvarez 2015).

10. Drutman 2015, 28.

11. Lipton and Williams 2016; Kinzer 2016.

12. Hertel-Fernandez 2014. Ferguson and Rogers (1986) date the political shift at this time, during the recession of 1973–1975. See also Mayer 2016, 73–90, and the description of the Grassroots Leadership Academy, a new Koch-funded initiative, in Parker and Haberman 2016.

13. Mills 1979; Ferguson and Rogers 1986.

14. Levy and Temin 2011; Neumann 2016.

15. Wilkerson 2010.

16. Wilkerson 2010; Logan and Parman 2015; Anderson 2016.

17. Piore and Safford 2006; Lee 2014.

18. Nixon 1969.

19. Phillips-Fein 2009, 322; Miller 2009, 64.

20. Hayek 1944; Temin and Vines 2014. One result of this shift in economic doctrine is a current push for a constitutional amendment to balance the federal budget each year (Wines 2016b).

21. Congressional Budget Office 2014.

22. Wigmore 1997.

23. Philippon and Reshef 2012.

24. Stevenson 2105, 2016; Bartlett 2013; Gornick and Milanovic 2015.

25. Lipton and Moyer 2015; Scheiber and Cohen 2015.

26. Zingales 2015. Here is an intriguing cross-section case; we admire Cuban artists and ball players because talented Cubans cannot go into finance.

27. Gelles 2015; Jones 2015, 35.

28. http://www.wid.world/#Database. Atkinson (2015, 38) puts the thresholds a bit higher than Jones: $400,000 for the top 1 percent and $150,000 for the top 10 percent.

29. Chozick 2015.

30. This is the median worker, in contrast to the median family of three described in the Pew Research Center report (Pew 2015).

31. Bureau of Labor Statistics 2015. The earnings variation between academic fields is echoed by variation within fields. The top 10 percent of university English teachers earn above $100,000 a year and are comfortably within the FTE sector (Fourcade, Ollion, and Algan 2015).

32. Santos and Rich 2015.

3   The Low-Wage Sector

1. Gelman et al. (2008, 71–73) note that prosperity leads people to vote Republican, but that race still has effects on voting in the South. Kuziemko and Washington (2015) say race is key. See also Woodward 1974; Anderson 2016.

2. Powell's secret memo probably had not come to light before his confirmation (Phillips-Fein 2009, 163; Jeffries 1994, 6; Alexander 2010).

3. Autor, Levy, and Murnane 2003. This segmentation of the labor market was anticipated by Reich (1991).

4. Krueger and Summers 1987.

5. Weil 2014.

6. Bewley 1999; Weil 2014; Isaac and Scheiber 2016; Kang 2016. Holzer disputed the data in figure 4, arguing that there are new jobs that fall in the middle. His examples are of service jobs that are performed in close proximity to the persons served. Several of these jobs appear to require college education, and they may pay enough to get workers into the FTE sector. Most of them appear to be in the low-wage sector, albeit at the upper end (Holzer and Lerman 2009; Holzer 2015).

7. Porter 2016.

8. Azar, Schmalz, and Tecu 2015.

9. Tirman 2015.

10. Acemoglu et al. 2016; Pierce and Schott 2016. The reduction of American manufacturing should have reduced labor earnings, but there was a small temporary rise.

11. Freeman 1995; Autor, Dorn, and Hanson 2013.

12. US Bureau of Labor Statistics 2016; International Labour Organization 2015.

13. Bosworth and Burtless 2016.

14. Goolsbee and Krueger 2015, 13. The two-tier wage system was abandoned in 2015, as the automobile companies became profitable again (Vlasic and Chapman 2015).

15. Board of Governors of the Federal Reserve System 2015, 2.

16. Katznelson 2005; Boustan 2010; Card, Mas, and Rothstein 2008. Recent research observes increasing segregation even before the Second World War and in both urban and rural settings. Residential segregation may have reached a peak after *Brown v. Board of Education*, but it did not start with it (Gerstle 1995; Logan and Parman 2015; Shertzer and Walsh 2016).

17. Wilson 1996, 42.

18. Cherlin 2014, 172–175.

19. The racial composition of figure 1 shows that roughly 90 percent of both black and Latino families are in the low-wage sector (Pew Research Center 2015). The Latino population is growing rapidly (Stepler and Brown 2016).

20. Caraley 1992.

21. Wilson 1996.

22. The *New York Times* covered this issue repeatedly. See Bosman 2016b, 2016c, 2016d; Bosman, Davey, and Smith 2016; Davey and Smith 2016a; Goodnough 2016; Goodnough, Davey, and Smith 2016.

23. Wilson 1996, 49; Mauer 2006; Glaze and Kaeble 2014.

24. Bonczar 2003. This estimate was derived from historical data for 2001, but it undoubtedly is still accurate today. The prison population has declined somewhat in recent years, but through the early release of inmates with long sentences, not from a reduction of arrest and conviction rates. Some blacks encouraged increased police attention to their neighborhoods to protect themselves (Fortner 2015). I doubt whether any of them foresaw how much drug laws would affect their communities.

25. Alexander 2010; Crutchfield and Weeks 2015.

26. Roeder, Eisen, and Bowling 2015; Gottschalk 2015; Lofstrom and Raphael 2016, 123.

27. "'Welfare Queen' Becomes Issue in Reagan Campaign" 1976. Reagan found a forty-seven-year-old welfare recipient named Linda Taylor using aliases to increase her benefits, and he greatly exaggerated the amount of money involved and number of aliases she used.

28. Davis 2015; Parker and Eder, 2016.

29. Agan and Starr 2016. In economics jargon, employers employ statistical discrimination when individual discrimination is disallowed.

30. Murray 2012.

31. Goffman 2014; Smallacombe 2006. Putnam (2000) differentiates bridging and bonding social capital. Bridging social capital is inclusive and extends to civic groups; bonding social capital is exclusive and restrictive. In poor

neighborhoods, people lack bridging social capital that can help them find education and jobs, but they have bonding social capital within family and church groups.

32. Current Population Survey, http://www.census.gov/hhes/www/cpstables/032015/pov/pov03_100.htm.

33. Wilson 2009; Putnam 2015.

34. Goffman 2014; Case and Deaton 2015; Tavernise 2016.

35. Gustafson 2009.

36. Edin 1997; Wacquant 2009.

37. Pinto 2015; Stockman 2015.

4   Transition

1. Harris and Todaro 1970.

2. Ferguson 2007.

3. Baily and Dynarski 2011; National Center for Education Statistics 2015.

4. Beasley 2011; Carey 2014; Bui and Miller 2016.

5. DiTomaso 2013.

6. Weerts and Ronca 2006; National Science Board 2012.

7. Mortenson 2012.

8. Dynarski 2015a.

9. Kinser 2006.

10. Cohen 2015b; Looney and Yannelis 2015.

11. Bernard 2015; Waldman 2016.

12. Consumer Financial Protection Bureau 2015; Morgenson 2015.

13. Dynarski 2016b.

14. Carey 2015. This story appears extreme, but it is hardly unique. John Acosta graduated from law school in Indiana in late 2015 and passed the bar exam on his first try. He is, however, over $200,000 in debt for his studies. The government will forgive the loan after twenty-five years if he cannot repay his debt, but the IRS probably will treat the forgiven amount as income, yielding a $70,000 tax bill on the eve of Acosta's retirement (Scheiber 2016b).

15. Krueger 2012.

5   Race and Gender

1. Coates 2015, 17–18.

2. Fields and Fields 2012, 283.

3. Boyer and Nissenbaum 1974.

4. Quotations from Handlin and Handlin 1950, 211, 216, 221–222. See also Galenson 1981; Isenberg 2016. Isenberg notes that some English immigrants were vagrants and criminals sent to America against their will.

5. Foner 1988; Woodward 1974.

6. Anderson 2016; Carl, 2016.

7. Margo 1985.

8. Agee and Evans 1941.

9. Johnson 1966; Katznelson 2005; Fairlie and Sundstrom 1999.

10. Warren 2015.

11. Alexander 2010; Bonczar 2003.

12. Ignatiev 1995; MacDonald 1999.

13. Brodkin 1998.

14. Pew Research Center 2015.

15. Alesina, Glaeser, and Sacerdote 2001.

16. Acharya, Blackwell, and Sen 2015.

17. Rankine 2015, 105–109. There are real examples where conviction was the result of arrests like this. The story of Derrick Hamilton, who studied law in prison and proved the innocence of some of his friends and finally himself appeared in *The New Yorker*. Gonnerman 2016.

18. Coates 2015.

19. Krantz 2016; Stack 2016b.

20. Covert 2015; Stack 2016a. The "20 minutes of action" quote is from the offending student's father's statement to the court.

21. Liptak 2016c.

22. Krugman, 2016b; Eckholm, 2016.

23. Kessler-Harris 2001, 246.

24. Blinder and Fausset 2016; Liptak 2016a; Siegel 2002; Greenhouse, 2016; Wines, 2016; Wines and Blinder, 2016.

25. Kuziemko and Washington 2015; Reid 2015.

26. Liptak 2016b. Oral arguments with photos of the marked notes can be found at https://www.supremecourt.gov/oral_arguments/argument_transcripts/14-8349_6537.pdf.

27. Kerber 1998, 305; Stewart 2016.

28. Miller 2016.

6   The Investment Theory of Politics

1. Luce 2015.

2. Dimon 2016.

3. Levinson 2006; Maier 2011.

4. Overton 2006.

5. Burnham 2015, 29, 35, 46.

6. Keyssar 2000, part I; Burnham 2010.

7. Katznelson 2013.

8. 570 US __ (2013); Overton 2006.

9. Hasen 2012; Wines and Fernandez 2016.

10. Thompson 2010.

11. Herszenhorn 2016. Trump speedily said his remarks had been misconstrued (Rappeport 2016).

12. http://www.whytuesday.org/.

13. Keyssar 2000; Kousser 1999, 2.

14. Keyssar 2000, 175.

15. Two kinds of actions are needed now. For the long run: adjustments in either the payments to recipients or the taxes that finance them, and possibly changes in both. For the short run: the government needs to loan Social Security funds to deal with immediate problems. The latter issue is straightforward. Just as the federal government loaned money to banks in the financial crash of 2008, one branch of the government needs to loan money to another to assure continuity of actions. The former, long-run issue is a question of public policy. Conservative politicians want to reduce benefits to restore a balance between taxes and payments for the next seventy-five years. Increasing the age at which recipients get Social Security benefits is one way to reduce benefits. Liberal politicians want to increase taxes to balance the system (Diamond and Orszag 2005; Hill 2016).

16. Bartels 2008, 177.

17. Bacevich 2016, 194, 244. Tony Blair sold the war to the British public in the same way (Ross 2016).

18. Ferguson 1995, chapter 1.

19. Ibid.

20. Bartels 2008, 265, 267, 289. Bartels reaffirmed this conclusion in a more recent book, saying, "Election outcomes are essentially random choices among the available parties—musical chairs" (Achen and Bartels 2016, 312).

21. Traugott 2016.

22. Ferguson, Jorgensen, and Chen 2013.

23. Ferguson, Jorgensen and Chen 2016.

24. Lee and Norden 2016.

25. Gilens and Page 2014.

26. Mayer 2016, 90.

7 Preferences of the Very Rich

1. http://www.forbes.com/forbes-400/list/.

2. Page, Bartels, and Seawright 2013, 56.

3. Ibid.

4. Freeland 2012, 5, 241.

5. Drutman 2013; Gold and Narayanswamy 2016.

6. Phillips-Fein 2009, 221–225.

7. Miller 2015, 64.

8. Kroll et al. 2014.

9. Norris 2014; Corkery 2016; Buettner and Bagli 2016.

10. Bagli 2016; Rattner 2016a; Frank 2016; Norris 2014; Sommer 2015; Cohen 2016b.

11. Zucman 2014, 2015, 35, 107; Lipton and Creswell 2016.

12. Sokol 2014. Obama, as the highest-ranking African American politician, was subject to implacable opposition to his policies and the indignity of politicians claiming his election was illegitimate because he was not born in the United States—a claim without a shred of evidence (Parker and Eder 2016; Barbaro 2016).

13. Mayer 2016, 9, 55, 86–87.

14. Mayer 2010, 2016, 280–285; Dwyer 2016.

15. Quoted in Mayer 2016, 123. Italics in the original.

16. Mayer 2016, chapter 4.

17. Mayer 2016, provides charts showing Kochtopus spending on politics and think tanks, 2009–2013, on the inside front and back covers of her book. See also Vogel 2015.

18. Full disclosure: The paper that gave rise to this book was supported by the Institute for New Economic Thinking.

8 Concepts of Government

1. Small-d democrats are members of a democracy. They should not be confused with large-d Democrats who are members of a political party.

2. *Bush v. Gore*, 531 US 98 (2000); *Shelby County v. Holder*, 570 US __ (2013); Ewald 2009; Scher 2011; Berman 2015.

3. Moss 2002.

4. See chapter 12.

5. These regulations have been eroded by the subcontracting described in chapter 3.

6. Barro 2015; Scheiber 2015, 2016a.

7. Rawls 1999.

8. Rattner (2016b) shows that this process is already under way.

9. See chapter 10.

10. Dawisha 2014.

11. Winters 2011.

12. Hacker and Pierson (2016) chastise us all for forgetting our history, but they only recall this small part of our long history and pay little attention to the important role of racecraft.

13. Overton 2006; Ewald 2009; Scher 2011; Berman 2015.

14. Bacevich 2016; Gerges 2016, 133.

15. Wang 2013; Daley 2016.

16. Scheindlin 2016.

17. Kar and Mazzone 2016.

18. Herszenhorn 2016a; Brittain and Horwitz 2016; Fandos 2016; Herszenhorn 2016b. Mayer 2016 shows on the inside front cover of her book that "the Network" funneled $6.6 million to the National Rifle Association. See also Greenhouse 2016a.

19. Corasaniti and Parker 2016; Gold and Narayanswamy 2016.

20. Mayer 2016, 90; Beard 2015, chapter 9.

9   Mass Incarceration

1. Williams 2016.

2. Fountain and Schmidt 2016.

3. Apuzzo 2016; Davey 2016b. A federal study of the Baltimore police found the same kind of bias that the Ferguson study found (Stolberg 2016).

4. Gottschalk 2015; Davey and Smith 2016b; Van Cleve 2016.

5. Tirman 2015; Bernstein 2009, 2016.

6. Edsall and Edsall 1991; Mauer 2006; Anderson 2016.

7. Western 2006, 78–79; Alexander 2010.

8. Kyckelhahn 2014; Carlson 2014.

9. Henrichson, Rinaldi, and Delaney 2015.

10. Swavolo, Riley, and Subramanian 2016; Keller and Pearce 2016.

11. Jones and Forman 2015.

12. Bonczar 2003; Tirman 2015.

13. Alexander 2010; Stuntz 2011; Edwards, Bunting, and Garcia 2013.

14. Charles Colton Task Force on Federal Corrections 2015; Eavis 2016; Hulse 2016.

15. *O'Conner v. Donaldson*, 422 US 563 (1975).

16. Sanders 2016.

17. Toner 1988; Edsall with Edsall 1991.

18. Bunton 2016; Pfaff 2016; Robertson 2016.

19. Weiser 2016; Schwartz 2016.

20. Hull 2009; Hinton, 2016.

21. Bernstein 2009, 2016. The Netflix series *Orange Is the New Black* featured a private takeover of a prison that has publicized the issues of mass incarceration and private prisons. And the federal Justice Department sent out a memo in August 2016 saying it would phase out the use of private prisons (Yates 2016).

22. Riggs 2012; Ashton and Petteruti 2011; Loewenstein 2016.

23. Ivory, Protess, and Bennett 2016; Hager and Santo 2016.

24. Burnham and Ferguson 2014.

25. Seelye 2016.

26. Stolberg and Eckholm 2016; Lichtblau 2016; Johnston 2016; Rubin 2016.

27. Harris 2016, xix and passim.

28. Wacquant 2009; Soss, Fording, and Schram 2011; http://www.census.gov/hhes/www/cpstables/032015/pov/pov03_100.htm.

10   Public Education

1. Schorr 1989.

2. Goldin 2006.

3. Goldin and Katz 2002; Temin 2002.

4. Goldstein 2014.

5. Allegretto and Mishel 2016.

6. Farley, Danziger, and Holzer 2000; Tribe and Matz 2014, 20.

7. Reardon and Bischoff 2011, 2016; Edsall 2016.

8. Temin 2002; Nocera 2015.

9. Goldin and Rouse 2000; Card and Giuliano 2014; Dynarski 2016a.

10. Johnson 2011. See also Clotfelter 2004.

11. Margo 1990.

12. Zernike 2015b, 2016a; Cohen 2016.

13. Bettinger 2005: Bifulco and Ladd 2006: Sass 2006; Kozol 2005; Nield and Balfanz 2006.

14. Dynarski 2015b; Taylor 2015.

15. Dobbie and Fryer 2013.

16. Mather, Correa, and Louttit 2016.

17. Zernike 2016b.

18. Fryer calls these practices "the five tenets." Others call them "No Excuses." The former consist of frequent teacher feedback, data-driven instruction, high-dosage tutoring, increased instructional time, a relentless focus on academic achievement. The latter emphasize discipline and comportment, traditional reading and math skills, instruction time, and selective teacher hiring. Common elements are the focus on increased instructional time and on academic achievement, identified by questions that mirror those for discipline and comportment. The two sets of practices identify similar schools (Dubner 2005; Fryer 2014; Dobbie and Fryer 2013; Angrist, Pathak, and Walters 2013).

19. Russakoff 2015.

20. Ibid., 76.

21. Ibid., 218; Schorr 1989.

22. Smeeding 2016.

23. Heckman, Pinto, and Savelyev 2013, 3–5; Reardon, Waldfogel, and Bassok 2016.

24. Schorr 1989; Kirp 2013; Jackson, Johnson, and Persico 2016. Connecticut may be about to follow New Jersey as courts try to adjust school spending to student needs (Harris 2016; Zernike 2016c).

25. Barnett et al. 2013.

26. Editorial Board 2016.

27. Delpit 2012.

28. Kirp 2013.

29. Goleman 1995, 2006; Harris 2016.

30. Schorr 1989, 191.

31. Consortium for Longitudinal Studies 1983; Garces, Thomas, and Currie 2002; Currie and Neidell 2007; Ludwig and Miller 2007; Heckman, Pinto, and Salvelyev 2013.

32. Currie and Thomas 2000.

33. Bush 2007; Head Start 2015.

34. Macur 2016; Dasgupta 2007, 31.

35. Reardon 2012; Porter 2015.

36. Abascal and Baldassarri 2015.

37. Lewis 2010; Levine et al. 2014.

11   American Cities

1. Jargowsky 2015, 13.

2. Caraley 1992.

3. Troesken 2006, 140.

4. Rocheleau 2016.

5. Bosman 2016a; Wines, McGeehan, and Schwartz 2016.

6. Schwartz 2016b.

7. Belkin 1999; Jargowsky 2015. Ferguson, Missouri, where a white policeman shot an unarmed young black man in 2014, was 75 percent white in 1990, but it had become two-thirds black by 2010 as white flight spread from inner cities to inner suburbs.

8. Newman 1972.

9. Wilson 1996, 2009; Murray 2012.

10. MacDonald 1999; Swarns 2015.

11. Goffman 2014.

12. Chetty, Hendren, and Katz 2016; Chyn 2016; Wolfers 2016.

13. Heckman 1989.

14. The eight criteria are capacity, condition, funding, future need, operation and maintenance, public safety, resilience, and innovation.

15. American Society of Civil Engineers 2013.

16. Northeast Corridor Commission 2015; Fitzsimmons and Chen 2015.

17. Forsberg 2010; Zernike 2015a.

18. Scharfenberg 2015. Kanter (2015) proposes high-tech solutions to our transport problems, arguing implicitly that they will help the FTE sector as well as the low-wage sector. However, they will require substantial expenditures, making them unlikely in the near future.

19. Dungea 2015; Vennochi 2015.

20. Stolberg and Fandos 2016; Fandos 2016b.

21. DeLong and Summers 2012; Authers 2015; Surowiecki 2016; Eavis 2015.

22. Cohen 2015a; Associated Press 2015; Dougherty 2016.

12 Personal and National Debts

1. Rajan 2010; Cynamon and Fazzari 2016.

2. Koo 2008. Unemployment has fallen, but the participation rate remains low.

3. Mian and Sufi 2014.

4. Special Inspector General for TARP 2015. The banks disputed the numbers in the report, but Morgenson (2015) supported the thrust of the report: "It appears that the program allowed big banks to run roughshod over borrowers again and again."

5. Barofsky 2012, 156. Now banks are selling troubled mortgages to hedge funds, which often foreclose and either sell the houses or rent them out at high rents with little maintenance (Dreier and Sen 2015; Goldstein 2015).

6. Gordon 2015; Summers 2015.

7. Temin and Vines 2014.

8. Krugman 2016; Federal Reserve Bank of St. Louis data (FRED), https://research.stlouisfed.org/fred2/series/LNS11300060.

9. Grunwald 2012.

10. Pear and Abelson 2016.

11. Alabama reacted particularly strongly to *Shelby County v. Holder* (570 US __ (2013). The state first required voters to have an ID such as a driver's license. It then closed the offices that issue driver's licenses in counties that are mostly black—claiming it was only cutting costs. These actions are being contested in court, but the outcome is uncertain (Bennett 2014; Cason 2015; New York Times Editorial Board 2015).

12. Rutenberg 2015.

13. Stiglitz and Bilmes 2008; Basevich 2016, 3–5. Basevich opened his military history of these wars with the statement, "Just as the American Revolution was about independence and the Civil War was about slavery, oil has always defined the raison d'être of the War on the Greater Middle East."

14. Gerges 2016, 8, 17.

15. Singer 2005; Basevich 2016, 278.

16. Kinzer 2016.

17. Schwartz 2016a; Irwin 2016.

13 Comparisons

1. Bourguignon 2015.

2. Piketty 2014.

3. Goos, Manning, and Salomons 2014.

4. Porter and Stern 2015; Atkinson 2015, 215.

5. Milanović 2016, 12–18.

6. The second decile of income in the United States was compared with the eighth decile in China. Milanović continued the quoted sentence to say, "and trying to disentangle their individual effects is futile" (Milanović 2016, 20, 35, 110).

7. Atkinson 2015, 3.

14 Conclusions

1. Case and Deaton 2015.

2. Anderson 2016; Confessore 2016.

3. Wright 2013.

4. Page, Bartels, and Seawright 2013; Ferguson 1995; Hacker and Pierson 2010; Gilens and Page 2014.

5. Autor 2015; Feinstein 1998.

6. Dewey 1935, 62; Piketty 2014, 481.

7. Heckman, Pinto, and Savelyev 2013.

8. Kremer 1993.

9. Dewey 1935, 66; Rawls 1999.

Appendix

1. Piketty 2014, 271–303.

2. Solow 1956.

3. Piketty 2014. Piketty focused on the capital-income ratio, β, while Solow concentrated on the capital-labor ratio, k. Readers need to be aware of this different notation to go back and forth between the two authors. Piketty's second law in his notation is $\beta = s/g$.

4. Kuznets 1955; Fogel 1987; Piketty 2014; Temin 2002. Fogel argued that Kuznets would have been surprised at the notoriety of his tentative effort to make sense of fragmentary evidence.

5. Goldsmith 1969; King and Levine 1993; Levine 2005.

6. Temin and Vines 2014; Zingales 2015.

7. Solow 1957.

8. Mincer 1958; Becker 1964.

9. Weill (2015) criticized Piketty for not including human capital.

10. Putnam 1993, 2000.

11. Hall and Jones 1999; Dasgupta 2007, 31. Hall and Jones referred to social infrastructure rather than social capital.

12. Piketty 2014, 119.

13. Others have criticized Piketty for these omissions (Weil 2015).

14. Piketty 2014, 20.

References

Abascal, Maria, and Delia Baldassarri. 2015. "Love Thy Neighbor? Ethnoracial Diversity and Trust Reexamined." *American Journal of Sociology* 121 (3) (November): 122–182.

Acemoglu, Daron, David Autor, David Dorn, Gordon H. Hanson, and Brandon Price. 2016. "Import Competition and the Great US Employment Sag of the 2000s." *Journal of Labor Economics* 34 (S1) (Part 2, January): S141–S198.

Acharya, Avichit, Matthew Blackwell, and Maya Sen. 2014. "The Political Legacy of American Slavery." Harvard Kennedy School Working Paper 14-057. http://papers.ssrn.com/sol3/papers.cfm?abstract_id=2538616. Accessed September 20, 2016.

Achen, Christopher H., and Larry M. Bartells. 2016. *Democracy for Realists: Why Elections Do Not Produce Responsible Government.* Princeton: Princeton University Press.

Agan, Amanda Y., and Sonja B. Starr. 2016. "Ban the Box, Criminal Records, and Statistical Discrimination: A Field Experiment." University of Michigan Law and Economic Research Paper 16-012. http://papers.ssrn.com/sol3/papers.cfm?abstract_id=2795795. Accessed September 20, 2016.

Agee, James, and Walker Evans. 1941. *Let Us Now Praise Famous Men.* Boston: Houghton Mifflin.

Alesina, Alberto, Edward Glaeser, and Bruce Sacerdote. 2001. "Why Doesn't the United States Have a European-Style Welfare State?" *Brookings Papers on Economic Activity* (Fall): 187–278. Also available as NBER Working Paper No. 8524.

Alexander, Michelle. 2010. *The New Jim Crow: Mass Incarceration in the Age of Colorblindness.* New York: New Press.

Alichi, Ali, Kory Kantenga, and Juan Solé. 2016. "Income Polarization in the United States." IMF Working Paper, WP/16/121, June.

Allegretto, Sylvia, and Lawrence Mishel. 2016. "The Teacher Pay Gap Is Wider than Ever." *Economic Policy Institute*, August 9. http://www.epi.org/publication/the-teacher-pay-gap-is-wider-than-ever-teachers-pay-continues-to-fall-further-behind-pay-of-comparable-workers. Accessed September 20, 2016.

American Society of Civil Engineers. 2013. *2013 Report Card for American Infrastructure*. http://www.infrastructurereportcard.org. Accessed September 20, 2016.

Anderson, Carol. 2016. *White Rage: The Unspoken Truth of Our Racial Divide*. New York: Bloomsbury.

Angrist, Joshua D., Parag A. Pathak, and Christopher R. Walters. 2013. "Explaining Charter School Effectiveness." *American Economic Journal: Applied Economics* 5 (4) (October): 1–27.

Apuzzo, Matt. 2016. "Department of Justice Sues Ferguson, Which Reversed Course on Agreement." *New York Times*, February 10.

Arsenault, Mark. 2016. "Globe Parts Ways with Home Delivery Company." *Boston Globe*, March 9.

Ashton, Paul, and Amanda Petteruti. 2011. "Gaming the System: How the Political Strategies of Private Prison Companies Promote Ineffective Incarceration Policies." Justice Policy Institute, Washington, DC, June.

Associated Press. 2015. "Obama Signs 5-Year Infrastructure Spending Bill." *New York Times*, December 4.

Atkinson, Anthony B. 2015. *Inequality: What Can Be Done?* Cambridge, MA: Harvard University Press.

Authers, John. 2015. "Infrastructure: Bridging the Gap." *Financial Times*, November 9.

Autor, David H. 2015. "Why Are There Still So Many Jobs? The History and Future of Workplace Automation." *Journal of Economic Perspectives* 29 (3) (Summer): 3–30.

Autor, David H., and David Dorn. 2013. "The Growth of Low-Skill Service Jobs and the Polarization of the US Labor Market." *American Economic Review* 103 (5) (August): 1553–1597.

Autor, David H., David Dorn, and Gordon H. Hanson. 2013. "The China Syndrome: Local Labor Market Effects of Import Competition in the United States." *American Economic Review* 103 (6): 2121–2168.

Autor, David H., Frank Levy, and Richard J. Murnane. 2003. "The Skill Content of Recent Technological Change: An Empirical Exploration." *Quarterly Journal of Economics* 118 (November): 1279–1333.

Azar, Jose, Martin C. Schmalz, and Isabel Tecu. 2015. "Anti-competitive Effects of Common Ownership." University of Michigan working paper, March 3. http://www.bc.edu/content/dam/files/schools/csom_sites/finance/Schmalz-031115.pdf. Accessed September 20, 2016.

Bacevich, Andrew J. 2016. *America's War for the Great Middle East: A Military History*. New York: Random House.

Bagli, Charles V. 2016. "How Donald Trump Built an Empire on $885 Million in Tax Breaks." *New York Times*, September 17.

Baily, Martha J., and Susan M. Dynarski. 2011. "Inequality in Postsecondary Education." In *Whither Opportunity? Rising Inequality, Schools, and Children's*

Life Chances, ed. Greg J. Duncan and Richard J. Murnane, 117–132. New York: Russell Sage Foundation.

Barbaro, Michael. 2016. "Donald Trump Clung to 'Birther' Lie for Years, and Still Isn't Apologetic." *New York Times*, September 16.

Barnett, W. Steven, Kwanghee Jung, Min-Jong Youn, and Ellen C. Freder. 2013. "Abbott Preschool Program Longitudinal Effects Study: Fifth Grade Follow-Up." National Institute for Early Education Research, Rutgers, New York, March 20. http://nieer.org/sites/nieer/files/APPLES%205th%20Grade.pdf. Accessed September 20, 2016.

Barro, Josh. 2015. "Thanks, Obama: Highest Earners' Tax Rates Rose Sharply in 2013." *New York Times*, December 30.

Bartels, Larry M. 2008. *Unequal Democracy: The Political Economy of the New Gilded Age.* New York: Russell Sage Foundation.

Bartlett, Bruce. 2013. "Exploring Mitt Romney's Taxes and Tax Plan." *New York Times*, August 21.

Barofsky, Neil. 2012. *Bailout: An Inside Account of How Washington Abandoned Main Street While Rescuing Wall Street.* New York: Free Press.

Beard, Mary. 2015. *SPQR: A History of Ancient Rome.* New York: W. W. Norton.

Beasley, Maya A. 2011. *Opting Out: Losing the Potential of America's Young Black Elite.* Chicago: University of Chicago Press.

Becker, Gary. S. 1964. *Human Capital: A Theoretical and Empirical Analysis with Special Reference to Education.* New York: Columbia University Press.

Belkin, Lisa. 1999. *Show Me a Hero.* Boston: Little, Brown.

Bennett, Jim, "Alabama Photo Voter ID Guide." 2014. Office of the Secretary of State, State of Alabama, March.

Berman, Ari. 2015. *Give Us the Ballot: The Modern Struggle for Voting Rights in America.* New York: Farrar, Straus and Giroux.

Bernard, Tara Siegel. 2015. "Judges Rebuke Limits on Wiping Out Student Loan Debt." *New York Times*, July 17.

Bernstein, Nina. 2009. "Immigrant Detainee Dies, and a Life Is Buried, Too." *New York Times*, April 2.

Bernstein, Nina. 2016. "Health Care at New Jersey Immigrant Jail Is Substandard, Watchdog Groups Say." *New York Times*, May 11.

Bettinger, Eric P. 2005. "The Effect of Charter Schools on Charter Students and Public Schools." *Economics of Education Review* 24 (April): 133–147.

Bewley, Truman. 1999. *Why Wages Don't Fall During a Recession.* Cambridge, MA: Harvard University Press, 1999.

Bickerton, Chris, and Alex Gourevitch. 2011. "Productivity, Inequality, Poverty." *The Current Moment*, August 18. https://thecurrentmoment.wordpress.com/2011/08/18/productivity-inequality-poverty/. Accessed September 22, 2016.

Bifulco, Robert, and Helen F. Ladd. 2006. "The Impact of Charter Schools on Student Achievement: Evidence from North Carolina." *Education Finance and Policy* 1 (Winter): 30–90.

Blinder, Alan, and Richard Fausset. 2016. "Federal Judge Upholds North Carolina Voter Rules." *New York Times*, April 25.

Board of Governors of the Federal Reserve System. 2015. "Report on the Economic Well-Being of U.S. Households in 2014." May. http://www .federalreserve.gov/econresdata/2014-report-economic-wel l-being-us-households-201505.pdf. Accessed September 22, 2016.

Bonczar, Thomas P. 2003. "Prevalence of Imprisonment in the U.S. Population, 1974–2001." U.S. Department of Justice, Bureau of Justice Statistics, Special Report. Washington, DC, August.

Bosman, Julie. 2016a. "Crumbling, Destitute Schools Threaten Detroit's Recovery." *New York Times*, January 20.

Bosman, Julie. 2016b. "Few Answers on When Flint Will Have Clean Water Again." *New York Times*, January 27.

Bosman, Julie. 2016c. "Flint's Former Manager Resigns as Head of Detroit Schools." *New York Times*, February 2.

Bosman, Julie. 2016d. "Many Flint Residents Are Desperate to Leave, But See No Escape." *New York Times*, February 4.

Bosman, Julie, Monica Davey, and Mitch Smith. 2016. "As Water Problems Grew, Officials Belittled Complaints from Flint." *New York Times*, January 20.

Bosworth, Barry, and Gary Burtless. 2016. "Later Retirement, Inequality in Old Age, and the Growing Gap in Longevity between Rich and Poor." *Economic Studies at Brookings*, January.

Bourguignon, François. 2015. *The Globalization of Inequality*. Princeton: Princeton University Press.

Boustan, Leah Platt. 2010. "Was Postwar Suburbanization 'White Flight'? Evidence from the Black Migration." *Quarterly Journal of Economics* 125 (February): 417–443.

Boyer, Paul, and Stephen Nissenbaum. *Salem Possessed: The Social Origins of Witchcraft*. Cambridge, MA: Harvard University Press, 1974.

Bradley Kar, Robin, and Jason Mazzone. "The Garland Affair: What History and the Constitution Really Say about President Obama's Powers to Appoint a Replacement for Justice Scalia." *New York University Law Review* 91 (May 2016): 53–114.

Brittain, Amy, and Dari Horwitz. "Justice Scalia Spent His Last Hours with Members of This Secretive Society of Elite Hunters." *Washington Post*, February 24, 2016.

Brodkin, Karen. *How Jews Became White Folks and What That Says about Race in America*. New Brunswick, NJ: Rutgers University Press, 1998.

Buettner, Russ, and Charles V. Bagli. "How Donald Trump Bankrupted His Atlantic City Casinos, But Still Earned Millions." *New York Times*, June 11, 2016.

Bui, Quoctrung, and Claire Cain Miller. 2016. "Why Tech Degrees Are Not Putting More Blacks and Hispanics into Tech Jobs." *New York Times*, February 25.

Bunton, Derwyn. 2016. "When the Public Defender Says, 'I Can't Help.'" *New York Times*, February 19.

Bureau of Labor Statistics. 2015. "Occupational Employment Statistics." http://www.bls.gov/oes/current/oes_nat.htm#19-0000. Accessed September 22, 2016.

Burnham, Walter Dean. 2010. *Voting in American Elections: The Shaping of the American Political Universe since 1788*. Bethesda, MD: Academic Press.

Burnham, Walter Dean. 2015. "Voter Turnout and the Path to Plutocracy." In *Polarized Politics; The Impact of Divisiveness in the US Political System*, ed. William Crotty, 27–69. Boulder, CO: Lynne Rienner.

Burnham, Walter Dean, and Thomas Ferguson. 2014. "Americans Are Sick to Death of Both Parties: Why Our Politics Is in Worse Shape Than We Thought." *Alternet*, December 18. http://www.alternet.org/americans-are-sick-death-both-parties-why-our-politics-worse-shape-we-thought. Accessed September 22, 2016.

Bush, George W. 2007. "President Bush Signs 'Improving Head Start for Schooling Readiness Act of 2007' into Law." The White House, Washington, DC, December. https://georgewbush-whitehouse.archives.gov/news/releases/2007/12/20071212-3.html. Accessed September 22, 2016.

Caraley, Demetrios. 1992. "Washington Abandons the Cities." *Political Science Quarterly* 107: 1–30.

Card, David, and Laura Giuliano. 2014. "Does Gifted Education Work? For Which Students?" NBER Working Paper No. 20453, September.

Card, David, Alexandre Mas, and Jesse Rothstein. 2008. "Tipping and the Dynamics of Segregation." *Quarterly Journal of Economics* 123 (February): 177–218.

Carey, Kevin. 2014. "When Higher Education Doesn't Deliver on Its Promise." *New York Times*, October 4.

Carey, Kevin. 2015. "Student Debt in America: Lend with a Smile, Collect with a Fist." *New York Times*, November 27.

Carl, Jeremy. 2016. "The Lawless Anti-White Identity Politics of the Democratic Party is on Full Display in Philly." *National Review*, August. www.nationalreview.com/node/438380/print. Accessed September 22, 2016.

Carlson, Andrew. 2014. "State Higher Education Finance." State Higher Education Executive Officers Association. http://www.sheeo.org/sites/default/files/project-files/SHEF_FY2014_EMBARGOED.pdf. Accessed September 22, 2016.

Case, Anne, and Angus Deaton. 2015. "Rising Morbidity and Mortality in Midlife among White Non-Hispanic Americans in the 21st Century." *Proceedings of the National Academy of Sciences of the United States of America* 112 (49) (December 8): 15078–15083.

Cason, Mike. 2015. "State to Close 5 parks, Cut Back Services and License Offices." *Alabama Media Group*, September. http://www.al.com/news/index .ssf/2015/09/state_announces_to_close_becau.html#incart_river_home. Accessed September 22, 2016.

Charles Colton Task Force on Federal Corrections. "Who Gets Time for Federal Drug Offenses? Data Trends and Opportunities for Reform." Urban Institute, Washington, DC, November 2015.

Cherlin, Andrew J. *Labor's Love Lost: The Rise and Fall of the Working-Class Family in America*. New York: Russell Sage Foundation, 2014.

Chetty, Raj, Nathaniel Hendren, and Lawrence Katz. "The Effects of Exposure to Better Neighborhoods on Children: New Evidence from the Moving to Opportunity Experiment." *American Economic Review* 106 (4) (2016): 855–902.

Chozick, Amy. 2015. "Middle Class is Disappearing, at Least from Vocabulary of Possible 2016 Contenders." *New York Times*, May 11.

Chyn, Eric. 2016. "The Long-Run Effect of Public Housing Demolition on Labor Market Outcomes of Children." Economics Department, University of Michigan, Ann Arbor, MI, March 27.

Clotfelter, Charles T. 2004. *After Brown: The Rise and Retreat of School Segregation*. Princeton: Princeton University Press.

CNN. DATE. "Poll: 'Obamacare' vs. 'Affordable Care Act.'" CCN Political Unit. http://politicalticker.blogs.cnn.com/2013/09/27/poll-obamacare-vs-affordable -care-act/. Accessed September 22, 2016.

Coates, Ta-Nehisi. *Between the World and Me*. New York: Spiegel and Grau, 2015.

Cohen, Patricia. 2015a. "Gasoline-Tax Increase Finds Little Support." *New York Times*, January 2.

Cohen, Patricia. 2015b. "For-Profit Colleges Accused of Fraud Still Receive U.S. Funds." *New York Times*, October 12.

Cohen, Patricia. 2016a. "A Rising Call to Promote STEM Education and Cut Liberal Arts Funding." *New York Times*, February 21.

Cohen, Patricia. 2016b. "States Vie to Shield the Wealth of the 1 Percent." *New York Times*, August 8.

Confessore, Nicholas. 2015. "A Wealthy Governor and His Friends Are Remaking Illinois." *New York Times*, November 29.

Confessore, Nicholas. 2016. "For Whites Sensing Decline, Trump Unleashes Words of Resistance." *New York Times*, July 13.

Congressional Budget Office. 2014. "The Distribution of Household Income and Federal Taxes, 2011." Washington, DC, November.

Consortium for Longitudinal Studies. 1983. *As the Twig is Bent ... Lasting Effects of Preschool Programs*. Hillsdale, NJ: Lawrence Erlbaum Associates.

Consumer Financial Protection Bureau. 2015. "Student Loan Servicing." September. http://files.consumerfinance.gov/f/201509_cfpb_student-loan -servicing-report.pdf. Accessed September 22, 2016.

Corkery, Michael. 2016. "Regulators Fear $1 Billion Cleanup Bill." *New York Times*, June 6.

Covert, Bryce. 2015. "Shutting Down Planned Parenthood Would Catapult Women into Poverty." *Nation*, December 23. http://www.thenation.com/article/ shutting-down-planned-parenthood-would-catapult-women-into-poverty/. Accessed September 22, 2016.

Cozick, Amy. 2015. "Middle Class Is Disappearing, at Least from Vocabulary of Possible 2016 Contenders." *New York Times*, May 11.

Corasaniti, Nick, and Ashley Parker. 2016. "G.O.P. Donors Shift Focus from Top of Ticket to Senate Races." *New York Times*, May 20.

Crutchfield and Weeks. 2015. "The Effects of Mass Incarceration on Communities of Color." *Issues in Science and Technology* 32 (1) (Fall): 46–51.

Currie, Janet, and Matthew Neidell. 2007. "Getting Inside the 'Black Box' of Head Start Quality: What Matters and What Doesn't." *Economics of Education Review* 26 (1) (February): 83–99.

Currie, Janet, and Duncan Thomas. 2000. "School Quality and the Longer Term Effects of Head Start." *Journal of Human Resources* 35 (4) (Autumn): 755–774.

Cynamon, Barry Z., and Steven M. Fazzari. 2016. "Inequality, the Great Recession, and Slow Recovery." *Cambridge Journal of Economics* 40 (2) (): 373–399.

Daley, David. 2016. *Rat F**ked: The True Story Behind the Secret Plan to Steal America's Democracy*. New York: Norton.

Dasgupta, Partha. 2007. *Economics: A Very Short Introduction*. Oxford: Oxford University Press.

Davey, Monica. 2016a. "With Fewer Members, a Diminished Political Role for Wisconsin Unions." *New York Times*, February 27.

Davey, Monica. 2016b "Ferguson Voters Give Split Result in Funding Police Overhaul." *New York Times*, April 6.

Davey, Monica, and Mitch Smith. 2016a. "Emails Reveal Early Suspicions of a Flint Link to Legionnaires' Disease." *New York Times*, February 4.

Davey, Monica, and Mitch Smith. 2016b. "Chicago Police Dept. Plagued by Systematic Racism, Task Force Finds." *New York Times*, April 13.

Davis, Julie Hirschfeld. 2015. "Obama's Twitter Debut, @POTUS, Attracts Hate-Filled Posts." *New York Times*, May 21.

Dawisha, Karen. 2014. *Putin's Kleptocracy: Who Owns Russia?* New York: Simon and Shuster.

DeLong, J. Bradford, and Lawrence H. Summers. 2012. "Fiscal Policy in a Depressed Economy." *Brookings Papers on Economic Activity* 44 (1) (Spring): 233–297.

Delpit, Lisa. 2012. *Multiplication Is for White People: Raising Expectations for Other People's Children*. New York: The New Press.

DeSilver, Drew. 2014. "For Most Workers, Real Wages Have Barely Budged for Decades." Pew Research Center, October 9. http://www.pewresearch.org/fact-tank/2014/10/09/for-most-workers-real-wages-have-barely-budged-for-decades/. Accessed September 22, 2016.

Dewey, John. 1935. *Liberalism and Social Action*. New York: Putnam.

Diamond, Peter A., and Peter R. Orszag. 2005. *Saving Social Security: A Balanced Approach*. Washington, DC: Brookings Institution Press.

Dimon, Jamie. 2016. "Why We're Giving Our Employees a Raise." *New York Times*, July 12.

DiTomaso, Nancy. 2013. *The American Non-Dilemma: Racial Inequality without Racism*. New York: Russell Sage Foundation.

Dobbie, Will, and Roland D. Fryer, Jr. 2013. "Getting beneath the Veil of Effective Schools: Evidence from New York City." *American Economic Journal: Applied Economics* 5 (4) (October): 28–60.

Doogan, Kevin. *New Capitalism? The Transformation of Work*. Cambridge: Polity Press, 2009.

Dreier, Peter, and Aditi Sen. 2015. "Hedge Funds: The Ultimate Absentee Landlords." *American Prospect* 25 (5) (Fall): 40–45. http://prospect.org/article/hedge-funds-ultimate-absentee-landlords-fall-preview. Accessed September 22, 2016.

Drutman, Lee. 2013. "The Political 1% of the 1% in 2012." *Sunlight Foundation Blog*, June 24, http://sunlightfoundation.com/blog/2013/06/24/1pct_of_the_1pct/. Accessed September 22, 2016.

Drutman, Lee. 2015. *The Business of America Is Lobbying*. New York: Oxford University Press.

Dubner, Stephen J. 2005. "Toward a Unified Theory of Black America." *New York Times*, March 20.

Dungea, Nicole. 2015. "Review Faults T on Maintenance, Disabled Riders." *Boston Globe*, December 31.

Dwyer, Jim. 2016. "What Happened to Jane Mayer When She Wrote about the Koch Brothers." *New York Times*, January 26.

Dylan, Bob. *Only a Pawn in Their Game*. Los Angeles: Warner Brothers, 1963.

Dynarski, Susan. 2015a. "New Data Gives Clearer Picture of Student Debt." *New York Times*, September 10.

Dynarski, Susan. 2015b. "Urban Charter Schools Often Succeed. Suburban Ones Often Don't." *New York Times*, November 20.

Dynarski, Susan. 2016a. "Why Talented Black and Hispanic Students Can Go Undiscovered." *New York Times*, April 8.

Dynarski, Susan. 2016b. "America Can Fix Its Student Debt Loan Crisis, Ask Australia." *New York Times*, July 10.

Eavis, Peter. 2015. "A Missed Opportunity of Ultra-Cheap Money." *New York Times*, December 17.

Eavis, Peter. 2016. "Debate over Prison Population Turns to the States." *New York Times*, April 12.

Eckholm, Erik. 2016. "Anti-Abortion Group Presses Ahead despite Recent Supreme Court Ruling." *New York Times*, July 9.

Edin, Kathryn J. 1997. *Making Ends Meet: How Single Mothers Survive Welfare and Low-Wage Work*. New York: Russell Sage Foundation.

Edin, Kathryn J., and H. Luke Shaefer. 2015. *$2.00 a Day: Living on Almost Nothing in America*. Boston: Houghton Mifflin Harcourt.

Editorial Board. 2015. "Gov. Christie's Toxic School Plan." *New York Times*, June 25.

Edsall, Thomas B. 2016. "How the Other Fifth Lives." *New York Times*, April 27.

Edsall, Thomas B., with Mary D. Edsall. 1991. *Chain Reaction: The Impact of Race, Rights and Taxes on American Politics*. New York: Norton.

Edwards, Ezekiel, Will Bunting, and Lynda Garcia. 2013. *The War on Marijuana in Black and White*. New York: American Civil Liberties Union.

Edwards, John. 2004. "Speech to the Democratic National Convention." July 28. http://www.washingtonpost.com/wp-dyn/articles/A22230-2004Jul28.html. Accessed September 22, 2016.

Eichengreen, Barry. *Exorbitant Privilege: The Rise and Fall of the Dollar and the Future of the International Monetary System*. New York: Oxford University Press, 2011.

Eligon, John. "A Question of Environmental Racism in Flint." *New York Times*, January 21, 2016.

Ewald, Alec C. *The Way We Vote: The Local Dimension of American Suffrage*. Nashville: Vanderbilt University Press, 2009.

Fairlie, Robert W., and William A. Sundstrom. 1999. "The Emergence, Persistence and Recent Widening of the Racial Unemployment Gap." *Industrial and Labor Relations Review* 52 (2) (January): 252–270.

Fandos, Nicholas. 2016a. "Garland Should Not Be Considered after Election, McConnell Says." *New York Times*, March 20.

Fandos, Nicholas. 2016b. "House Members Refuse Washington Subway System's Pleas for More Funds." *New York Times*, April 13.

Farley, Reynolds, Sheldon Danziger, and Harry J. Holzer. 2000. *Detroit Divided*. New York: Russell Sage Foundation.

Feinstein, Charles H. 1998. "Pessimism Perpetuated: Real Wages and the Standard of Living during and after the Industrial Revolution." *Journal of Economic History* 58 (September): 625–659.

Ferguson, Ronald F. 2007. *Towards Excellence with Equity: An Emerging Vision for Closing the Achievement Gap*. Cambridge, MA: Harvard Education Press.

Ferguson, Thomas. 1995. *Golden Rule: The Investment Theory of Party Competition and the Logic of Money-Driven Political Systems.* Chicago: University of Chicago Press.

Ferguson, Thomas, Paul Jorgensen, and Jie Chen. 2013. "Party Competition and Industrial Structure in the 2012 Elections: Who's Really Driving the Taxi to the Dark Side?" *International Journal of Political Economy* 42 (2) (Summer): 3–41.

Ferguson, Thomas, Paul Jorgensen, and Jie Chen. 2016. "How Money Drives US Congressional Elections." Institute of New Economic Thinking Working Paper No. 48 (August 1). https://www.ineteconomics.org/ideas-papers/research-papers/how-money-drives-us-congressional-elections?p=ideas-papers/research-papers/how-money-drives-us-congressional-elections. Accessed September 20, 2016.

Ferguson, Thomas, and Joel Rogers. 1986. *Right Turn: The Decline of the Democrats and the Future of American Politics.* New York: Hill and Wang.

Fields, Karen E., and Barbara J. Fields. 2012. *Racecraft: The Soul of Inequality in American Life.* New York: Verso.

Fitzsimmons, Emma G., and David W. Chen. 2015. "Aging Infrastructure Plagues Nation's Busiest Rail Corridor." *New York Times,* July 26.

Fogel, Robert W. 1987. "Some Notes on the Scientific Methods of Simon Kuznets." NBER Working Paper No. 2461, December.

Foner, Eric. 1988. *Reconstruction: America's Unfinished Revolution, 1863–77.* New York: Harper and Row.

Forsberg, Mary E. 2010. "A Hudson Tunnel That Goes One Way." *New York Times,* October 27.

Fortner, Michael Javen. 2015. "The Real Roots of the '70s Drug Laws." *New York Times,* September 28.

Fourcade, Marion, Etienne Ollion, and Yann Algan. 2015. "The Superiority of Economists." *Journal of Economic Perspectives* 29 (1) (Winter): 89–113.

Fountain, Henry, and Michael S. Schmidt. 2016. "'Bomb Robot' Takes Down Dallas Gunman, But Raises Enforcement Questions." *New York Times,* July 8.

Frank, Robert. 2016. "One Top Taxpayer Moved, and New Jersey Shuddered." *New York Times,* April 30.

Freeland, Chrystia. 2012. *Plutocrats: The Rise of the New Global Super-Rich and the Fall of Everyone Else.* New York: Penguin.

Freeman, Richard A. "Are Your Wages Set in Beijing?" *Journal of Economic Perspectives* 9 (3) (Winter 1995): 15–32.

Fryer, Roland D., Jr. "Injecting Charter School Best Practices into Traditional Public Schools: Evidence from Field Experiments." *Quarterly Journal of Economics* 129 (3) (2014): 65–93.

Galenson, David W. 1981. *White Servitude in Colonial America: An Economic Analysis.* New York: Cambridge University Press.

Garces, Eliana, Duncan Thomas, and Janet Currie. 2002 "Longer-Term Effects of Head Start." *American Economic Review* 92 (4) (September): 999–1012.

Gelles, David. "For the Highest Paid C.E.Os, the Party Goes On." *New York Times*, May 16, 2015.

Gelman, Andrew. 2008. *Red State, Blue State, Rich State, Poor State: Why Americans Vote the Way They Do*. Princeton: Princeton University Press.

Gerges, Fawaz A. 2016. *ISIS: A History*. Princeton: Princeton University Press.

Gerstle, Gary. 1995. "Race and the Myth of the Liberal Consensus." *Journal of American History* 80 (2) (September): 579–586.

Gilens, Martin, and Benjamin I. Page. 2014. "Testing Theories of American Politics: Elites, Interest Groups, and Average Citizens." *Perspectives on Politics* 12 (3) (September): 564–581.

Glaze, Lauren E., and Danielle Kaeble. 2014. "Correctional Populations in the United States, 2013." US Department of Justice, Bureau of Justice Statistics, Bulletin. Washington, DC, December.

Goffman, Alice. 2014. *On the Run: Fugitive Life in an American City*. Chicago: University of Chicago Press.

Gold, Martea, and Anu Narayanswamy. 2016. "The New Gilded Age: Close to Half of All Super-PAC Money Comes from 50 Donors." *Washington Post*, April 15.

Goldin, Claudia. 1990. *Understanding the Gender Gap: An Economic History of American Women*. New York: Oxford University Press.

Goldin, Claudia. 2006. "The Quiet Revolution That Transformed Women's Employment, Education, and Family." *American Economic Review* 96 (2) (May): 1–12.

Goldin, Claudia, and Lawrence F. Katz. 2002. "The Power of the Pill: Oral Contraceptives and Women's Career and Marriage Decisions." *Journal of Political Economy* 110 (August): 730–770.

Goldin, Claudia, and Lawrence F. Katz. 2008. *The Race between Education and Technology*. Cambridge, MA: Harvard University Press.

Goldin, Claudia, and Cecilia Rouse. 2000. "Orchestrating Impartiality: The Impact of 'Blind' Auditions on Female Musicians." *American Economic Review* 90 (4) (September): 715–741.

Goldsmith, R. W. 1969. *Financial Structure and Development*. New Haven: Yale University Press.

Goldstein, Dana. 2014. *The Teacher Wars: A History of America's Most Embattled Profession*. New York: Doubleday.

Goldstein, Matthew. 2015. "As Banks Retreat, Private Equity Rushes to Buy Troubled Home Mortgages." *New York Times*, September 28.

Goleman, Daniel. 1995. *Emotional Intelligence: Why It Can Matter More Than IQ*. New York: Bantam Books.

Goleman, Daniel. 2006. *Emotional Intelligence: The New Science of Human Relationships*. New York: Bantam Books.

Gonnerman, Jennifer. 2016. "Home Free: How a New York State Prisoner

Became a Failhouse Lawyer, and Changed the System." *New Yorker*, June 20, 40–49.

Goodnough, Abby. 2016. "Legionnaires' Outbreak in Flint Was Met with Silence." *New York Times*, February 22.

Goodnough, Abby, Monica Davey, and Mitch Smith. 2016. "When the Water Turned Brown." *New York Times*, January 23.

Goolsbee, Austan D., and Alan B. Krueger. 2015. "A Retrospective Look at Rescuing and Restructuring General Motors and Chrysler." *Journal of Economic Perspectives* 29 (2) (Spring): 3–24.

Goos, Maarten, Alan Manning, and Anna Salomons. 2014. "Explaining Job Polarization: Routine-Biased Technical Change and Offshoring." *American Economic Review* 104 (8) (August): 2509–2526.

Gordon, Robert J. 2015. "Secular Stagnation: A Supply-Side View." *American Economic Review* 105 (5) (May): 54–59.

Gornick, Janet C., and Branko Milanovic. 2015. "Income Inequality in the United States in Cross-National Perspective: Redistribution Revisited." Luxembourg Income Study Center Research Brief (1/2015), May 4.

Gottschalk, Marie. 2015. *Caught: The Prison State and the Lockdown of American Politics*. Princeton: Princeton University Press.

Grunwald, Michael. 2012. *The New New Deal: The Hidden Story of Change in the Obama Era*. New York: Simon and Shuster.

Gustafron, Kaaryn. 2009. "The Criminalization of Poverty." *Journal of Criminal Law and Criminology* 99 (3) (Spring): 643–716.

Hacker, Jacob S., and Paul Pierson. 2010. *Winner-Take-All Politics: How Washington Made the Rich Richer—and Turned Its Back on the Middle Class*. New York: Simon & Schuster.

Hacker, Jacob S., and Paul Pierson. 2016. *American Amnesia: How the War on Government Led Us to Forget What Made America Prosper*. New York: Simon and Schuster.

Hager, Eli, and Alysia Santo. 2016. "Private Prisoner Vans' Long Road of Neglect." *New York Times*, July 6.

Hall, E. Robert, and Charles I. Jones. 1999. "Why Do Some Countries Produce So Much More Output per Worker than Others?" *Quarterly Journal of Economics* 114 (February): 83–116.

Handlin, Oscar, and Mary F. Handlin. 1950. "Origins of the Southern Labor System." *William and Mary Quarterly* 7 (April): 199–222.

Harris, Alexes. 2016. *A Pound of Flesh: Monetary Sanctions as Punishment for the Poor*. New York: Russell Sage Foundation.

Harris, Elizabeth. 2016a. "Where Nearly Half of Pupils are Homeless, School Aims to Be Teacher, Therapist, even Santa." *New York Times*, June 6.

Harris, Elizabeth A. 2016b. "Judge, Citing Inequality, Orders Connecticut to Overhaul Its School System." *New York Times*, September 7.

Harris, John R., and Michael P. Todaro. 1970. "Migration, Unemployment and Development: A Two-Sector Analysis." *American Economic Review* 60: 126–142.

Hasen, Richard L. 2012. *The Voting Wars: From Florida 2000 to the Next Election Meltdown.* New Haven: Yale University Press.

Head Start. 2015. "Introduction to Monitoring." Early Childhood Learning and Knowledge Center, Administration for Children and Families, U.S. Department of Health and Human Services, Washington, DC, November. https://eclkc.ohs.acf.hhs.gov/hslc/grants/monitoring/intro-to-monitoring.html. Accessed September 22, 2016.

Heckman, James, Rodrigo Pinto, and Peter Savelyev. 2013. "Understanding the Mechanisms Through which an Influential Early Childhood Program Boosted Adult Outcomes." *American Economic Review* 103 (6) (October): 2052–2086.

Henrichson, Christian, Joshua Rinaldi, and Ruth Delaney. 2015. "The Price of Jails: Measuring the Taxpayer Cost of Local Incarceration." Vera Institute of Justice, May. https://www.vera.org/publications/the-price-of-jails-measuring-the -taxpayer-cost-of-local-incarceration. Accessed September 22, 2016.

Herszenhorn, David M. 2016a. "G.O.P. Senators Say Obama Supreme Court Pic Will Be Rejected." *New York Times,* February 23.

Herszenhorn, David M. 2016b. "Wisconsin Race Frames Dispute over Supreme Court." *New York Times,* March 24.

Herszenhorn, David M. 2016. "Paul Ryan Calls Donald Trump's Attack on Judge 'Racist'" But Backs Him Still." *New York Times,* June 7.

Hertel-Fernandez, Alexander. 2014. "Who Passes Business's 'Model Bills'? Policy Capacity and Corporate Influence in U.S. Politics." *Perspectives on Politics* 12 (3) (September): 583–602.

Hill, Steven. 2016. *Expand Social Security Now!* Boston: Beacon Press.

Hinton, Elizabeth. 2016. *From the War on Poverty to the War on Crime: The Making of Mass Incarceration in America.* Cambridge, MA: Harvard University Press.

Holzer, Harry J., 2015. "Job Market Polarization and U.S. Worker Skills: A Tale of Two Middles." Economic Studies at Brookings, April.

Holzer, Harry J., and Robert I. Lerman. 2009. "The Future of Middle-Skill Jobs." Center on Children and Families, CCF Brief #41, Brookings Institution, Washington, DC.

Hull, Elizabeth A. 2009. "Our 'Crooked Timber': Why Is American Punishment So Harsh?" In *Criminal Disenfranchisement in an International Perspective,* ed. Alec Ewald and Brandon Bottinghaus, 136–164. New York: Cambridge University Press.

Hulse, Charles. 2016. "Why Washington Couldn't Pass a Crime Bill Both Parties Backed." *New York Times,* September 16.

Ignatiev, Noel. 1995. *How the Irish Became White.* New York: Routledge.

Irwin, Neil. 2016. "The Economic Expansion Is Helping the Middle Class, Finally." *New York Times*, September 13.

Isaac, Mike, and Noam Scheiber. 2016. Uber Settles Cases with Concessions, but Drivers Stay Freelancers." *New York Times*, April 21.

Isenberg, Nancy. 2016. *White Trash: The 400-Year Untold History of Class in America*. New York: Viking.

Ivory, Danielle, Ben Protess, and Kitty Bennett. 2016. "When You Dial 911 and Wall Street Answers." *New York Times*, June 25.

Jackson, C. Kirabo, Rucker C. Johnson, and Claudia Persico. 2016. "The Effect of School Spending on Educational and Economic Outcomes: Evidence from School Finance Reforms." *Quarterly Journal of Economics* 131 (1) (February): 157–218.

Jargowsky, Paul A. 2015. "The Architecture of Segregation: Civil Unrest, the Concentration of Poverty, and Public Policy." Issue Brief. The Century Foundation, August 9.

Jeffries, John C., Jr. 1994. *Justice Lewis F. Powell, Jr.* New York: Scribner's.

Johnson, Lyndon B. 1966. "To Fulfill These Rights." In *Public Papers of the Presidents of the United States: Lyndon B. Johnson, 1965*, Vol. II, 635–640. Washington, DC: Government Printing Office.

Johnson, Rucker C. 2011. "Long-Run Impacts of School Desegregation and School Quality on Adult Attainment." NBER Working Paper No. 16664, January.

Johnston, Katie. 2016. "Western Mass. Prisoner Rehabilitation Program Lauded." *Boston Globe*, June 20.

Jones, Charles I. 1997. "On the Evolution of the World Income Distribution." *Journal of Economic Perspectives* 11 (3) (Summer): 19–36.

Jones, Alexander, and Benjamin Forman. 2015. "Exploring the Potential for Pretrial Innovation in Massachusetts." MassINC (Massachusetts Institute for a New Commonwealth) Policy Brief, September.

Jones, Charles I. 2015. "Pareto and Piketty: The Macroeconomics of Top Income and Wealth Inequality." *Journal of Economic Perspectives* 29 (1) (Winter): 29–46.

Kang, Cecilia. 2016. "No Driver? Bring It On: How Pittsburgh Became Uber's Testing Ground." *New York Times*, September 10.

Kanter, Rosabeth Moss. 2015. *Move: Putting America's Infrastructure Back in the Lead*. New York: Norton.

Katznelson, Ira. 2005. *When Affirmative Action Was White: An Untold History of Racial Inequality in Twentieth-Century America*. New York: Norton.

Katznelson, Ira. 2013. *Fear Itself: The New Deal and the Origins of Our Time*. New York: Norton.

Kaufman, Dan. 2016. "The Destruction of Progressive Wisconsin." *New York Times*, January 16.

Keller, Josh, and Adam Pearce. 2016. "This Small Indiana County Sends More People to Prison than San Francisco and Durham, N.C., Combined. Why?" *New York Times*, September 2.

Kerber, Linda K. 1998. *No Constitutional Right to Be Ladies*. New York: Hill and Wang.

Kessler-Harris, Alice. 2001. *In Pursuit of Equity: Women, Men, and the Quest for Economic Citizenship in 20th Century America*. New York: Oxford University Press.

Keyssar, Alexander. 2000. *The Right to Vote: The Contested History of Democracy in the United States*. Revised edition. New York: Basic Books.

King, R. G., and Ross Levine. 1993. "Finance and Growth: Schumpeter Might Be Right." *Quarterly Journal of Economics* 108: 717–738.

Kinser, Kevin. 2006. *From Main Street to Wall Street: The Transformation of For-Profit Higher Education*. ASHE Higher Education Report, Vol. 31, No. 5. San Francisco: Jossey-Bass.

Kinzer, Stephen. 2016. "Frustrating the War Lobby." *Boston Globe*, September 18.

Kirp, David L. 2013. *Improbable Scholars: The Rebirth of a Great American School System and a Strategy for America's Schools*. Oxford: Oxford University Press.

Komlos, John. 2016. "Growth of Income and Welfare in the U.S., 1979–2011." NBER Working Paper No. 22211, April.

Koo, Richard. 2008. *The Holy Grail of Economics*. Singapore: Wiley.

Kousser, J. Morgan. 1999. *Colorblind Injustice: Minority Voting Rights and the Undoing of the Second Reconstruction*. Chapel Hill: University of North Carolina Press.

Kozol, Jonathan. 2005. *The Shame of the Nation: The Restoration of Apartheid Schooling in America*. New York: Crown.

Krantz, Laura. 2016. "WPI Says Student Partly Responsible for Assault." *Boston Globe*, June 7.

Kremer, Michael. 1993. "Population Growth and Technological Change, One Million B.C. to 1990." *Quarterly Journal of Economics* 108 (3) (August): 681–716.

Kroll, Andy, et al. 2014. "A Brief History of Big Oil Tax Breaks for Oil Companies." *Mother Jones*, April 14. http://www.motherjones.com/politics/2014/04/oil-subsidies-energy-timeline. Accessed September 22, 2016.

Krueger, Alan B. 2012. "The Rise and Consequences of Inequality." Speech by the chairman of the Council of Economic Advisers, January 12.

Krueger, Alan B., and Lawrence H. Summers. 1987. "Reflections on the Structure of Labor Markets." In *Unemployment and the Structure of Labor Markets*, ed. Kevin Lang and Jonathan Leonard, 17–47. Oxford: Blackwell.

Krugman, Paul. 2016a. "Remembrances of Booms Past." *New York Times*, May 23.

Krugman, Paul. 2016b. "States of Cruelty." *New York Times,* August 29.

Kuziemko, Ilyana, and Ebonya Washington. 2015. "Why Did the Democrats Lose the South? Bringing New Data to an Old Debate." NBER Working Paper No. 21703, November.

Kuznets, Simon. 1955. "Economic Growth and Income Inequality." *American Economic Review* 45 (1) (March): 1–28.

Kyckelhahn, Tracy. 2014. "State Corrections Expenditures, FY 1982–2010." United States Department of Justice, Bureau of Justice Statistics, revised, April 30. http://www.bjs.gov/content/pub/pdf/scefy8210.pdf. Accessed September 22, 2016.

Lee, Chisun, and Lawrence Norden. 2016. "The Secret Power Behind Local Elections." *New York Times,* June 25.

Lee, Sophia Z. 2014. *The Workplace Constitution: From the New Deal to the New Right.* New York: Cambridge University Press.

Levine, Ross. 2005. "Finance and Growth: Theory and Evidence." *In Handbook of Economic Growth,* vol I, part A, ed. Philippe Aghion and Steven N. Durlauf. 865–934. Amsterdam: Elsevier.

Levine, Sheen S. Evan P. Apfelbaum, Mark Bernard, Valerie L. Bartelt, Edward J. Zajac, and David Stark. 2014. "Ethnic Diversity Deflates Price Bubbles." *Proceedings of the National Academy of Sciences of the United States of America* 111 (52) (December 30): 18524–18529.

Levinson, Stanford. 2006. *Our Undemocratic Constitution: Where the Constitution Goes Wrong (and How We the People Can Correct It).* New York: Oxford University Press.

Levy, Frank, and Peter Temin. 2007. "Inequality and Institutions in 20th Century America." National Bureau of Research Working Paper 13106, May.

Levy, Frank, and Peter Temin. 2011. "Inequality and Institutions in 20th Century America." In *Economic Evolution and Revolution in Historical Times,* ed. Paul Rhode, Joshua Rosenbloom, and David Weiman, 357–386. Stanford: Stanford University Press.

Lewis, Michael. 2010. *The Big Short: Inside the Doomsday Machine.* New York: Norton.

Lewis, W. Arthur. 1954. "Economic Development with Unlimited Supplies of Labour." *Manchester School* 22:139–191.

Lichtblau, Eric. 2016. "U.S. to Curb Queries on Criminal Histories of Government Job Seekers." *New York Times,* April 29.

Liptak, Adam. 2016a. "Justices Leave Texas Voter ID Law Intact, with a Warning." *New York Times,* April 29.

Liptak, Adam. 2016b. "Supreme Court Finds Racial Bias in Jury Selection for Death Penalty Case." *New York Times,* May 23.

Liptak, Adam. 2016c. "Supreme Court Strikes Down Texas Abortion Restrictions." *New York Times,* June 27.

Lipton, Eric, and Julie Creswell. 2016. "Panama Papers Show How Rich United States Clients Hid Millions Abroad." *New York Times*, June 5.

Lipton, Eric, and Liz Moyer. 2015. "Hospitality and Gambling Interests Delay Closing of Billion-Dollar Tax Loophole." *New York Times*, December 20.

Lipton, Eric, and Brooke Williams. 2016. "How Think Tanks Amplify Corporate America's Influence." *New York Times*, August 7.

Loewenstein, Antony. 2016. "Private Prisons Are Cashing In on Refugees' Desperation." *New York Times*, February 25.

Lofstrom, Magnus, and Steven Raphael. 2016. "Crime, the Criminal Justice System, and Socioeconomic Inequality." *Journal of Economic Perspectives* 30 (2) (Spring): 103–126.

Logan, Trevon, and John Parman. 2015. "The National Rise in Residential Segregation." NBER Working Paper No. 20934, February.

Looney, Adam, and Constantine Yannelis. 2015 "A Crisis in Student Loans? How Changes in the Characteristics of Borrowers and in the Institutions They Attended Contributed to Rising Loan Defaults." *Brookings Papers on Economic Activity* (Fall): 1–89.

Luce, Edward. 2015. "Forecasting the World in 2016." *Financial Times*, December 31.

Ludwig, Jens, and Douglas L. Miller. 2007. "Does Head Start Improve Children's Life Chances? Evidence from a Regression Discontinuity Design." *Quarterly Journal of Economics* 122 (1) (February): 159–208.

MacDonald, Michael Patrick. 1999. *All Souls: A Family Story from Southie.* New York: Ballantine.

Macur, Juliet. 2016. "Before Kris Jenkins' Shot, There Was Ryan Arcidiacono's Pass." *New York Times*, April 5.

Maier, Pauline. 2011. *Ratification: The People Debate the Constitution, 1787–1788.* New York: Simon and Shuster.

Margo, Robert A. 1985. *Disenfranchisement, School Finance, and the Economics of Segregated Schools in the United States South, 1880–1910.* New York: Garland.

Margo, Robert A. 1990. *Race and Schooling in the South, 1880–1950: An Economic History.* Chicago: University of Chicago Press.

Mather, Victor, Carla Correa, and Meghan Louttit. 2016. "U.S. Women Jump, Spin and Soar to Gymnastics Gold." *New York Times*, August 9.

Mauer, Marc. 2006. *The Race to Incarcerate.* New York: New Press.

Mayer, Jane. 2010. "Covert Operations: The Billionaire Brothers Who Are Waging a War against Obama." *New Yorker*, August 30.

Mayer, Jane. 2016. *Dark Money: The Hidden History of the Billionaires behind the Rise of the Radical Right.* New York: Doubleday.

Mian, Atif, and Amir Sufi. 2014. *House of Debt: How They (and You) Caused the Great Recession and How We Can Prevent It from Happening Again.* Chicago: University of Chicago Press.

Milanović, Branko. 2016. *Global Inequality: A New Approach for the Age of Globalization*. Cambridge, MA: Harvard University Press.

Miller, Claire Cain. 2016. "As Women Take Over a Male-Dominated Field, the Pay Drops." *New York Times*, March 18.

Miller, Edward H. 2009. *Nut Country: Right-Wing Dallas and the Birth of the Southern Strategy*. Chicago: University of Chicago Press.

Mills, D. Quinn. 1979. "Flawed Victory in Labor Law Reform." *Harvard Business Review* 57 (3): 92–102.

Mincer, Jacob. 1958. "Investment in Human Capital and Personal Income Distribution." *Journal of Political Economy* 66 (4) (August): 281–302.

Minow, Martha. 2003. "Public and Private Partnerships: Accounting for the New Religion." *Harvard Law Review* 115 (5) (March): 1229–1284.

Morgenson, Gretchen. 2015. "A Student Loan System Stacked against the Borrower." *New York Times*, October 9.

Mortenson, Thomas G. 2012. "State Funding: A Race to the Bottom." American Council on Education, Winter. http://www.acenet.edu/the-presidency/columns-and-features/Pages/state-funding-a-race-to-the-bottom.aspx. Accessed September 22, 2016.

Moss, David A. 2002. *When All Else Fails: Government as the Ultimate Risk Manager*. Cambridge, MA: Harvard University Press.

Murray, Charles. 2012. *Coming Apart: The State of White America, 1960–2010*. New York: Crown.

National Center for Education Statistics. 2015. "Postsecondary Attainment: Differences by Socioeconomic Status." http://nces.ed.gov/programs/coe/indicator_tva.asp. Accessed September 22, 2016.

National Science Board. 2012. "Diminishing Funding and Rising Expectations: Trends and Challenges for Public Research Universities." http://www.nsf.gov/nsb/sei/companion2/files/nsb1245.pdf. Accessed September 22, 2016.

Neal, Larry. 2015. *A Concise History of International Finance: From Babylon to Bernanke*. New York: Cambridge University Press.

Newman, Oscar. 1972. *Defensible Space: Crime Prevention through Urban Design*. New York: Macmillan.

New York Times Editorial Board. 2015. "Alabama Puts Up More Hurdles for Voters." *New York Times*, October 8.

Nield, Ruth C., and Robert Balfanz. 2006. "An Extreme Degree of Difficulty: The Educational Demographics of Urban Neighborhood High Schools." *Journal of Education for Students Placed at Risk* 11 (April): 123–141.

Nixon, Richard. 1969. "Address to the Nation on Domestic Programs." *The American Presidency Project*, ed. Gerhard Peters and John T. Woolley, August 8. http://www.presidency.ucsb.edu/ws/?pid=2191. Accessed September 22, 2016.

Nocera, Joe. 2015. "Zuckerberg's Expensive Lesson." *New York Times*, September 8.

Norris, Floyd. 2014. "Made in the U.S.A., But Banked Overseas." *New York Times*, September 25.

Northeast Corridor Commission. 2015. "Five-Year Capital Plan, Fiscal Years 2016–2020." http://www.nec-commission.com/reports/nec-five-year-capital-plan-fy-2016-2020/. Accessed September 22, 2916.

Overton, Spencer. 2006. *Stealing Democracy: The New Politics of Voter Suppression*. New York: Norton.

Page, Benjamin I., Larry M. Bartels, and Jason Seawright. 2013. "Democracy and the Policy Preferences of Wealthy Americans." *Perspectives on Politics* 11 (March): 51–73.

Pamuk, Orhan. 2015. *A Strangeness in My Mind*. New York: Knopf.

Parker, Ashley, and Steve Eder. 2016. "*Inside the Six Weeks* Donald Trump Was a Nonstop 'Birther.'" *New York Times*, July 2.

Parker, Ashley, and Maggie Haberman. 2016. "With Koch Brothers Academy, Conservatives Settle in for Long War." *New York Times*, September 6.

Pear, Robert, and Reed Abelson. 2016. "As Insurers Like Aetna Balk, U.S. Makes New Push to Bolster Health Care Act." *New York Times*, August 18.

Pew Research Center. 2015. "The American Middle Class Is Losing Ground: No Longer the Majority and Falling Behind Financially." December 9. http://www.pewsocialtrends.org/2015/12/09/the-american-middle-class-is-losing-ground/. Accessed September 22, 2016.

Pfaff, John. 2016. "A Mockery of Justice for the Poor." *New York Times*, April 29.

Philippon, Thomas, and Ariell Reshef. 2012. "Wages and Human Capital in the U.S. Finance Industry: 1909–2006." *Quarterly Journal of Economics* 127 (November): 1551–1609.

Phillips-Fein, Kim. 2009. *Invisible Hands: The Businessmen's Crusade Against the New Deal*. New York: Norton.

Pierce, Justin R., and Peter K. Schott. 2016. "The Surprisingly Swift Decline of US Manufacturing Employment." *American Economic Review* 106 (7) (July): 1632–1662.

Piketty, Thomas. 2014. *Capital in the Twenty-First Century*. Cambridge, MA: Harvard University Press.

Pinto, Nick. 2015. "The Bail Trap." *New York Times*, August 13.

Piore, Michael J., and Sean Stafford. 2006. "Changing Regimes of Workplace Governance, Shifting Axes of Social Mobilization and the Challenge to Industrial Relations Theory." *Industrial Relations* 45 (3) (July): 299–325.

Porter, Eduardo. 2015. "Education Gap between Rich and Poor Is Growing Wider." *New York Times*, September 22.

Porter, Eduardo. 2016. "With Competition in Tatters, the Rip of Inequality Widens." *New York Times*, July 12.

Porter, Michael, and Scott Stern. 2015. "Social Progress Index." *Social Progress Imperative*. http://www.socialprogressimperative.org/global-index/. Accessed September 22, 2016.

Powell, Lewis. 1971. "The Powell Memo (also known as the Powell Manifesto)." August 23. http://reclaimdemocracy.org/powell_memo_lewis/. Accessed September 22, 2016.

Putnam, Robert D. 1993. *Making Democracy Work: Civic Traditions in Modern Italy*. Princeton: Princeton University Press.

Putnam, Robert D. 2000. *Bowling Alone: The Collapse and Revival of American Community*. New York: Simon and Schuster.

Putnam, Robert D. 2015. *Our Kids: The American Dream in Crisis*. New York: Simon and Schuster.

Rajan, Radhuram. 2010. *Fault Lines: How Hidden Fractures Still Threaten the World Economy*. Princeton: Princeton University Press.

Rankine, Claudia. 2015. *Citizen: An American Lyric*. Minneapolis, MN: Greywolf Press.

Rappeport, Alan. 2016. "Donald Trump Says His Remarks on Judge Were 'Misconstrued.'" *New York Times*, June 7.

Rattner, Steven. 2016a. "Donald Trump and Art of the Tax Loophole." *New York Times*, May 1.

Rattner, Steven. 2016b. "Long Lines at Airports? You Ain't Seen Nothing Yet." *New York Times*, July 8.

Rawls, John. 1999. *A Theory of Justice*. Cambridge, MA: Harvard University Press.

Reardon, Sean F. 2012. "The Widening Academic Achievement Gap between the Rich and the Poor." *Community Investments* 24 (Summer): 19–30.

Reardon, Sean F., and Kendra Bischoff. 2011. "Income Inequality and Income Segregation." *American Journal of Sociology* 116 (4) (January): 1092–1153.

Reardon, Sean F., and Kendra Bischoff. 2016. "The Continuing Increase in Income Segregation, 2007–2012." Stanford Center for Education Policy Analysis, March. http://cepa.stanford.edu/content/continuing-increase-income-segregation-2007-2012. Accessed September 22, 2016.

Reardon, Sean F., Jane Waldfogel, and Daphna Bassok. 2016. "The Good News about Educational Inequality." *New York Times*, August 26.

Reeves, Richard V. 2015. "The Dangerous Separation of the American Middle Class." Social Mobility Memos, Brookings Institution, September 3. http://www.brookings.edu/blogs/social-mobility-memos/posts/2015/09/03-separation-upper-middle-class-reeves. Accessed September 22, 2016.

Reeves, Richard V., and Nathan Joo. 2015. "Not Just the 1%: Upper Middle Class Income Separation." Social Mobility Memos, Brookings Institution, September 10. http://www.brookings.edu/blogs/social-mobility-memos/posts/2015/09/10-not-just-1-percent-income-reeves. Accessed September 22, 2016.

Reich, Robert B. 1991. *The Work of Nations: Preparing Ourselves for 21*st*-Century Capitalism.* New York: Knopf.

Reid, Joy-Ann. 2015. *Fracture: Barack Obama, the Clintons and the Racial Divide.* New York: HarperCollins.

Riggs, Mike. 2012. "Four Industries Getting Rich off the Drug War." Reason. com, April 22. http://reason.com/archives/2012/04/22/4-industries-getting-rich -off-the-drug-w/2. Accessed September 22, 2016.

Rocheleau, Matt. 2016. "A List of All of the Boston Schools with Recent Lead Concerns." *Boston Globe*, August 17.

Robertson, Campbell. 2016. "In Louisiana, the Poor Lack Legal Defense." *New York Times*, March 19.

Roeder, Oliver, Lauren-Brooke Eisen, and Julia Bowling. 2015. *What Caused the Crime Decline?* New York: Brennan Center for Justice at NYU.

Ross, Carne. 2016. "Chilcot Report: How Tony Blair Sold the War." *New York Times*, July 6.

Rubin, Robert E. 2016. "How to Help Former Inmates Thrive." *New York Times*, June 3.

Russakoff, Dale. 2015. *The Prize: Who's in Charge of America's Schools.* Boston: Houghton Mifflin Harcourt.

Rutenberg, Jim. 2015. "Voting Rights Act, a Dream Undone." *New York Times*, August 2.

Saez, Emmanuel, and Gabriel Zucman. 2016. "Wealth Inequality in the United States since 1913: Evidence from Capitalized Income Tax Data." *Quarterly Journal of Economics* 131 (2) (May): 519–578.

Sanders, Eli. 2016. *While the City Slept: A Love Lost to Violence and a Young Man's Descent into Madness.* New York: Viking.

Santos, Fernanda, and Motoko Rich. 2015. "Recession, Politics and Policy Stretch Arizona School Budgets." *New York Times*, June 5.

Sass, Tim R. 2006. "Charter Schools and Student Achievement in Florida." *Education Finance and Policy* 1 (Winter): 91–122.

Scharfenberg, David. 2015. "MBTA Repair Bill up to $7.3b, and May Rise, Panel Says." *Boston Globe*, August 31.

Scheiber, Noam. 2015. "Justice in Taxes, Most Likely Short-Lived." *New York Times*, December 31.

Scheiber, Noam. 2016a. "White House Increases Overtime Eligibility by Millions." *New York Times*, May 17.

Scheiber, Noam. 2016b. "The Law School Bust." *New York Times*, June 19.

Scheiber, Noam, and Patricia Cohen. 2015. "For the Wealthiest, a Private Tax System that Saves Them Billions." *New York Times*, December 29.

Scheindlin, Shira A. 2016. "America's Trial Court Judges: Our Front Line for Justice." *New York Times*, May 7.

Scher, Richard K. 2011. *The Politics of Disenfranchisement: Why Is It So Hard to Vote in America?* Armonk, NY: M. E. Sharpe.

Schorr, Lisbeth B. 1989. *Within Our Reach: Breaking the Cycle of Disadvantage.* New York: Random House.

Schwartz, Nelson D. 2014. "The Middle Class Is Steadily Eroding, Just Ask the Business World." *New York Times,* February 2.

Schwartz, Nelson D. 2016a. "In an Age of Privilege, Not Everyone Is in the Same Boat." *New York Times,* April 23.

Schwartz, Nelson D. 2016b. "Why Corporate America Is Leaving the Suburbs for the City." *New York Times,* August 1.

Seelye, Katherine Q. 2016. "Massachusetts Chief's Tack in Drug War: Steer Addicts to Rehab, Not Jail." *New York Times,* January 24.

Shertzer, Allison, and Randall P. Walsh. 2016. "Racial Sorting and the Emergence of Segregation in American Cities." NBER Working Paper No. 22077, March.

Siegel, Reva B. 2002. "She the People: The Nineteenth Amendment, Sex Equality, Federalism, and the Family." *Harvard Law Review* 115 (4): 948–1046.

Singer, Peter W. 2005. "Outsourcing War." *Foreign Affairs,* March/April. https://www.foreignaffairs.com/articles/2005-03-01/outsourcing-war. Accessed September 22, 2016.

Smallacombe, Patricia Stern. 2006. "Rootedness, Isolation, and Social Capital in an Inner-City White Neighborhood." In *Social Capital in the City: Community and Civil Life in Philadelphia,* ed. Richardson Dilworth, 177–195. Philadelphia: Temple University Press.

Smeeding, Timothy M. 2016. "Gates, Gaps, and Intergenerational Mobility: The Importance of an Even Start." In *The Dynamics of Opportunity in America: Evidence and Perspective,* ed. Irwin Kirsch and Henry Braun. New York: Springer ebooks.

Smith, Mitch. 2016. "Michigan: Emergency Declared over Flint's Water." *New York Times,* January 5.

Sokol, Jason. 2014. *All Eyes Are Upon Us: Race and Politics from Boston to Brooklyn.* New York: Basic Books.

Solow, Robert M. 1956. "A Contribution to the Theory of Economic Growth." *Quarterly Journal of Economics* 70 (February): 65–90.

Solow, Robert M. 1957. "Technical Change and the Aggregate Production Function." *Review of Economics and Statistics* 39 (3) (August): 312–320.

Sommer, Jeff. 2015. "Pfizer Didn't Need an Inversion to Avoid Paying U.S. Taxes." *New York Times,* November 25.

Soss, Joe, Richard C. Fording, and Sanford F. Schram. 2011. *Disciplining the Poor: Neoliberal Paternalism and the Persistent Power of Race.* Chicago: University of Chicago Press.

Special Inspector General for TARP (Troubled Asset Relief Program). 2015.

Quarterly Report to Congress, July 29. http://www.sigtarp.gov/Quarterly%20
Reports/July_29_2015_Report_to_Congress.pdf.

Stack, Liam. 2016a. "Florida Governor Signs Law to Cut Funding for Abortion
Clinics." *New York Times*, March 25.

Stack, Liam. 2016b. "Light Sentence for Brock Turner in Stanford Rape Case
Draws Outrage." *New York Times*, June 6.

Steinfeld, Robert J. 1991. *The Invention of Free Labor: The Employment
Relation in English and American Law and Culture, 1350–1870*. Chapel Hill:
University of North Carolina Press.

Steinfeld, Robert J. 2001. *Coercion, Contract, and Free Labour in the
Nineteenth Century*. Cambridge: Cambridge University Press.

Stevenson, Alexandra. 2015. "For Top 25 Hedge Fund Managers, a Difficult
2014 Still Paid Well." *New York Times*, May 5.

Stevenson, Alexandra. 2016. "Hedge Funds Faced Choppy Waters in 2015, but
Chiefs Cashed In." *New York Times*, May 10.

Stepler, Renee, and Anna Brown. 2016. "Statistical Picture of Hispanics in the
United States." Pew Research Center, April 19. http://www.pewhispanic.org/
2016/04/19/statistical-portrait-of-hispanics-in-the-united-states-key-charts/.
Accessed September 22, 2016.

Stewart, Amy. 2016. "Female Officers Save Lives." *New York Times*, July 26.

Stiglitz, Joseph E. 2012. *The Price of Inequality*. New York: Norton.

Stiglitz, Joseph E., and Linda Bilmes. 2008. *The Three Trillion Dollar War: The
Trues Cost of the Iraq Conflict*. New York: Norton.

Stockman, Farah. 2015. "Sex, Drugs, and Racist Policing in Rutland, VT."
Boston Globe, August 27.

Stolberg, Cheryl. 2016. "Findings of Police Bias in Baltimore Validate What
Many Have Long Felt." *New York Times*, August 10.

Stolberg, Sheryl Gay, and Erik Eckholm. 2016. "Virginia Governor Restores
Voting Rights to Felons." *New York Times*, April 22.

Stolberg, Sheryl Gay, and Nicholas Fandos. 2016. "Washington Metro, 40 and
Creaking, Stares at a Midlife Crisis." *New York Times*, April 3.

Stuntz, William J. 2011. *The Collapse of American Criminal Justice*. Cambridge,
MA: Harvard University Press.

Summers, Lawrence H. 2015."Demand Side Secular Stagnation." *American
Economic Review* 105 (5): 60–65.

Surowiecki, James. 2016. "System Overload." *New Yorker*, April 18.

Swarns, Rachel L. 2015. "Biased Lending Evolves, and Blacks Face Trouble
Getting Mortgages." *New York Times*, October 30.

Swavolo, Elizabeth, Kristine Riley, and Ram Subramanian. 2016. "Overlooked:
Women and Jails in an Era of Reform." Vera Institute of Justice, August. https://
www.vera.org/publications/overlooked-women-and-jails-report. Accessed
September 22, 2016.

Tavernise, Sabrina. 2016. "Disparity in Life Spans of the Rich and the Poor Is Growing." *New York Times*, February, 12.

Taylor, Kate. 2015. "At a Success Academy Charter School, Singling Out Pupils Who Have 'Got to Go.'" *New York Times*, October 29.

Temin, Peter. 1999. "The American Business Elite in Historical Perspective." In *Elites, Minorities, and Economic Growth*, ed. Elise S. Brezis and Peter Temin. 19–39. Amsterdam: Elsevier.

Temin, Peter. 2002. "The Golden Age of Economic Growth Reconsidered." *European Review of Economic History* 6 (April): 3–22.

Temin, Peter. 2002. "Teacher Quality and the Future of America." *Eastern Economic Journal* 28 (Summer): 285–300.

Temin, Peter. 2016. "The American Dual Economy: Race, Globalization and the Politics of Exclusion." *International Journal of Political Economy* 45 (2) (Summer): 1–40.

Temin, Peter, and David Vines. 2013. *The Leaderless Economy: Why the World Economic System Fell Apart and How to Fix It*. Princeton: Princeton University Press

Temin, Peter, and David Vines. 2014. *Keynes: Useful Economics for the World Economy* . Cambridge, MA: MIT Press.

Thompson, Heather Ann. 2010. "Why Mass Incarceration Matters: Rethinking Crisis, Decline, and Transformation in Postwar American History." *Journal of American History* 97 (3) (December): 703–734.

Tirman, John. 2015. *Dream Chasers: Immigration and the American Backlash*. Cambridge, MA: MIT Press.

Toner, Robin. 1988. "Prison Furloughs in Massachusetts Threaten Dukakis Record on Crime." *New York Times*, July 5.

Traugott, Michael W. 2016. "Americans: Major Donors Sway Congress More than Constituents." Gallup, June 1–5. http://www.gallup.com/poll/193484/americans-major-donors-sway-congress-constituents.aspx?g_source=Politics&g_medium=newsfeed&g_campaign=tiles. Accessed September 22, 2016.

Tribe, Laurence, and Joshua Matz. 2014. *Uncertain Justice: The Roberts Court and the Constitution*. New York: Henry Holt.

Triffin, Robert. 1961. *Gold and the Dollar Crisis: The Future of Convertibility*. New Haven: Yale University Press.

Troesken, Werner. 2006. *The Great Lead Water Pipe Disaster*. Cambridge, MA: MIT Press.

US Bureau of Labor Statistics. 2016. "Nonfarm Business Sector: Labor Share (PR85006173)." FRED, Federal Reserve Bank of St. Louis. http://fred.stlouisfed.org/series/PR85006173. Accessed September 12, 2016.

Van Cleve, Nicole Gonzalez. 2016. "Chicago's Racist Cops and Racist Courts." *New York Times*, April 14.

Vennochi, Joan. 2015. "The T's Haves and Have-Nots." *Boston Globe*, December 17.

Vlasic, Bill, and Mary M. Chapman. 2015. "U.A.W. Contracts Change Math for Detroit Automakers." *New York Times*, November 24.

Vogel, Kenneth P. 2015. "The Koch Intelligence Agency." Politico, November 18. http://www.politico.com/story/2015/11/the-koch-brothers-intelligence -agency-215943. Accessed September 22, 2016.

Wacquant, Loïc. 2009. *Punishing the Poor: The Neoliberal Government of Social Insecurity*. Durham, NC: Duke University Press.

Waldman, Annie. 2016. "In New Jersey Student Loan Program, Even Death May Not Bring a Reprieve." *New York Times*, July 3.

Wang, Sam. 2013. "The Great Gerrymander of 2012." *New York Times*, February 2.

Warren, Elizabeth. 2015. "Speech on Racial Inequality." Edward M. Kennedy Institute for the United States Senate, September 27. http://www.warren.senate .gov/?p=press_release&id=967. Accessed September 22, 2016.

Weets, David J., and Justin M. Ronca. 2006. "Examining Differences in State Support for Higher Education: A Comparative Study of State Appropriations for Research Universities." *Journal of Higher Education* 77 (November–December): 935–967.

"'Welfare Queen' Becomes Issue in Reagan Campaign." 1976. *New York Times*, February 15.

Weil, David N. 2014. *The Fissured Workplace: Why Work Became So Bad for So Many and What Can Be Done to Improve It*. Cambridge, MA: Harvard University Press.

Weil, David N. 2015. "Capital and Wealth in the Twenty-First Century." *American Economic Review* 105 (5) (May): 34–37.

Weiser, Benjamin. 2016. "Rich Defendants' Request to Judges: Lock Me Up in a Gilded Cage." *New York Times*, June 1.

Western, Bruce. 2006. *Punishment and Inequality in America*. New York: Russell Sage Foundation.

Wigmore, Barrie A. 1997. *Securities Markets in the 1980s: The New Regime, 1979–1984*. New York: Oxford University Press.

Wilkerson, Isabel. 2010. *The Warmth of Other Suns: The Epic Story of America's Great Migration*. New York: Random House.

Williams, Timothy. 2016. "Number of Women in Jail Has Grown Far Faster than That of Men, Study Says." *New York Times*, August 17.

Wilson, William Julius. 1996. *When Work Disappears: The World of the New Urban Poor*. New York: Knopf.

Wilson, William Julius. 2009. *More than Just Race: Being Black and Poor in the Inner City*. New York: Norton.

Wines, Michael. 2016a. "Federal Judge Bars North Dakota from Enforcing Restrictive Voter ID Law." *New York Times*, August 1.

Wines, Michael. 2016b. "Inside the Conservative Push for States to Amend the Constitution." *New York Times*, August 22.

Wines, Michael, and Lizette Alvarez. 2015. "Council of Conservative Citizens Promotes White Primacy, and G.O.P. Ties." *New York Times*, June 22.

Wines, Michael, and Alan Blinder. 2016. "Federal Appeals Court Strikes Down North Carolina Voter ID Requirement." *New York Times*, July 29.

Wines, Michael, and Manny Fernandez. 2016. "Stricter Rules for Voter IDs Reshape Races." *New York Times*, May 1.

Wines, Michael, Patrick McGeehan, and John Schwartz. 2016. "Schools Nationwide Still Grapple with Lead in Water." *New York Times*, March 26.

Winters, Jeffrey A. 2011. *Oligarchy*. Cambridge: Cambridge University Press.

Wolfers, Justin. 2016. "Growing Up in a Bad Neighborhood Does More Harm than We Thought." *New York Times*, March 25.

Woodward, C. Vann. 1974. *The Strange Career of Jim Crow*. New York: Oxford University Press.

Wright, Gavin. 2013. *Sharing the Prize: The Economics of the Civil Rights Revolution in the American South*. Cambridge, MA: Harvard University Press.

Yates, Sally Q. 2016. "Reducing Our Use of Private Prisons" Memo sent by Sally Q. Yates, Deputy Attorney General, to the acting director of the Federal Bureau of Prisons, August 18. https://www.justice.gov/opa/blog/phasing-out-our-use-private-prisons. Accessed September 22, 2016.

Zernike, Kate. 2015a. "Amtrak Official Says Rail Delays May Become 'Norm.'" *New York Times*, August 10.

Zernike, Kate. 2015b. "Obama Administration Calls for Limits on Testing in Schools." *New York Times*, October 24.

Zernike, Kate. 2016a. "Test Scores Show a Decline in Math among High School Seniors." *New York Times*, April 27.

Zernike, Kate. 2016b. "A Sea of Charter Schools in Detroit Leaves Students Adrift." *New York Times*, June 28.

Zernike, Kate. 2016c. "An F-Minus for America's Schools from a Fed-Up Judge." *New York Times*, September 8.

Zingales, Luigi. 2015. "Does Finance Benefit Society?" Presidential Address to the American Finance Association, January. Also available as NBER Working Paper No. 20894, January.

Zucman, Gabriel. 2014. "Taxing across Borders: Tracking Personal Wealth and Corporate Profits.'" *Journal of Economic Perspectives* 29 (4) (Fall): 121–148.

Zucman, Gabriel. 2015. *The Hidden Wealth of Nations: The Scourge of Tax Havens*. Chicago: University of Chicago Press.

Index

industrialization and, 155
Massachusetts and, 105
neoliberalism and, 17, 21–22
Powell and, 21
Reagan and, 22
taxes and, 174n15
Libertarian Review journal, 84
Lincoln, Abraham, 51, 87
Loans
 bankruptcy and, 90
 education, 137
 forgiving, 172n14
 government, 49, 174n15
 nonperforming, 139
 redlining and, 34, 53
 S&L crisis and, 17
 Social Security and, 174n15
 student, 43–45, 137, 140, 172n14
 writing down, 158
Lobbying, 15, 18, 24, 44, 83, 110–111
Low-wage sector
 African Americans and, 27–29,
  34–40, 50–54, 153–154, 171n19
 bargaining power and, 31
 birth of, 27
 capital and, 29, 32, 39, 42–45
 cities and, 130, 135–136
 college and, 29, 122
 company boundaries and, 29–30
 competition and, 31–34, 103
 concepts of government and, 89, 92
 cross-country comparison and,
  147–150
 debt and, 137–143
 Democrats and, 154
 demographics of, 10
 discrimination and, 38, 153
 disengagement and, 35, 117
 dual economy and, 4, 8, 9–13
 federal grants and, 35
 financial crisis of 2008 and, 38
 401(k) plans and, 33–34
 FTE (finance, technology, and
  electronics) sector and, 11–13, 25,
  27–29, 32–37, 153–155, 170n6
 Great Gatsby Curve, The, and, 46
 Great Migration and, 27–29, 34–35

 health care and, 154
 hourglass job profile and, 28–29
 housing and, 34, 153
 ignored needs of, 80, 135, 142,
  153–155
 immigrants and, 27–28, 32, 35, 153
 independent contractors and, 31, 52,
  65
 industry and, 28–34
 infrastructure issues and, 157–158
 Investment Theory of Politics and,
  62, 65–70, 75
 labor and, 27–40, 44, 103
 Latinos and, 35, 38–39, 55, 153–154,
  171n19
 Lewis model and, xiv, 28, 36, 103
 literacy tests and, 65–66
 mass incarceration and, 38, 101,
  103, 105, 107, 112–114, 153–154,
  156
 middle class and, 38
 mortgages and, 34
 North and, 27–29, 32, 34
 pensions and, 31, 33, 69
 police and, 39–40
 poll taxes and, 58, 65
 poverty and, 27, 35, 39–40
 public education and, 115, 117,
  119–128, 130, 153–154, 160,
  170n6
 race and, 49, 55, 153–154
 reform for, 156–159
 Republicans and, 154, 170n1
 retirement and, 11, 25, 29, 33–34, 45,
  90, 141, 156, 172n14
 segregation and, 27, 34
 service workers and, 29–30
 slavery and, 27
 social capital and, 39, 153
 Social Security and, 69–70
 South and, 27–29, 34–35, 142,
  170n1
 subcontractors and, 30–31, 57
 taxes and, 31, 36
 transition and, 11, 41–46
 unemployment and, 34, 37, 157
 unions and, 28–29, 32–34